Lecture Notes in Computer Science   2261
Edited by G. Goos, J. Hartmanis, and J. van Leeuwen

Springer

Berlin
Heidelberg
New York
Barcelona
Hong Kong
London
Milan
Paris
Tokyo

Felix Naumann

Quality-Driven Query Answering for Integrated Information Systems

 Springer

Series Editors

Gerhard Goos, Karlsruhe University, Germany
Juris Hartmanis, Cornell University, NY, USA
Jan van Leeuwen, Utrecht University, The Netherlands

Author

Felix Naumann
IBM Almaden Research Center
650 Harry Road, San Jose, CA 95123, USA
E-mail: felix@almaden.ibm.com

Dissertation der Humboldt Universität zu Berlin
Tag der mündlichen Prüfung: 19. Dezember 2000

Referent: Prof. Dr. Johann-Christoph Freytag, Humboldt Universität zu Berlin
Referent: Prof. Myra Spiliopoulou, Handelshochschule Leipzig
Referent: Prof. Gio Wiederhold, Stanford University

Cataloging-in-Publication Data applied for

Die Deutsche Bibliothek - CIP-Einheitsaufnahme

Naumann, Felix:
Quality driven query answering for integrated information systems /
Felix Naumann. - Berlin ; Heidelberg ; New York ; Barcelona ; Hong Kong ;
London ; Milan ; Paris ; Tokyo : Springer, 2002
   (Lecture notes in computer science ; 2261)
   ISBN 3-540-43349-X

CR Subject Classification (1998): H.3, H.2, H.4, I.2.11, C.2.4, F.2.2

ISSN 0302-9743
ISBN 3-540-43349-X Springer-Verlag Berlin Heidelberg New York

Springer-Verlag Berlin Heidelberg New York
a member of BertelsmannSpringer Science+Business Media GmbH

http://www.springer.de

© Springer-Verlag Berlin Heidelberg 2002
Printed in Germany

Typesetting: Camera-ready by author, data conversion by Boller Mediendesign
Printed on acid-free paper   SPIN: 10846092   06/3142   5 4 3 2 1 0

Foreword

The Internet and the World Wide Web (WWW) are becoming more and more important in our highly interconnected world as more and more data and information is made available for online access. Many individuals and governmental, commercial, cultural, and scientific organizations increasingly depend on information sources that can be accessed and queried over the Web. For example, accessing flight schedules or retrieving stock information has become common practice in today's world. When accessing this data, many people assume that the information accessed is accurate and that the data source can be accessed reliably.

These two examples clearly demonstrate that not only the information content is important, the **information about the quality of the data** becomes an even more crucial and critical aspect for individuals and organizations when they make plans or take decisions based on the results of their queries. More precisely, having access to information of known quality becomes critical for the well-being and indeed for the functioning of modern industrialized societies.

Surprisingly, despite the urgent need for clear concepts and techniques to judge and value quality and for technology to use such (meta) information, very few scientific results are known and available. Few approaches are known to use quality measures for accessing and querying information over the Web. Only a limited number of products on the IT market address this burning problem.

With this book Dr. Felix Naumann is one of the first to address the topic of querying data with quality in a systematic and comprehensive way from a database point of view. His two-step approach reflects his clear understanding of the problem as well as the solutions required for "real-world" settings. As a basis he first describes the various "properties" of information quality (IQ) by more specific – and technically sound – quality measures before introducing ranking algorithms to select Web sources for access. In the second part of his book, Dr. Naumann focuses on "quality-driven" query answering, in particular on query planning using the different quality criteria. Again, the solutions presented reflect Dr. Naumann's desire not to come up with *any* solution, but rather to design algorithms that could be used in "real world" systems, a goal he greatly achieves. His particular focus on completeness of data, a very important aspect for "real-world" scenarios, together with the designed algorithms, is another highlight of this book. The careful reader will notice – despite the many technical details – that

Dr. Naumann's in-depth treatment of completeness provides the insight into the problem necessary for such an important topic.

In summary, the approach and systematic treatment of information quality taken in this book and the way Dr. Naumann describes problems and solutions makes this book valuable for both researchers and practitioners who are interested in gaining a better understanding of the issues and solutions available in the context of information quality. The in-depth presentation of the algorithms and techniques is enlightening to students and a valuable resource for computer scientists as well as for business people. I predict that in the years ahead this book will provide the "road map" for others in this area both in research and development.

November 2001   Johann-Christoph Freytag

Preface

Research and business is currently moving from centralized databases towards information systems integrating distributed, autonomous data sources. With it, research focus has shifted from traditional query optimization to the field of query planning. Query planning is the problem of finding query execution plans across distributed, heterogeneous, overlapping, and autonomous data sources. We argue that for such data sources the main discriminator for different query execution strategies is no longer response time, as it is for database queries, but – more generally – the *information quality* (IQ) of the result. This thesis investigates the usage of IQ-criteria to improve the answering of user queries against integrated information systems. We discuss what kind of IQ-metadata is necessary, how it can be acquired, and – most importantly – how it can be used to improve the quality of query results and the performance of query planning algorithms. A simple application for these research issues is a meta-search engine that uses existing search engines as its distributed data sources. Other examples include stock information systems, travel guides, and distributed molecular biology databases.

The thesis has three main parts. Part I lays the foundation for the problem of querying Web data sources and shows why IQ-reasoning is helpful. We describe the mediator–wrapper architecture and show how to describe sources and user queries using the concept of the universal relation. Several application examples serve as rationale throughout the thesis.

Part II introduces our model of information quality. We present a comprehensive set of IQ-criteria together with score assessment methods. Each data source is rated by a set of IQ-criteria, such as completeness, understandability, or accuracy. To compare data sources and query plans qualitatively using multiple criteria, we present appropriate ranking methods, which aggregate IQ-criterion scores to an overall quality value.

Part III puts information quality to work by combining query planning with IQ-reasoning. We revise the conventional query planning goal of finding all plans for a query: The new goal is to find the best N plans and use a quality model to quantify the term 'best'. We present two algorithms to solve this problem. The first acts as an add-on to any given query planning algorithm, the second explicitly integrates IQ-reasoning into the planning process, thereby speeding up query planning itself. Next, we part from the conventional query planning paradigm of finding different plans for a query, each with a different result. The usage of new outerjoin-type merge operators to combine sources enables a reduction of the paradigm to finding a single, best plan. We concentrate on the completeness criterion describing the amount of data returned by a plan and present two families of optimization algorithms for different real world situations. All algorithms are evaluated using a simulation testbed.

The main contribution of the thesis is the comprehensive integration of information quality reasoning and query planning. Research has recognized the importance of quality reasoning, but, to the best of our knowledge, IQ-reasoning for query planning has not been adequately addressed before.

Acknowledgments

I thank my advisors Prof. Johann Christoph Freytag, Prof. Myra Spiliopoulou, and Prof. Hans-Joachim Lenz for their constant support, frequent meetings, and useful advice. Prof. Freytag offered a great research environment that was a pleasure to work in and turned three years of research into rewarding results and an enjoyable time. Myra introduced me to database research, had the first inkling that quality-reasoning is a promising research topic, and guided my research in many meetings. Prof. Lenz helped find different perspectives on my work and never hesitated to plunge into the depths of my research. Also, I thank Prof. Gio Wiederhold for an extensive and valuable discussion and for reviewing this thesis.

The Graduate School for Distributed Information Systems supported this thesis financially and – more importantly – through regular discussions and evaluation by its professors and students. Among the many students of the graduate school to whom I am grateful for three wonderful years, I point out Ulf Leser and André Bergholz. Due to Ulf, my research was particularly enjoyable and successful, through much help, many discussions, and having a great time together. André was an important constant for my research and university life, leading the path I was to follow.

Working with the dbis team at the Humboldt University has been good fun. Ulrike Sholz and Heinz Werner were especially patient and helpful. Mike Stillger gave superb guidance for an inexperienced colleague – thanks Mike. I thank Ramana Yerneni and Prof. Hector Garcia-Molina for an enlightening stay at Stanford University, Claudia Rolker who I have yet to meet, and finally Julia Böttcher and Daniel Tonn for our successful projects.

Last but not least, Anneke, my parents, and my sister supported me and put up with me all along.

This research was supported by the German Research Society, Berlin-Brandenburg Graduate School in Distributed Information Systems (DFG grant no. GRK 316).

August 2001   *Felix Naumann*

Contents

1 Introduction

The development of the Internet—especially the World Wide Web—has made it possible to access a multitude of data sources on almost any given topic. Web directories guide users to these sources, search engines let users discover sources previously unknown to them, and a huge number of Web sites act as data sources and provide the actual data. Most often, a user may choose between many alternative sources and source combinations to obtain the desired information item. This choice is advantageous but also time-consuming. It is advantageous to choose the most renowned, the fastest, or the most accurate sources. But it is time-consuming to come to this choice through trial and error. And it is even more time-consuming to access several sources in a row if the desired information is not provided by a single source, but is spread across those sources.

Consider search engines as data sources. Most users have chosen their favorite search engine, possibly based on personal experience in response time, relevancy of the results, ranking method, usability, etc. However, users might miss just the right Web page, simply because that page was not yet indexed or ranked sufficiently high by the search engine of choice. Meanwhile, this Web page might have already been indexed by other search engines. The user might turn to one of these and may eventually find the wanted Web page. A meta-search engine solves this problem by simultaneously querying multiple search engines with the user's keywords. The results of the different engines are integrated to a combined response to the user. The drawback is that a quality-unaware meta-search engine uses engines of mixed quality, for instance, they return dead links.

Integrated access to data that is spread over multiple, distributed, autonomous, and heterogeneous data sources is an important problem for information consumers in many areas. Wherever there is more than one alternative data source to choose from, this choice yields advantages and disadvantages. Apart from search engines there are many other scenarios:

- Bargain finders are services that search the Internet for different offers for the same product and allow comparison shopping in a browser. Choosing the sources to go to is one of the most important tasks of bargain finders. Also, data about the products must be integrated to present a more complete description to the user.

F. Naumann: Quality-Driven Query Answering, LNCS 2261, pp. 3-10, 2002.

- Many stock exchanges publish stock quotes online. This stock information service is also provided by many Internet portals, such as the Yahoo Web site or AOL financial services. Additionally, there are numerous data sources for business specific data such as company profiles, size, etc. Examples are the Wall Street Journal Web site or the online services of CNN. The quality of these sources varies widely. Many sources delay stock quote data by a certain amount of time; sources often require payments; some sources have a high reputation, others do not. Finding out which sources have the desired information and which of these sources has the highest quality is a difficult task.
- There is an abundance of Web-based telephone and email directories that can be integrated to increase the chance of finding a person (white pages) or company (yellow pages).
  Reasoning about their quality can identify large sources, sources with much additional data about a person like address and email, source with up-to-date data, etc. Integration of the sources using this metadata can greatly enhance the final result and help filter out duplicates.
- In the scope of the Human Genome Project many Web-based molecular biology information systems have emerged. One of the current goals of the project is to integrate these sources [27].
  Considering quality criteria like accuracy, correct annotation, or timeliness in this process increases the overall quality of the integration result.

In the Web age, source selection, information integration, and information filtering are important tasks to shield information consumers from data overflow, data errors, or simply low quality data. This thesis introduces an innovative solution to perform these tasks by reasoning about the quality of the sources and of the information they provide. The results of this thesis apply to most any integrated information system, but the problems we solve are most apparent for systems integrating Web data sources.

1.1 Centralized Databases Vs. the World Wide Web

The information system paradigm shift—from central database management systems (DBMSs) to distributed multidatabase systems and finally to virtual, integrated World Wide Web information systems—has moved attention from *query processing* to what we call *query planning*.

Query processing is concerned with efficiently answering a user query to a single- or multidatabase. In this context efficiency means speed. If not the speed of answering one query efficiently, it is the speed of the overall running system that is optimized. Many researchers and developers have designed sophisticated algorithms, index structures, etc., to enhance database performance. All those techniques have the same goal: Find a single query execution plan that provides the user with the correct and complete query result in an efficient manner. Query planning on the other hand is concerned with finding *all* correct query execution plans across different, autonomous sources that together form the complete result.

Completeness and correctness in a DBMS are defined with regard to the content of the underlying database. A relational DBMS should respond to a query with *only* those tuples that match the query (correctness) and with *all* the tuples that match the query (completeness). The underlying assumptions are that the database contains only correct data and that it contains all relevant data (closed world assumption). For instance, corporate users of an customer database assume that all customer data is correct and that data about all customers is actually stored within the database. Typical users will not doubt the data provided, and they will not turn to other databases suspecting that there is more customer data stored elsewhere.

In general, these completeness and correctness assumptions do not hold for Web data sources in an open world, quite the contrary: A search engine will never have indexed *every* available Web page on the World Wide Web (WWW); stock information systems do not provide data on every stock; Web-based telephone directories only store data about some people, but never cover all telephone networks. That is, Web data sources are usually not complete. Correctness is also never guaranteed: Web pages may change after a search engine has indexed them; stock information systems purposely return delayed and thus incorrect stock quotes; etc.

Of course, DBMSs may also contain incorrect data; of course DBMSs may also not have all available data. However, compared to Web data sources, the owner of a DBMS has the power to change this situation. If there are inaccurate data, one can correct them, if data is missing, one can insert it. If the overall quality of the system is low, one can take measures to increase the quality aspects that are amiss. Web data sources on the other hand are autonomous. If completeness and correctness or the overall information quality are not satisfying, there is usually nothing the integrating system can do about it.

1.2 Information Quality on the Web

The World Wide Web (WWW) can be regarded as an enormous pool of data sources. It is made up of numerous, independent, and autonomous Web sites, i.e., independent, autonomous data sources. The Inktomi search engine website reports about 5 million distinct websites in their Web page database as of february 2000 [131], while covering about one tenth of the Web [101]. The overall number of Web pages is reported to be over 1 billion [101]. Regardless of their content, these sources display large differences in the quality of the information they present.

Examples of poor information quality. Web data sources might be up-to-date or outdated, accurate or inaccurate, partial or complete, costly or free, fast or slow, comprehensible or unclear. Experienced Web users will have come across sources to which any combination of the mentioned quality adjectives can be applied. Most often, information quality (IQ) is not as high as one could wish or would expect, e.g.,

- due to the dynamics of the Web, search engine results often point to Web pages that no longer exist. Also, the inability of search engines to find relevant pages is source for much confusion and disappointment.
- many stock information systems are cluttered with data and thus incomprehensible. Also, such systems often charge high amounts of money for the data, rendering them unsuitable for many users.
- molecular biology information systems on the Web are very slow, because the searches require complex computations, such as sequence alignment with the BLAST algorithm [4], in many cases users must wait hours for their results. Also, they are outdated quickly by new experiments.

When sources store similar content, quality aspects, such as the ones mentioned before, constitute the main difference between them. These observations and others, such as those in [23, 132, 134, 84], give rise to the following axiom:

Information quality is the main discriminator of Web data sources, and information quality reasoning should be used to improve integrated query results.

Reasons for poor information quality. In an information system spanning multiple, distributed, and autonomous data sources, information quality can suffer problems that are intrinsic to any architecture of an integrated information system as well as various technical problems of such a system.

Web data sources are autonomous from the integrators point of view. The providers of the data have control over their source content and how they describe it. From a users point of view, a good data source provides useful information on a well-defined topic. The content, its origin, and further metadata should be described understandably, the content should be as comprehensive as possible. Only then can the user access the source purposefully and confidently. A source with poor quality will not describe its content and will have incomplete data on various topics. The user can only guess if the source should be accessed. In a WWW setting these problems are inevitable. To make use of all available data, a system that integrates Web data sources must access all available sources and must deal with the poor quality of the results.

Due to autonomy, source accessibility varies. Some sources allow full query capability, some provide only simple HTML-forms. Thus, not all available data can actually be used to answer queries. Source quality depends on source accessibility.

Also due to source autonomy, sources tend to be heterogeneous in various aspects: Sources use different data models, have different semantics, such as attribute names, different scope, different structures, etc. This heterogeneity decreases the quality of an integrated result. For instance, source attributes may be mapped incorrectly to attributes of the integrated result or integrity constraints of two sources may be contradicting.

Finally, technical reasons diminish the quality of data sources and the quality of integrated results: Sources usually present their data as an HTML-document. The structure of the result is confined to the ability of HTML to represent data. Because HTML is a layout-oriented language it is not adequate—to describe contents, it only describes the representational structure. Also, an intrinsic reason for diminished quality is the fact that data transfer is not immediate but via some network and HTTP protocol. Users must wait for data; the longer a user must wait, the lower is the perceived quality of the information. Finally, data on the Web is used by an international audience. Apart from the different perception of information quality by each individual, what is qualitatively good for some people is poor for others. Recognizing and identifying these and further quality issues is a first step towards quality-driven query answering in integrated information systems.

1.3 Problem Definition

This thesis addresses the problem of satisfyingly answering user queries against a given global schema of an integrated information system. Given a set of data sources and an information demand from a user, we develop methods for information quality reasoning to (i) identify the best sources to answer the query, (ii) efficiently and effectively combine those sources to a best plan, and (iii) integrate the plan results in the best possible way. We divide this general problem statement of quality-driven query answering into several subproblems:

Description of data sources and user queries. Users pose queries against the global, integrated schema of the integrated information system. To successfully match data sources to these user queries, both must be described in a compatible way. Source descriptions must be flexible enough to bridge as many types of heterogeneity as possible, so that as many sources as possible can be included in the system. User queries must be expressed in a way that enables a system to match them to appropriate sources.

Information integration. Data from autonomous and heterogeneous sources may overlap in the real world entities they represent and in the data they provide about them. Therefore, an integrated information system must be able to identify different representations of the same entity, and must resolve conflicts in the actual data.

Definition of query plan and result. To be able to respond to user queries in a meaningful and useful way, it is necessary to define what must be in the result, how it can be obtained, and how we represent the query result.

Data model issues, such as the granularity of the result, and representational issues, such as the format of the result, play an important role.

Definition of information quality. We interpret terms like "satisfying answer" and "best results " in the general problem statement as a query response of high information quality (IQ). To assess and maximize the information quality of an answer, an IQ-measure is necessary.

Assessment of IQ-criteria. Most IQ-criteria are difficult to assess. Some criteria are highly subjective like "understandability", the scores for others are hidden by the source like "completeness", some scores are outdated quickly, etc. To have IQ-scores ready for IQ-reasoning, a general assessment methodology is necessary.

Merging IQ-criteria. To obtain answers to user queries it is often necessary to query multiple data sources and combine the results. To calculate IQ-scores of the combined result, the individual IQ-scores of the sources must be combined by some merge-function. The merged scores should reflect the quality of the combined data as accurately as possible.

Multiple criterion ranking. We assess sources and plans with multiple IQ-criterion scores. The criteria are measured in different ranges, units, and scales. Additionally, a user weighting may assign different importance to criteria. To determine a ranking of sources or plans or to find the best source or plan, the scores must be aggregated to an overall quality score.

Efficient and effective planning. Once the sources are described, the IQ-scores are assessed, and the user query is stated, we must efficiently find the best plan or set of plans to answer the query. The plan should be effective, in that it optimizes the information quality of the result, possibly under a cost constraint. The algorithms to find these plans should be as efficient as possible.

We address and solve each of these problems during the course of this thesis.

1.4 Thesis Outline

The main contribution of this thesis is the application of IQ-reasoning to the problem of query answering in integrated information systems. Parts I and II introduce these two aspects respectively, Part III combines both under different planning paradigms. Here, we outline the thesis by summarizing each chapter and citing publications where these ideas and results have been presented.

Part I – Querying the Web

Chapter 1: Introduction This chapter has motivated and stating the problem of satisfyingly answering user queries in integrated information systems. Data sources on the Web are particularly prone to display poor information quality, making it necessary to analyze and improve the information quality of query results in integrated systems. We divided this general problem into several subproblems, which will be solved in the course of this thesis.

Chapter 2: Integrating Autonomous Information Sources We define the architecture in more detail in and introduce their components—mediators and wrappers. The chapter presents the universal relation as a means to describe sources participating in such a system and to formulate user queries against the system. Furthermore, it describes application domains that serve as examples throughout the thesis.

Part II – Information Quality

Chapter 3: Information Quality Criteria We claim that user needs might be expressed by a set of information quality criteria, and that user satisfaction can be expressed by determining information quality scores for each criterion for the information at hand. The chapter presents a comprehensive list of IQ-criteria with definitions and assessment methods. This chapter benefits from contributions in [96] and [97].

Chapter 4: Quality Ranking Methods To aggregate multiple criteria scores an integrated information system must solve the *multi-attribute decision-making* (MADM) problem. The goal of MADM is to find a total ranking of "entities"—in our case data sources and query plans—based on scaled scores for multiple, weighted criteria. Chapter 4 presents this problem, along with five methods to solve it. The chapter discusses advantages and disadvantages of the methods for the particular problem of query answering and compares the methods through a detailed analysis. In [90] and [92] we presented some of the contributions of this chapter. The ranking methods of this chapter are an important tool for the algorithms of Chapter 5.

Part III – Quality-driven Query Answering

Chapter 5: Quality-driven Query Planning This chapter integrates query planning and information quality reasoning. We define the problem of finding the qualitatively best plans for a user query using multiple IQ-criteria. To this end, we develop a quality model for query plans, which mimics cost models in conventional query optimizers. A three-phase approach selects the best plans after a conventional planning phase. Then, the chapter presents an improved approach, which integrates the phases of the first algorithm into a single phase. This approach uses a branch & bound algorithm using quality scores as bounds. Our evaluation shows a high speed-up compared to existing algorithms. The two approaches were presented in [95] and [71], respectively.

Chapter 6: Query Planning Revisited We revisit our conventional model of query planning and uncover shortcomings. To adapt this model to real world situations and enable more powerful planning, we introduce three new merge operators to combine sources in plans—the join-merge, the left outerjoin-merge, and the full outerjoin-merge operators. Using these operators, we shift the goal of query planning from finding a set of best plans to finding the best set of plans, enabling algorithms to find a single, globally optimal solution, instead of multiple, locally optimal plans. The last section of this chapter redefines query plans using the new operators and establishes the search space of all plans.

Chapter 7: Completeness of Data Following the new query planning paradigm, this chapter concentrates on the completeness criterion. This chapter formally defines completeness as a combination of coverage measuring the number of real world entities represented in a source, and density measuring the amount of data per represented entity. Completeness is one of the most important IQ-criteria for the integration of Web information systems—gaining high completeness is a main goal of integration. We show how to calculate completeness of query plans, i.e., how to calculate completeness across the new merge operators. Finally, the chapter shows several properties of the measures that allow an algebraic reordering of the operators for conventional query optimization. The completeness criterion was dealt with thoroughly in [93] and [91].

Chapter 8: Completeness-driven Query Optimization This chapter covers the problem of maximizing the completeness of responses to user queries. First, the chapter introduces a cost model and formally defines the problem of maximizing completeness under a cost constraint, and it shows that the problem is NP-complete. The chapter studies several special cases of the problem, gives algorithms for each and shows the performance of the algorithms with the help of simulation experiments. The chapter presents results published in [136] and [94].

Part IV – Discussion

Chapter 9: Conclusion The final chapter summarizes and discusses the main contributions of this thesis. Additionally, we suggest further research problems where IQ-reasoning is helpful. The chapter concludes with an appeal to let IQ-reasoning pervade integrated information systems.

2 Integrating Autonomous Information Sources

Emerging network technologies have made a profound impact on the design of information systems. On the one hand, data now can be partitioned and duplicated across a local or world wide network forming distributed database management systems. On the other hand, data can be integrated from different autonomous sources. Such sources may be heterogeneous in their data model, their schema, their structure, etc. The goal of an integrated information system is to allow users integrated, read-only, and run-time access to the data of multiple sources, hiding distribution and heterogeneity. Figure 2.1 shows the general layout of such a system. Multiple data sources are connected to an integrated information system. Users pose queries against this system. Because data is stored locally at the sources, the system must distribute the query appropriately across them. The sources return data on request to the integrated system. Thereby, the integrated information system must solve the following problems, among others:

- Sources are be technically, syntactically, and structurally heterogeneous.
- The integrating system must provide a homogeneous, single user interface to enable users to pose queries.
- The integrating system must be able to match a user query with appropriate sources using source descriptions.

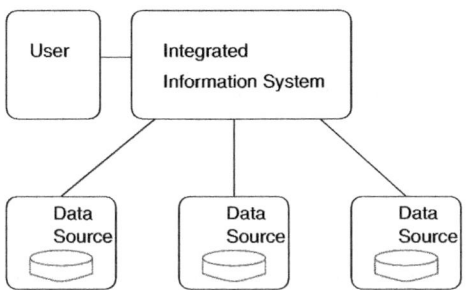

Fig. 2.1. The general architecture of an integrated information system

In the following sections, we introduce mediator-based information systems as one architecture for such a system. First, we describe the general architecture consisting of a mediator and wrappers to access sources. Then,

F. Naumann: Quality-Driven Query Answering, LNCS 2261, pp. 11-25, 2002.

we concentrate on the tasks of the mediator and describe the global schema of the mediator, and our solution to source description and user query formulation. Finally, we characterize data overlap between the sources, present possible applications for integrated information systems, and review related work.

2.1 The Mediator-Wrapper Architecture

The mediator-wrapper architecture was proposed by Wiederhold to allow integrated access to multiple, autonomous data sources (see Figure 2.2) [133]. Because the sources are autonomous, they may be distributed across a network and heterogeneous in technical, syntactical, and semantical aspects. A mediator-based information system comprises wrappers, which hide technical and syntactical heterogeneity from the mediator, and a mediator, which additionally hides semantical heterogeneity from the user.

Data sources store their data in different ways, for instance, in a database or as flat files. The data is exported over the Internet through a query interface. Each data source is wrapped by one or more source-specific wrapper components, which offer a query interface hiding the particular data model, access path, and interface technology of the source. Wrappers are used by a *mediator*, which offers users an integrated access through its global schema. The user poses queries against the global schema of the mediator, the mediator distributes the query to appropriate wrappers. The wrappers transform the queries so they are understandable and executable by the data source they wrap, collect the results, and return them to the mediator. Finally, the mediator integrates the results as a user response.

In this thesis we concentrate on the tasks of the mediator. Wrapper construction and deployment are discussed for instance in [114, 116]. We base our approach on the relational model as canonical data model, i.e., wrappers export a local relational schema, the mediator stores a global relational schema. We assume the global schema to be given. Schema integration, i.e., the task of finding a global schema, given a set of local schemata, is discussed for instance in [8, 55].

2.2 The Universal Relation

Users of a mediator-based information system communicate with the mediator by posing queries against its global schema. We assume that this schema consists of relations and attributes. Relations store tuples that represent real world entities. A tuple consists of a set of attribute values, one of which is a globally consistent and unique ID—the primary ID. Thus, if two data sources store tuples with the same ID, the tuples represent the same real world entity. The values of the other attributes need not be consistent across sources.

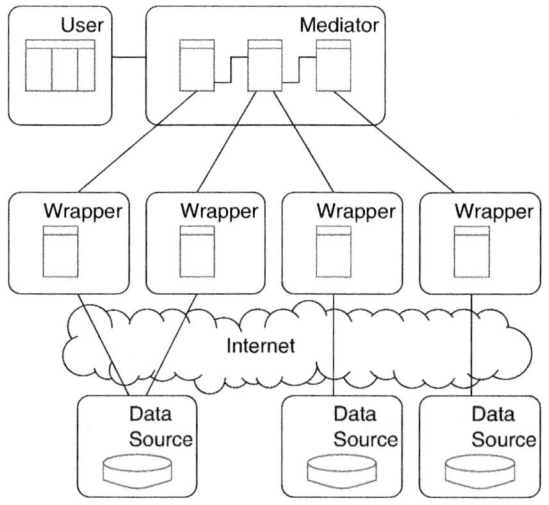

Fig. 2.2. The mediator-wrapper architecture

We call the set of tuples of a relation R the *extension* of R, and the set of attributes of R the *intension* of R. The extensions of relations of the global schema do not exist physically at the mediator, but reside at the participating data sources.

Relations may contain foreign ID-attributes, thus forming relationships between entities. Due to the autonomy of the sources, we can make no assumptions about referential integrity. For the same reason, we cannot require that ID-attributes are keys from the mediators point of view—the sources may store conflicting data about an entity. Together we have three disjoint types of attributes: primary IDs, foreign IDs, and ordinary attributes. To reflect the reality of many Web data sources, we allow all attribute values other than the ID to be `null`. A `null` value denotes missing or unknown data.

Example 2.2.1. Figure 2.3 shows an exemplary global schema at the mediator. It contains three relations, each with an underlined primary ID, and two relationships, which we identify by using the same attribute names. So for instance, attribute a_3 in relation R_1 is a foreign ID for the primary ID of R_2. This global schema serves as an example throughout the thesis.

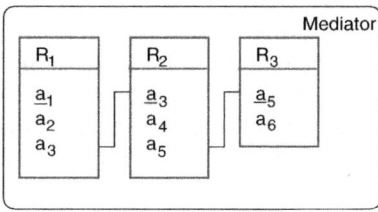

Fig. 2.3. The global schema of the mediator

We propose the universal relation as a means to describe sources and user queries. The original universal relation model "aims at achieving complete access path independence in relational databases by relieving the user of the need for logical navigation among relations" [78]. Instead of revealing the global schema with its relations to the user, the relations are combined to a single, universal relation. The access path independence holds twofold for integrated information systems: First, the user must no longer formulate joins between relations, the joins are implicit in the universal relation. Second, the user need not specify which data sources are used to fill the global relations with data. The sources are selected automatically in the planning process.

Definition 2.2.1 (Universal Relation). *Let A be the set of all attributes of the global schema, i.e., the union of all attributes of global relations. Then the universal relation UR is the relation consisting of all attributes A.*

Following Maier et al., we make the usual *universal relation scheme assumption* and *unique role assumption* for the universal relation [78].

Definition 2.2.2 (Universal Relation Scheme Assumption). *If an attribute name appears in two or more places in the global schema, it refers to the same property of real world entities in each place.*

Simply put, the universal relation scheme assumption ensures that attribute names are not homonyms. E.g., an attribute 'volume' in a global schema of a stock information system cannot be used for both stock trading volume and company turnover. Renaming attributes and adapting source wrappers accordingly can ensure this assumption.

Definition 2.2.3 (Unique Role Assumption). *For each set of attributes there is a unique relationship between them.*

The unique role assumption is more restrictive. It states that the graph of the global schema cannot be cyclic. So for instance, relation R_3 of our example cannot additionally include any of the attributes $a_1 - a_4$. Such cycles can be resolved by replacing one of the attributes in the cycle with two distinct attributes in the global schema of the mediator. Also, the unique role assumption implies that the graph of the global schema is *connected*. That is, all relations must be interconnected by ID–foreign ID relationships. Under these assumptions the extension of UR is clear without ambiguity. A full discussion on universal relations and their implications is in [126].

We use the concept of the universal relation (i) to describe sources and (ii) as a user interface to formulate queries. We define both aspects as subsets of the attributes of the universal relation in the following sections. This approach restricts our model to simple yet expressive source descriptions and user queries.

Our method of source description is expressive enough to cover most Web data sources as we show by typical examples for integration applications.

Simultaneously, our source descriptions are simple enough to avoid notorious query planning problems that arise when sources can be expressed as views containing joins.

The universal relation as a query interface is expressive enough to allow the same user queries as they would be posed to the Web sources themselves through HTML-forms. Simultaneously, the interface is simple enough to allow casual users to formulate queries. The user only selects a set of attributes and possibly specifies some selection conditions; joins between the underlying relations are included automatically.

To represent the universal relation, the underlying relations, sources providing data for the relations, and user queries, we present the *UR-tableau*. A UR-tableau is a table similar to the table of the universal relation *UR* itself and is shown in Table 2.1.

Table 2.1. The UR-tableau

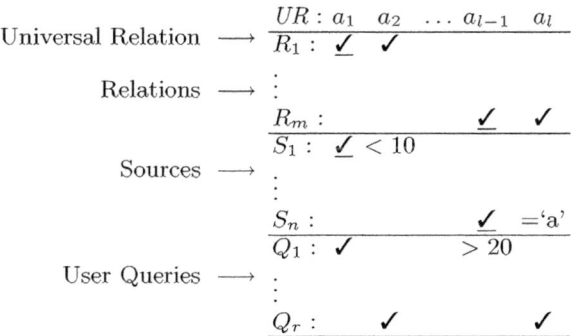

The columns of a UR-tableau represent the attributes of *UR*. The rows however do not represent tuples but rather entire tuple sets. The tuples represented by relation R_i are shown as a row R_i where all attributes of the relations are marked '✓' in the corresponding column. ID-attributes are underlined: '✓'. The tuples represented in a source S_i are shown as a row S_i, again with '✓' marks for the attributes that are exported by the source. Again, we underline ID-attributes. Additionally, we can include conditions on attributes of the sources. Instead of marking the attribute in the UR-tableau, we note the condition in the corresponding column. A condition implies a mark. Finally, the tuples requested by a user query are represented in the same way as sources. In the following sections, we discuss these concepts in more detail and give examples.

Example 2.2.2. Table 2.2 shows the UR-tableau with attributes $a_1, \ldots, a_6$, and relations R_1, R_2, and R_3, corresponding to the global schema of Figure 2.3.

Table 2.2. UR-tableau combining three relations

UR	a_1	a_2	a_3	a_4	a_5	a_6
R_1 :	✓	✓	✓			
R_2 :			✓	✓	✓	
R_3 :					✓	✓

2.2.1 Source Description

The global schema exists only virtually; data is physically scattered over a set of distributed and heterogeneous data sources. We cannot expect that those sources conform to the structure of the global schema. Nor is it feasible to adapt the global schema whenever new sources are added or sources cease to exist. An easy plug-in and plug-out of data sources is of utmost importance in a highly dynamic environment, such as the WWW. The interfaces of the sources might range from simple HTML-forms, to a CORBA interface, or a full SQL-interface. Wrappers take care of these technical heterogeneities and export data understandable by the mediator and conforming to the global schema of the mediator.

To enable this flexibility, we model sources as views on the global schema. This approach is called the local-as-view approach as opposed to the global-as-view approach, where relations of the global schema are modeled as views against the schemata of the sources. For convenience we use the term 'source' but usually mean the corresponding source view on UR describing the source. We assume that a source exports attributes of only one global relation. If a source provides data for different global relations, we model this source as two or more different views. It is not necessary that a source exports the entire set of attributes of a relation—we only require the ID-attribute. The view may contain selections on the attribute values:

Definition 2.2.4 (Source view). *Let UR be the universal relation with attribute set A, and let R be a relation of the global schema with attribute set $A_R \subseteq A$. Then a source S for R exporting attribute set A_S with $A_S \subseteq A_R$ is described as*

$$S[A_S] \leftarrow R[A_R], \ C,$$

where C is a conjunction of selection conditions on attributes $a_i \in A_S$. Conditions have the form "$a_i \ \theta \ const$", where $\theta \in \{<, >, \leq, \geq, =\}$.

Of course, we do not require that different sources define views on different global relations. Instead, many sources may feed data for the same relation, i.e., we assume a one to many relationship between relations and sources.

The local-as-view approach relieves us of the problem of schema integration [70]. Instead of integrating a schema from the local schemata of the data sources in a bottom-up fashion, we can assume that a global schema suiting the users is given. Thus, there is no need to integrate given schemata, rather, one must find source providing data for our schema in a top-down fashion.

Example 2.2.3. Table 2.3 shows the UR-tableau of the previous example, with five sources that provide data for *UR*. Sources must have a mark for exactly one ID-attribute, and further marks only for attributes of the same relation. We can see that sources S_1 and S_2 provide data for R_1, sources S_3 and S_4 for R_2, and source S_5 for R_3. The descriptions of S_3 and S_4 specify a selection on a_4. Note that some sources do not export all attributes of a relation.

Table 2.3. Universal relation with five sources.

UR	a_1	a_2	a_3	a_4	a_5	a_6
R_1 :	✓	✓	✓			
R_2 :			✓	✓	✓	
R_3 :					✓	✓
S_1 :	✓	✓	✓			
S_2 :	✓	✓				
S_3 :				✓ > 10		
S_4 :				✓ > 50	✓	
S_5 :					✓	✓

2.2.2 User Queries

A user query Q is a set of attributes from *UR*, where attributes possibly carry selection conditions.

Definition 2.2.5 (User Query). *Let A be the set of attributes of the universal relation UR. Then a user query is*

$$Q[A_Q] \leftarrow UR, C,$$

where $A_Q \subseteq A$ and C is a conjunction of selection conditions on attributes $a_i \in A_Q$. Conditions have the form "$a_i \; \theta \; const$", where $\theta \in \{<, >, \leq, \geq, =\}$.

When formulating a query, the user needs not perceive the underlying relations of *UR*. Note that attributes can be selected from the entire set and are not restricted to a certain relation like sources views. Users can arbitrarily select attributes of *UR* and add selection conditions. As Gupta pointed out recently, most users of commercial Web sites are unwilling or unable to formulate complex queries and joins [54]. Using *UR* as user interface has the advantage that queries are easy to formulate using a Query-By-Example interface. In particular, no joins have to be formulated. The restrictions implied by the universal relation facilitate the explanation of the main ideas of this thesis, because they restrict the set of possible queries: No relation occurs more than once in a query, only predefined joins are used, there are no conditions on attributes that are not projected, etc. Even though such complex queries do occur, they are not common in real life situations. Maier et al.

argue that users have in mind basic relationships for every set of attributes
[78]. These relationships are reflected in the design of the universal relation.

Example 2.2.4. Table 2.4 shows the previous UR-tableau with four exemplary user queries. User queries can have marks on any attribute of the UR-
tableau.

Table 2.4. Universal relation with three user queries.

UR	a_1	a_2	a_3	a_4	a_5	a_6
$Q_1:$		✓		✓		
$Q_2:$	✓	< 10		✓		✓
$Q_3:$	✓	> 10		< 40		
$Q_4:$	✓				✓	

When answering user queries, we make assumptions regarding the special
semantics of the queries. We assume that users of integrated information
systems have—among others—three requirements (R.1, R.2, R.3) and we
present three corresponding concessions/relaxations (C.1, C.2, C.3).

R.1 The user expects only *correct* results, i.e., only tuples where all selection
predicates hold true. For example, a user of a search engine expects *only*
such Web pages that contain the specified keywords.

C.1 The user accepts tuples where attribute values are *close* to their selection
condition. For example, a user querying for cars with a price lower then
$10,000 might also find cars for $10,500 agreeable in the result. Or the
results of a search engine can be extended by allowing their plurals or
using a thesaurus.

R.2 The user expects the result to be *extensionally complete*, i.e., contain
all correct tuples accessible by the integrated system. A user of a stock
information system asking for quotes with a day trade volume of more
than 1 billion expects *all* quotes for which this is true.

C.2 The user accepts *extensionally incomplete* answers in the presence of
constrained resources. If, for any reason, the extensionally complete answer cannot be returned, the best possible answer should be returned.
We define the term "best" later. A user of a search engine usually does
not demand the entire result set but is satisfied with, say, ten Web pages.
However, the result should consist of the Web pages best matching the
keywords of the query.

R.3 The user expects the result to be *intensionally complete*, i.e., contain all
attributes of the query and contain non-`null` values in all the attributes.
For example, a user of a stock information system asking for stock quotes
of certain companies expects tuples where no data is missing.

C.3 The user accepts *intensionally incomplete* answers or answers with *missing values*—a partial answer is better than no answer. A user of a stock

information service asking for companies whose stock quotes have risen more than 10 percent today along with a company profile is at least partially satisfied with tuples without the profile. Of course, those tuples for which the profile *is* available should be listed first, but others might still be a helpful part of the result.

Consider a query against a search engine on the Web. A user enters a keyword and typically receives 10 links to Web pages that are ranked highest among, say 10,000 links of the result. R.1 requires that only Web pages appear in the result that actually contain the keyword. C.1 would allow pages that contain not the exact keyword but a synonym or the plural form. R.2 requires all Web pages matching the keyword. This is usually not possible, because search engines are unable to keep up with the size and growth of the Web. However search engines are capable of returning an excessive amount of pages. C.2 takes this fact, and the inability of the user to scan 10,000 pages in a reasonable amount of time, into account. Instead of the complete result, C.2 asks for the best results. For search engines best results are the results that are most relevant to the user. Finally, R.3 requires all attributes of the query to appear in the result. So if a user asked for the language of the result pages, a search engine should return this information. C.3 concedes that this is not possible if the search engine does not store such data.

In this thesis we ignore concession C.1 and only return tuples that are correct. Although the integration of fuzzy correctness into our model of source description and user query processing as suggested by the concession is entirely possible, it is beyond the scope of this thesis.

Our query planning mechanisms take the other requirements and concessions into account (i) when deciding which sources should participate in answering the query, and (ii) when deciding how to combine the participating sources.

2.3 Information Overlap

Simultaneous gathering of data from multiple sources bears two advantages: We collect more data, and we collect more detailed data. Consider integrating data from several Web search engines. Search engines take keywords as a query and return URLs (links) together with some information about the linked Web page, such as title and size. Usage of more than one search engine covers larger parts of the Web and thus provides more links; for those links that are provided by more than one engine, we can hope for complementing attributes, i.e., one source returns the size of the linked Web page, another the language of the page, etc.

Generally speaking, data sources overlap in two ways: extensionally and intensionally. The extensional overlap between two sources is the set of real world entities that are represented in both sources. The intensional overlap between two sources is the set of attributes both sources provide.

Example 2.3.1. Consider the sources of Table 2.3 (page 17). Sources S_1 and S_2 extensionally overlap in those tuples where the value for a_1 is the same. Intensionally they overlap in attributes a_1 and a_3. Data conflicts arise for values of a_3 when the two sources store different values for the same real world entity identified by a_1. The extensional overlap of S_1 and S_3 are the tuples that have the same value for a_3, their intensional overlap is only a_3.

To make use of overlap and to integrate data in a meaningful and useful way, we must recognize identical entities represented in different sources (object identification), and we must be able to resolve any data conflicts between values (conflict resolution).

2.3.1 Object Identification

Integrating data from different sources requires that different representations of identical real world entities are identified as such [62]. This process is called object identification. Object identification is difficult, because the available knowledge about the objects under consideration may be incomplete, inconsistent, and sparse. A particular problem occurs if no natural IDs exist. For instance, the URL of a Web page is a natural ID for the page. A meta-search engine can use the URL of reported hits to find and integrate duplicates. On the other hand, a used car typically has no natural ID. An integrated information system for used cars has no easy way of finding identical cars being advertised in different data sources.

Object identification in the absence of IDs, which is essentially the same problem as duplicate detection, record linkage, or object fusion [98, 100, 105], is typically approached by statistical methods, for instance, using rough set theory [139]. To avoid the difficulties of object identification, we require that each tuple in a source has a unique ID-attribute, and that tuples gathered from different sources are identical if and only if their ID is identical. Although this requirement may seem strong, it is true for many domains: Web pages have the URL, stocks have a ticker symbol, books have an ISBN, persons have a passport number, etc.

2.3.2 Conflict Resolution

Once different tuples have been identified as representing the same entity, the data about them can be integrated. In general, a result, which is integrated from tuples of different sources, contains tuples where

1. some attribute value is not provided by any of the sources,
2. some attribute value is provided by exactly one source,
3. some attribute value is provided by more than one source.

In the first case, it is obvious how the result is merged—because the sources do not provide a value, the tuple in the result has no value either. In the second case, there is also no data conflict; thus, when constructing the result, the one attribute value can be used for the result tuple. Depending on the type of attribute and the type of sources, the fact that the data is missing in some sources can be taken into account as well, when determining the final attribute value.

The third case demands special attention. Several sources compete in filling the result tuple with an attribute value. If all sources provide the same value, that value can be used in the result. If this is not the case, there is a data conflict and a *resolution function* must determine what value shall appear in the result table.

Definition 2.3.1 (Resolution function). *Let D be an attribute domain and $D^+ := D \cup \bot$, where $\bot$ represents the null value. A resolution function f is an associative function $f : D^+ \times D^+ \to D^+$ with*

$$f(x,y) := \begin{cases} \bot & \text{if } x = \bot \text{ and } y = \bot \\ x & \text{if } y = \bot \text{ and } x \neq \bot \\ y & \text{if } x = \bot \text{ and } y \neq \bot \\ g(x,y) & \text{else} \end{cases}$$

where $g : D \times D \to D$. Function g is an internal associative resolution function.

Internal resolution functions are of various types, depending on the type of attribute, the usage of the value, and many other aspects [64, 137]. A simple resolution function might concatenate the values and annotate them with the source that provided the value. Especially conflicts in textual attributes may be resolved in this way. Here, the integration is not completely transparent, and users are given the opportunity to resolve the conflict by their own means. Notice that resolution functions need not only depend on the two conflicting attribute values. A resolution function could additionally depend on some date attribute of the sources and favor the most recent value.

In this thesis we do not develop resolution functions for the various attributes and attribute types. Instead, we assume a resolution function to be given whenever data conflicts occur.

2.4 Applications

We present two application domains in more detail, which we use to guide intuition and to show applicability of our approach throughout the thesis. Our examples draw from the world of search engines and stock information systems.

2.4.1 Meta-search Engines

Meta-search engines, such as MetaCrawler [82] or SavvySearch [118], are systems that integrate existing search engines. The global schema of a meta-search engine has only one relation. We show the corresponding UR-tableau in Table 2.5. The global ID of this relation is the URL of Web pages; other attributes include title, description, size, etc. Search engines, such as AltaVista [2] or Google [48], are each represented by a view. National search engines, such as Web.de [130], are modeled as views with a selection on the language of a Web page.

Table 2.5. Universal relation for a meta-search engines

UR	URL	title	descr.	date	size	lang.	categ.	rank
R_1:	✓	✓	✓	✓	✓	✓	✓	✓
Google:	✓	✓	✓		✓		✓	
AltaVista:	✓	✓	✓			✓		
Web.de:	✓	✓	✓			'= ger.'		✓

2.4.2 Stock Information Systems

A *meta stock information system* typically comprises more than one relation. For instance, many services combine stock data with company profiles in the global schema. We show the corresponding UR-tableau in Table 2.6. Examples for Web sources providing stock data are the Web servers of the stock exchanges, for instance the New York Stock Exchange or the London Stock Exchange servers [99, 77], online brokers, such as e*trade [40], and Internet portals, such as the Yahoo or AltaVista finance pages [3, 135]. Also, there are many online sources for company profiles, such as Merrill Lynch or Hoovers [81, 57]. Typically, these sources take the company name as input and return recent financial analysis of the company, press releases, and the like.

Table 2.6. Universal relation for an integrated stock information service

UR	symb.	quote	date	high	low	vol.	name	profile	news
R_1:	✓	✓	✓	✓	✓	✓	✓		
R_2:							✓	✓	✓
NYSE:	✓	✓	✓	✓	✓	✓	✓		
e*trade:	✓	✓	✓	✓	✓	✓	✓		
Yahoo:	✓	✓	✓			✓	✓		
Hoovers:							✓	✓	
Merrill Lynch:							✓	✓	✓

2.5 Related Work

Related work for this chapter draws from two areas—designing an architecture for distributed information systems and describing autonomous sources wrt. a global data model and schema.

2.5.1 Architectures for Distributed Information Systems

Özsu and Valduriez identified three dimensions of distributed information systems [104]:

- The degree of distribution across a network, such as local area network or the Internet. For this thesis the distribution and underlying network are not important[1].
- The degree of autonomy of the local sources. In this thesis we assume total autonomy of the local sources, i.e., the sources determine what data they export, how they export it, and of what quality the data is.
- The degree of heterogeneity of the local sources. Due to their autonomy, we assume sources to be heterogeneous. In this thesis we do not deal with heterogeneity other than suggesting the universal relation as a means to describe sources and user queries. Wrappers hide further heterogeneity.

To take into account these new dimensions for database systems, the architecture of such systems changed from the three level architecture for centralized DBMS, also known as the ANSI/SPARC architecture [125], to a five level architecture for federated DBMS [120]. The two additional schema levels allow for transformation and filtration of the data from local sources, so they can be integrated according to a global, federated schema. Sheth and Larson give an overview of architectures for federated database systems [120]. The authors give a taxonomy of federated systems with the main distinction of whether there is a federated schema. Leser suggests to expand their classification including mediator-based information systems as federated information systems with a federated schema, comprising non-database components with restricted capabilities and read-only access [70]. These properties apply to the integrated information systems discussed in this thesis.

The mediator-wrapper architecture was proposed by Wiederhold as a conceptual framework for the integration of distributed and heterogeneous data sources [133]. The tasks of the different components were substantiated for the project on intelligent information integration (I3) [5]. It has since found broad acceptance in many research projects.

---

[1] In fact, all results apply to multiple databases on one machine.

2.5.2 Source Description

Many research projects embrace the problem of integrating autonomous data sources. The Stanford-IBM Manager of Multiple Information Sources (TSIM-MIS) [22], the Information Manifold (IM) [75], and the Services and Information Management for decision Systems (SIMS) [6] are prominent examples.

To integrate data sources we must describe (i) their content and (ii) their processing capability. Given local schemata of the wrappers or sources and a global schema of the mediator, Hull identified two approaches to source description [58]: the global schema is described as a set of views against the local schemata (global-as-view), or the local schemata are described as views against the global schema (local-as-view). With the help of views, we are able to describe both content and capability of sources.

A source description of the TSIMMIS system has the form *head:–tail* where *head* describes objects of the mediator, and *tail* describes conditions that source objects must meet [106]. Thus, the system adapts the global-as-view concept where the global schema is built from the available local schemata.

The IM and the SIMS projects adapt the local-as-view paradigm where the global schema is independent of the source schemata. A source description of the IM has the form $R \subseteq Q$ where R represents tuples returned by a source relation and Q represents tuples obtained by a conjunctive query (view) against the global schema [74]. This approach makes maintenance of systems simple: Building a wrapper involves not much more than formulating the appropriate views—sources can be plugged in and out of the system without interference with the mediator.

Our approach to source description is similar, although we restrict the source views to views against the universal relation. Thus, source description (and user queries) are less powerful, but we avoid the difficult problems of finding correct plans for a query as described by Levy et al. [74]. We chose the local-as-view approach for this thesis, because in the ever changing Web environment high adaptability and an easy plug-in plug-out of sources is necessary. Also, the autonomy of data sources makes it impractical to model the global schema after the sources as the global-as-view approach does. Leser suggests a compromise between the two approaches [70]. Query correspondence assertions match views against the global schema with views against the local schemata.

Allowing `null` values in the relational data model was proposed by Codd [26] as a means to denote an unknown, missing, or non-existent value. Date offers a thorough discussion of opportunities and problems with `null` values [29]. With the pervasion of Web data sources, considering `null` values and unsure or inconsistent values has become more important than ever. For instance, Liu and Ling present a Web data model for partial and inconsistent data [76].

2.6 Summary

In this chapter we established the mediator-wrapper architecture as the basis of our integration approach, we discussed methods to deal with data overlap that occurs when integrating data, and we gave several application examples for our approach. The main contribution of this chapter is our method of using the universal relation both for source description and as a user interface, expressed through the newly introduced UR-tableau. The universal relation constitutes a balance between expressiveness and simplicity that perfectly suits our approach of including information quality reasoning in the integration of autonomous data sources.

3 Information Quality Criteria

Information quality (IQ) is one of the main discriminators of data and data sources on the Web. As we have seen in the previous sections, the autonomy of Web data sources renders it necessary and useful to consider their quality when accessing them and integrating their data.

Low information quality is one of the most pressing problems for consumers of information integrated from autonomous sources. This statement is true for the entire range from casual users of Web information services to decision makers using an intranet to obtain data from different departments. Poor IQ may have considerable social and economic impact [128]. Also, the result of the integration process is directly influenced by data quality. A large company has reported that up to 60 percent of the data integrated to their data warehouse was unusable due to the poor quality of the input data [103]. The autonomy of Web data sources prevents information consumers from directly controlling the quality of the data they receive. Users must resort to analyzing the quality of the data once it is retrieved and use the analysis for future queries. Research has recognized the importance of analyzing information quality for many different applications [128, 112], and many techniques have been proposed to improve and maintain quality of individual data sources [127]. As a result, several projects have emerged to find a measure for information quality.

General definitions for information quality are "fitness for use" [124], "meets information consumers needs" [111], or "user satisfaction" [32]. These definitions are just as non-operational as Pirsigs: "Even though quality cannot be defined, you know what it is" [108]. Rather, we conceive quality as an aggregated value of multiple IQ-criteria. With this definition information quality is flexible regarding the application domain, the sources, and the users, because the selection of criteria can be adapted accordingly. Also, assessing scores for certain aspects of information quality and aggregating these scores is easier than immediately finding a single global IQ-score.

In the following we give a comprehensive set of IQ-criteria with definitions and we review related projects; we examine how and which IQ-criterion scores can be assessed automatically and for which criteria user input is necessary.

F. Naumann: Quality-Driven Query Answering, LNCS 2261, pp. 29–50, 2002.
© Springer-Verlag Berlin Heidelberg 2002

3.1 Information Quality Criteria for the Web

Information quality is a combination of IQ-criteria as defined in the following. These definitions are proposals formulated in the most general way to allow for different interpretation depending on applications, data sources, and users. We point out criteria that play an especially important role for integrated Web information systems. Notice that many criteria are not independent and typically not all criteria should be used at the same time. Rather, an application specific selection of criteria helps to identify qualitatively good data and simultaneously reduces assessment cost. We discuss this issue and give examples after the definitions.

3.1.1 IQ-criteria

We classify IQ-criteria into four sets:

- *Content-related* criteria concern the actual data that is retrieved. The properties represented by these criteria are intrinsic to the data.
- *Technical* criteria measure aspects that are determined by the soft- and hardware of the source, the network, and the user.
- *Intellectual* criteria are subjective aspects of the data source. For calculations we shall later project these properties to properties of the data in the source.
- *Instantiation-related* criteria concern the presentation of the data, i.e, the current instance of the information as it is provided.

After a brief definition and description of each criterion and a discussion on its relevancy for information systems integrating Web sources, we give a short list of synonyms that were used by various authors to express the same criterion. The criteria and synonyms were compiled from [7, 23, 60, 95, 111, 132, 128]. They are summarized in Table 3.2 (page 39).

Content-Related Criteria.

Accuracy is the quotient of the number of correct values in a source and the overall number of values in the source. A value is an instance of an attribute. For our context accuracy is the percentage of data without *data errors*, such as non-unique keys or out of range values. Mohan et al. give a list of possible data errors [85].

Increasing accuracy is a main goal of many research efforts. Accuracy is often used synonymously with data quality, as opposed to information quality. For us, data quality or accuracy is only one aspect of the overall information quality, which includes the entire set of criteria in this list.

Considering the accuracy criterion in a Web information system setting has the same importance as for traditional databases. Accuracy is one of the main intrinsic properties of data. Incorrect data is hard to detect, useless, and in many cases even harmful.

Synonyms: data quality, error rate, correctness, reliability, integrity, precision

Completeness is the quotient of the number of non-null values in a source and the size of the universal relation introduced in Chapter 2. The size of the universal relation is the number of attributes of the universal relation, multiplied with the number of tuples if all available sources were queried. The number of non-null values in a source is then the number of values a source can insert into the universal relation.

In Chapter 7 we analyze this criterion in great depth and apply it to several application domains. In Chapter 8 we perform optimization to maximize completeness.

Completeness is of great importance in information systems that integrate multiple data sources. One of the main goals for integration is to increase completeness: Querying only one source typically gives only one part of the result. Querying another source provides another, possibly overlapping part. The more sources we query, the more complete the result is.

Synonyms: coverage, scope, granularity, comprehensiveness, density, extent

Customer support is the amount and usefulness of human help via email or telephone. This criterion is closely related to the documentation criterion described next. It is one part of an overall help system to guide users in understanding and using data, in effect turning it into information. Depending on the type of support, one part of the measure could be the average waiting time for a response. Another, more difficult part to be assessed, is how useful the help is. For a discussion on the importance of this criterion, see the documentation criterion below, where the same arguments apply.

Documentation is the amount and usefulness of documents with metadata. For Web data sources documentation usually is in the form of "help"-links that lead to Web pages that explain the provided data. A simple measure counts the number of words in the documentation. Issues of usefulness and understandability are already covered by other criteria. We extend the scope of those IQ-scores to the documentation part of the source, e.g., the understandability of the documentation is measured elsewhere.

The importance of the documentation criterion depends on the application: Often the presentation of data is self-describing and it is not necessary to measure how well a source documents its data. For instance, this is the case for search engines. On the other hand, there are domains where integration and use of the source is not possible without good documentation. Molecular biology information sources have great problems with synonyms and homonyms and other types of heterogeneity [69]. Without a good documentation, query results are prone to misunderstanding.

Synonyms: clarity of definition, traceability

Interpretability is the degree to which the information conforms to the technical ability of the consumer. Technical abilities include languages spoken, units understood, etc. A highly interpretable source must also provide clear and simple definitions of all elements of the information. In this sense interpretability is similar to documentation and understandability.

A data source with a high interpretability is more easy to include in a mediated system, but the criterion plays a less important role once the source is successfully wrapped. In integrated information systems, interpretability of a source is not as important as other criteria, because we assume that any interpretability problems are hidden by wrappers and the mediator. The wrappers of a source, specified by a domain expert, can already convert units to suit the user, text can be automatically translated at least to a useful extent, etc. It is then up to the wrapper to present the integrated information in an interpretable way.

Synonyms: clarity of definition, simplicity

Relevancy (or relevance) is the degree to which the provided information satisfies the users need. Relevancy is a standard criterion in the field of information retrieval [117]. There, a document or piece of data is considered to be relevant to the query, if the keywords of the query appear often and/or in prominent positions in the document. That is, word counting techniques guide the relevance measure [52].

The importance of relevancy as a criterion depends on the application domain. For instance, for search engines relevancy is quite important, i.e., returned Web page links should be as relevant as possible, even though this precision is difficult to achieve. For instance, a query for the term "jaguar" at any Web search engine retrieves document links both for the animal and the automobile. If the user had the animal in mind, the links to automobile sites should have been considered as not relevant. The use of ontologies can solve such problem to some extent [31]. In other application domains, relevancy is implicitly high. For instance, a query for IBM stock quotes in an integrated stock information systems only returns relevant results, namely IBM stock quotes. The reason for this discrepancy is the definition of the domain: Search engines have the entire WWW as a domain and thus provide much data that is of no interest to the user. The domain of a stock information system is much more clear cut and much smaller, so a query is less likely to produce irrelevant results.

For our purposes we reduce the relevancy criterion to a correctness criterion. If a result is correct with respect to the user query, we assume that it is also relevant. If it is not relevant, the user query was either incorrect with respect to what the user had in mind, or it was not specific enough.

Synonyms: domain precision, minimum redundancy, applicability, helpfulness

Value-Added is a criterion that measures the amount of monetary benefit the use of the data provides. This criterion is typical for decision-support type of information systems, for which cost-benefit-calculations are undertaken. The value-added criterion must be considered when there is cost involved to obtain the data and when the nature of the data is yet unknown.

Often value-added cannot be attributed to the source of the data, but only to the data itself. A stock information system provides stock quotes, but cannot influence them and thus cannot increase "value-addedness"; a search engine has no influence on how useful its results are. For this reason this criterion is not considered for Web data sources.

Technical Criteria.

Availability of a data source is the probability that a feasible query is correctly answered in a given time range[1]. Availability is a technical measure concerning hardware and software of the source and the network connections between user, mediator, wrappers, and sources. Typically, availability also depends on the time of day and day of the week due to different usage patterns of the data source.

Availability is an important criterion for Web data sources: Query execution in integrated systems is especially vulnerable to low availability, because usually all participating sources of a query execution plan must be available in order for the query to be executed correctly. Availability is influenced by time-of day and week-dependent network congestion; world-wide distribution of servers; highly concurrent usage; denial-of-service attacks; planned maintenance interruptions; etc. In Section 8.2 we pay special attention to the availability criterion and

---

[1] In the following, we assume that a source either delivers its complete response or no response at all. A partial response, which may occur if the system breaks down during transmission, is counted as no response.

propose algorithms that dynamically adapt their optimization strategy in case of an unavailable source.

Synonyms: accessibility, technical reliability, retrievability, performability

Latency is the amount of time in seconds from issuing the query until the first data item reaches the user. If the result of the query is only one data item, e.g., one stock quote, latency is equal to response time (see below).

Latency is an important criterion in Web information system settings for two reasons: Information is sent over the Internet using the internet protocol (IP). This protocol sends data packaged in chunks of up to 64 kilobyte. If the entire response has a larger size, the first package might be displayed before further packages arrive. Additionally, many sources withhold some of the result and only return the first part. For instance, search engines typically return only the first 10 links. If the users desires more results, another query must be submitted. The second reason for the importance of latency is that in many applications the user is only interested in the first part of the data or only in an overview of the result. Again, search engines are a good example. Often, the first 10 results are enough to satisfy the user, especially if the results are ranked well. For many other applications, not the actual result, but the number of results is the only interest of the user. Consider a user querying a stock information system for companies whose stocks have risen more than 50 percent during the last year. In many cases, not the actual companies but their number is of interest.

Synonyms: Often response time and latency are used synonymously.

Price is the amount of money a user has to pay for a query. Commercial data sources usually either charge on a subscription basis for their data or on a pay-per-query or pay-per-byte basis. Often there is a direct tradeoff between price and other IQ-criteria. For example, free stock information services provide stock quotes with some delay (usually 15 minutes) while subscription systems provide the quotes in realtime. Also there may be a hidden cost in retrieving data: Users spend time online paying for the Internet connection and users are exposed to advertisements.

Considering price is important if at least one integrated data source charges money for data. It is common opinion that the World Wide Web has prospered due to its free information services. Information sources earn money by displaying advertisement. Experts predict a change towards high quality data sources that charge money for their services [33], rendering the price criterion more and more important.

Synonyms: query value-to-cost ratio, cost-effectivity

Quality of Service (QoS) is a measure for transmission and error rates of Web sources. A typical problem in QoS research is to guarantee a certain QoS for the transmission of a video or audio stream, so that no interruptions disturb the reception. Thus, the Quality of Service criterion is particularly interesting for sources that provide such streaming video or audio.

Synonyms: performability, throughput

Response time measures the delay in seconds between submission of a query by the user and reception of the complete response from the data source. The score for this criterion depends on unpredictable factors, such as network traffic, server workload etc. Another factor is the type and complexity of the user query. Again this cannot not be predicted, however, it can be taken into account once the query is posed and a query execution plan is developed. Finally, the technical equipment of the information server plays a role as well. However, in WWW settings network delay usually dominates all other factors.

Response time is the main and often sole criterion for traditional database optimizers. Even though for Web data sources it is just one aspect among many other IQ-criteria, it is still of high significance. Because of frequent time-outs and unknown availability of sources, users waiting a long time for a response from a source are more prone to abort the query than database users. This cancelation can be prevented by low latency, which gives users at least some results early on. Another reason for the importance of low response time is the potential competition on the Web. With many alternative sites the users quickly switches from one source to another to find the desired information. An integrated system, such as a meta-search engine, avoids this effect, but must also consider response time when deciding which sources to use to answer a query.

Synonyms: performance, turnaround time, latency

Security is the degree to which data is passed privately from users to the data source and back. Security covers technical aspects, such as cryptography, secure login etc., but also the possibility of anonymization of the user and authentification of the data source by a trusted organization. Most Web data sources publish a privacy policy to show that they are concerned with the topic.

The importance of security is application domain dependent: Users of search engines typically are not concerned about privacy—quite the contrary: The meta-search engine MetaCrawler provides the MetaSpy utility that allows users to watch queries as they are passed to the engine [83]. In other application domains users are very sensitive towards security: Users typically prefer their stock quote lookups to be secure; complex queries against molecular biology information systems can already spell out a valuable idea.

Synonyms: privacy, access security

Timeliness is the average age of the data in a source. The unit of timeliness depends on the application: for some applications seconds are appropriate, for others days are sufficiently precise. Here, the age of data is not the time between creation of the data and now, but the time between the last update or verification of the data and now. For instance, the timeliness of search engines is their update-frequency, i.e., the frequency with which they re-index Web pages, and not the age of the Web page itself. For stock information systems, timeliness is a measure for the delay with which stock quotes are presented. Typical free services have a 15 minute delay between the occurrence of a quote and its delivery to the user.

Timeliness is arguably one of the most important criteria for Web data sources. The main advantage of the Internet over traditional data sources like newspapers or journals is its ability to provide new data instantly and world-widely. A main reason for users to turn to WWW information services is to obtain up-to-date data. For search engines, high timeliness for instance means less dead links, for stock information systems high timeliness allows quicker reactions to changes on the stock market.

Synonyms: up-to-date, freshness, currentness

Intellectual Criteria.

Believability is the degree to which the data is accepted as correct by the user. In a sense, believability is the expected accuracy. Therefore, it can be determined by the same unit as accuracy, but generally, the believability criterion is influenced by many other factors so that a generic "grade" is more appropriate.

When querying autonomous data sources, believability is an important criterion. Apart from simply providing data, a source must convince the user that its data is "accepted or regarded as true, real, and credible" [128].

Synonyms: error rate, credibility, trustworthiness

Objectivity is the degree to which data is unbiased and impartial. The criterion score mainly depends on the affiliation of the information provider. Also, the criterion is strongly related to the verifiability criterion: The more verifiable a source is, the more objective it is. Again, objectivity is measured by some grade as there is no "real" unit for this criterion.

Objectivity is an important criterion if users fear malice of the data source. This fear could be approached by simply not using a data source with low objectivity or at least by verifying the data. For example, search engines display biased data for two reasons: (i) Web pages indexed by the search engine add certain keywords to their page to be ranked higher for searches. A popular example is to repeat the word "sex" thousands of times on a Web page. (ii) Search engines may be paid by Web site providers to intentionally rank their pages higher than others overriding the standard ranking algorithm employed by the search engine. Stock quotes on the other hand can easily be verified, so bias is not likely and thus, objectivity is not an important criterion for that domain.

Reputation is the degree to which the data or its source is in high standing. For instance, the Yahoo stock quote service might have a higher reputation than that of some off shore bank; the CNN news server might have a higher reputation than that of the Phoenix Gazette. Reputation increases with a higher level of awareness among the users. Thus, older, long-established data sources typically have a higher reputation.

The reputation criterion is important for some applications. For instance, we observed that most biologists prefer certain molecular biology sources over others, because of their higher reputation. Also, people tend to trust data from their own institute more than external data, as they also tend to prefer well-known sources.

Synonyms: credibility

Instantiation-Related Criteria.

Amount of data is the size of the query result, measured in bytes. Whenever appropriate, amount can also be measured as the number of result tuples. For instance, the number of links search engines return for a single request typically varies from 10 to 100. When querying a stock information service, for company profiles, amount is the length of the profile in bytes.

The importance of the amount criterion depends on the type of query. In a query for a stock quote of a certain company the amount of data returned is of no importance—it is simply a number. However, in a query for all data on a company including profiles, press releases etc, amount might be quite important.

Synonyms: essentialness

Representational conciseness is the degree to which the structure of the data matches the data itself. Search engines typically have a high conciseness—their main results are lists of links, which are represented as such. Molecular biology information systems on the other hand often have a low conciseness with incomprehensible data formats, many abbreviations, and unclear graphical representations. In our context of a mediator-wrapper architecture, representational conciseness is only of marginal importance. Wrappers extract the data from the sources and restructure them according to the global schema of the mediator. Any representational inconciseness should be caught by the wrapper and hidden from the user. Note however, representational conciseness is a measure for the complexity and stability of a wrapper. The less concise the representation is, the more difficult it is to build a wrapper around the source, to the degree that parts or the entire data cannot be extracted. Low conciseness regarding previous data makes a wrapper highly unstable, i.e, the wrapper must be maintained and updated frequently.

Synonyms: attribute granularity, occurrence identifiability, structural consistency, appropriateness, format precision

Representational consistency is the degree to which the structure of the data conforms to previously returned data. Because we review multiple sources, we extend this definition to not only compare compatibility with previous data but also with data of other sources. Thus, representational consistency is also the degree to which the structure of the data conforms to that of other sources. We assume wrappers to deliver a relational export schema that is always consistent with the global schema against which users query. Hence, representational consistency is a criterion to measure the work of the wrapper measured in seconds necessary to parse files, transform units and scales or translate identifiers into canonical object names.

Synonyms: integrity, homogeneity, value consistency, portability, compatibility

Understandability is the degree to which the data can be easily comprehended by the user. Thus, understandability measures how well a source presents its data, so that the user is able to comprehend its semantic value. Understandability is measured as a grade.

Understandability is only marginally important for the mediated information systems for the same reason as representational conciseness. A wrapper extracts data from the data source and transforms it according to the relational schema of the mediator. Any good or poor understandability is lost in this process. However, there are application domains or types of data, where the understandability score is retained. For instance, the understandability of a news article remains the same, independent of any representational changes. Also, graphics typically are not changed by the wrapper or mediator, so their understandability remains unchanged as well.

Synonyms: ease of understanding

Verifiability is the degree and ease with which the data can be checked for correctness. When data is mistrusted, it should be verified with the help of a, if possible unbiased, third party. Verifiability is high if either the data source names the actual source of the data, or if it points to a trusted third party source where the data can be checked for correctness. Note, that verifiability differs from believability in that verification can find a data correct or incorrect, while belief trusts the data without checking.

Verifiability is an important factor if the mediated system includes sources with a low believability or reputation. Especially Web data sources may suffer low scores in these criteria, because they have not had the time to establish a good reputation.

Synonyms: naturalness, traceability, provability

3.1.2 Criterion Selection for Web Information Systems

From the long list of IQ-criteria only a few should be selected for concrete implementations of a mediated system. The more criteria are selected, the more incomprehensible the source and plan selection process is to the user, and the more difficult IQ-assessment is, but also the more solid is the foundation of IQ-reasoning. The choice, which criteria to use, depends on several factors:

Application As already pointed out for several criteria, some are more important for a particular domain, others less. In Table 3.1 we give exemplary criterion sets for the two applications of our examples.

Users The main goal of using IQ-reasoning is to satisfy the user. Therefore, it
    is important to let users participate in the process of selecting the criteria
    that are used to predict user satisfaction.
Provider A provider of an integrated system can influence the choice of cri-
    teria to implement a certain policy. For instance, a provider might decide
    to offer a free service using only data sources free of charge. Then the
    price criterion is not used, despite the existence of sources with different
    prices.
Assessment A system should use only those IQ-criteria that it can accurately
    assess. If assessment is inaccurate, the criterion is useless and its use can
    even be counterproductive.

Example 3.1.1. We show selected criteria for the two application examples of
mediated information systems introduced earlier. Table 3.1 shows IQ-criteria
for search engines and for stock information systems.

Table 3.1. IQ-criteria for two information system domains.

Search Engine

Accuracy	Quality of the result ordering
Timeliness	Update frequency of the search engine
Availability	Percentage of time the search engine is "up"
Completeness	Percentage of the Web that the search engine has indexed
Latency	Time until first Web link reaches user
Redundancy	Number of redundant links in the search result
Response time	Time until the complete response reaches the user

Stock Information System

Availability	Percentage of time the information system is "up"
Completeness	Percentage of listed companies
Objectivity	Affiliation of source
Price	Amount of money charged per query
Response time	Time until the complete response reaches the user
Security	Privacy facilities of the source
Timeliness	Artificial delay of stock quotes

3.1.3 Related Work

This section reviews several projects concerned with information quality.
Some provide research from a global viewpoint and define IQ in a very general way. Others have focused either on certain quality aspects or on certain
application domains for IQ. All reviewed projects have in common that IQ is
defined as a set of quality criteria, i.e., that quality comprises many facets.
Instead of listing a criterion catalog in each section, we summarize in Table 3.2 the IQ-criteria used by the projects. Actual criterion names slightly
differ, but we have adapted them appropriately.

TDQM. Total Data Quality Management is a project at MIT, aimed at providing an empirical foundation for data quality. Wang and Strong have empirically identified fifteen IQ-criteria regarded by data consumers as the most important [128]. Their framework has already been used effectively in industry and government. To the best of our knowledge their work is the only empirical study in this field, and has thus been used as a research basis for other projects, such as the DWQ project (see below).

DWQ. Data Warehouse Quality (DWQ) is an ESPRIT funded project to analyze the meaning of data quality for data warehouses, and to produce a formal model of information quality to enable design optimization of data warehouses [60]. The approach is based on the empirical studies in [128]. However, the focus lies on data warehouse specific aspects, such as the quality of aggregated data. The authors develop a model for IQ-metadata management in a data warehouse setting.

Notions of Service Quality. Weikum distinguishes system-centric, process-centric, and information-centric criteria [132]. The authors set of criteria was put together in an informal, visionary manner with no claim for completeness. However from our perspective, Weikum does mention several new criteria, such as 'latency', which play an increasingly important role in new information systems, especially in WWW settings. The author discusses each criterion thoroughly, again in an informal manner.

SCOUG. Measurement of the quality of databases was the subject of the Southern California Online User Group (SCOUG) Annual Retreat in 1990. The brainstorming session resulted in a checklist of criteria that fall into ten broad categories [7]. These criteria are the most referenced ones within the database area. Although the focus lies on the evaluation of database performance (including categories like documentation and customer training) its similarity to our quality measures is obvious.

Chen et al. With a focus on Web query processing, Chen et al. propose a set of quality criteria from an information server viewpoint [23]. In their setting, a user can specify quality requirements along with the query. Under heavy workload, the WWW information server must then simultaneously process multiple queries and still meet the quality requirements. To this end, the authors present a scheduling algorithm that is based on time-relevant criteria, such as response time or "network delay". The authors only briefly discuss the other IQ-criteria.

Redman. In his book, intended as a guideline for information managers, Redman justifies the need of considering data quality in almost any organization through many examples [111]. The author gives guidelines on how to recognize poor data quality, how to improve it, and how to maintain quality control measures within an organization.

Redman distinguishes three IQ-criterion categories, each consisting of several criteria. The first aspect comprises quality dimensions as the user perceives the information. The second dimension covers the quality of the actual data, and the third dimension addresses quality issues of presenting the data.

Table 3.2. Criterion catalogs for information quality

Category	IQ Criteria	TDQM [128]	DWQ [60]	Wei-kum [132]	SCOUG [7]	Chen [23]	Red-man [111]
Content-related Criteria	Accuracy	✓	✓	✓	✓	✓	✓
	Completeness	✓	✓	✓	✓	✓	✓
	Customer Support				✓		
	Documentation				✓		
	Interpretability	✓	✓				✓
	Relevancy	✓	✓			✓	✓
	Value-Added	✓			✓		
Technical Criteria	Availability	✓	✓	✓	✓		✓
	Latency			✓		✓	
	Price			✓	✓		
	Quality of service			✓	✓		
	Response time			✓		✓	
	Security	✓	✓	✓			
	Timeliness	✓	✓	✓	✓	✓	✓
Intellectual Criteria	Believability	✓	✓	✓	✓		
	Objectivity	✓					
	Reputation	✓	✓				
Instantiation related Criteria	Amount of data	✓				✓	✓
	Repr. conciseness	✓					✓
	Repr. consistency	✓	✓	✓	✓		✓
	Understandability	✓					
	Verifiability				✓		✓

3.2 Information Quality Assessment

Information quality assessment is the process of assigning numerical values (IQ-scores) to IQ-criteria. An IQ-score reflects one aspect of information quality of a set of data items. Usually this set represents an entire data source, but it might be useful to assign scores to certain parts of data sources as well. We are aware of the difficulties of numerically expressing certain criteria. But because not the absolute IQ-scores are of importance, but rather their relative values, we believe that our numerical approach is reasonable. In this section we show that it is also feasible.

IQ-assessment is rightly considered difficult, and most research approaches to information quality lack methods or even suggestions on how to assess the quality scores in the first place.

1. Many IQ-criteria are of subjective nature and can therefore not be assessed automatically, i.e., independently and without help of the user.
2. Information sources often do not publish useful (and possibly compromising) quality metadata. Many sources even take measures to hinder IQ-assessment, and one must assume that data sources actively find ways to improve the perceived information quality without improving the quality itself.
3. If the amount of data in a source is large, assessment of the entire data set is impeded. In these cases, sampling techniques are necessary, decreasing the precision of the assessed scores [102].
4. Information from autonomous sources is subject to sometimes drastic changes in content and quality.

The most precise source for IQ-scores could be the data sources themselves, if they were willing to accurately assess them. However, this IQ-metadata is rarely available, especially if the source is in competition with other sources. Therefore, methods must be developed that independently assess IQ-metadata in an efficient manner. Assessment should be automated as much as possible but still be as user- or expert-guided as necessary. Users and experts could be independent assessors or the persons that will consume the data.

In the following, we classify IQ-criteria by the source of their IQ-scores. For each class we discuss general IQ-assessment issues and give specialized examples. We regard one valuable source for IQ-scores in more detail: metadata provided by the data sources. Finally, we review related work on IQ-assessment.

3.2.1 An Assessment-Oriented Classification

We identify three classes that partition IQ-criteria according to the possible sources of the criterion scores. Quality of information is influenced by three main factors: the perception of the user (the subject of a query), the data itself (the object of a query), and the process of accessing the data (the predicate of a query). Each of the three can provide IQ-metadata, i.e., each can deliver IQ-scores for certain IQ-criteria.

The user: Arguably, the user is the most important source for IQ-metadata. Ultimately, it is the user who decides whether some data is qualitatively good or not. Users can provide valuable input, especially for subjective criteria like understandability. Instead of the actual user of the data, independent persons might undertake the assessment.

Existing assessment methods *solely* rely on users to provide IQ-scores
[129, 12]. At the same time, obtaining user input is time consuming or
even impossible. We show that user input is only necessary for few criteria.

The data source: For many criteria the data source itself is the origin of IQ-
scores. Sometimes the sources supply criterion scores—voluntarily, such
as the price, or involuntarily, such as completeness. Because the source
provides data, it automatically provides some metadata that can be used
for IQ-scores.

The query process: The process of accessing data is a source for IQ-scores.
Criteria such as response time can be automatically assessed during the
query process without input from the user or from the data source.

The three sources for IQ-metadata correspond to three assessment-oriented
IQ-criteria classes as shown in Figure 3.1.

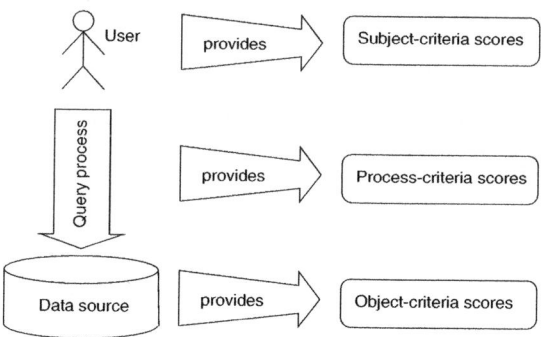

Fig. 3.1. Three sources of IQ-
criterion scores

Subject-criteria: Information quality criteria are subject-criteria, if their
scores can only be determined by individual users based on their personal views, experience, and background. Thus, the source of their scores
is the individual user. Subject-criteria have no objective, globally accepted score.

Object-criteria: The scores of object-criteria can be determined by a careful
analysis of data. Thus, the source of their scores is the data itself.

Process-criteria: The scores of process-criteria can only be determined by the
process of querying. Thus, the scores cannot be fixed, but may vary from
query to query.

Table 3.3 lists all IQ-criteria within their class and gives assessment methods for each criterion. We explain these methods in more detail in the following section.

Table 3.3. Classification of IQ-metadata criteria

Assessment Class	IQ-Criterion	Assessment Method
Subject-Criteria	Believability	user experience
	Concise representation	user sampling
	Interpretability	user sampling
	Relevancy	continuous user assessment
	Reputation	user experience
	Understandability	user sampling
	Value-Added	continuous user assessment
Object-Criteria	Completeness	parsing, sampling
	Customer Support	parsing, contract
	Documentation	parsing
	Objectivity	expert input
	Price	contract
	Security	parsing
	Timeliness	parsing
	Verifiability	expert input
Process-Criteria	Accuracy	cleansing techniques
	Amount of data	continuous assessment
	Availability	continuous assessment
	Consistent representation	parsing
	Latency	continuous assessment
	Quality of service	continuous assessment
	Response time	continuous assessment

3.2.2 Assessment Methods

Assessing IQ-criteria is a difficult task. Assessment should be as precise as possible, but also as practical as possible. Imprecise assessment can either result in retrieval of low quality data or can lead to avoidance of high quality data. Impractical assessment either results in inaccurate assessment or leads to undue assessment time and cost.

– Precision: An IQ-score should reflect reality as precisely as possible. The problem arises first with the definition of the criterion. Only a precisely defined criterion can be assessed precisely. Further problems are distinct to the criterion class:
  – Subject-criteria: Scores for subject-criteria are only precise for individual users, never for an entire group. An obstacle is the amount of time a user will invest for IQ-assessment. The more time a user spends assessing different criteria, the more precise the scores are.
  It is difficult to identify units for subject-criteria. For instance, understandability does not have an obvious unit, other than some grade. The units must be intuitive, uncomplicated, and well-described. Only then is the user able to assign proper and appropriate scores. Also, the range of the criterion scores must be clear to the user. If they are not known to the user, the scores will be askew.

- Object-Criteria: The precision of object-criteria is particularly vulnerable to layout and format changes of the data source, because the scores can only be assessed once the object of the query (the data) has been extracted from the result. Due to the size of many sources, sampling techniques must be used. Their precision strongly depends on the sample size and the sampling technique itself.
- Process-Criteria: Scores of process-criteria are especially prone to imprecision, because the query process depends on many factors, such as the query, the time of day, etc. Typically the precision of the scores declines over time—they are the most precise at the time they are determined.

If the data of a source can be partitioned into sets with heavily diverging IQ-scores, the views describing this source should be split according to this partitioning. Each of the new views then receives individual IQ-scores with a higher precision. A stock information system specializing in new market stocks could be modeled as two views: One view for the new market section, and one view for the rest. The first view in this case would have higher IQ-scores.

- Practicality: An assessment method should be as practical as possible. Inscrutable algorithms for IQ-reasoning are not trusted by users, because their correctness cannot be proven. Any assessment method should by understood by the user and should be easy to adapt to new sources and new requirements.
  - Subject-criteria: Users will not spend much time on IQ-assessment. A simple questionnaire must be enough, possibly with default scores. If users change their mind about the assessment of a source, an update of the scores must also be as practical as possible.
  - Object-criteria: Assessing object-criteria should neither be too costly nor too time consuming, especially if the methods must be applied on a regular basis to keep the scores up-to-date.
  - Process-criteria: For process-criteria, the same arguments apply as for object-criteria, and even more so. Process-criteria are—by definition—assessed during a query process. If this method is too time-consuming, the entire query process is delayed and the user is not satisfied.

Assessing Subject-Criteria. An integrated information system must keep individual IQ-score profiles for each user for all subject criteria. When assessing subject-criteria it is especially important to

- supply users with an exact definition of the criterion they are assessing. The definition should be concise, comprehensible, and non-ambiguous. The definition may be made up of several subcriteria; for example, to define understandability, the subcriteria language, structure, and graphical layout can be mentioned to guide the user.
- give the range the score should be in.
- provide examples of typical good and poor cases to guide the user.

The only way a system can support assessment is by providing default values as guidelines to users. If the user is not willing or able to provide individual scores, the default scores can be used. Either a system administrator provides the default scores, or the average score of other users is given.

In Table 3.3 we mention three methods of assessing subject-criteria—user experience, user sampling, and continuous user assessment. All three methods should be supported by a well-designed questionnaire.

User experience: For the user experience method, users must apply their experience and knowledge about the sources. This may include hear-say, experiences with the source itself, news reports, etc.

User sampling: To apply this method the user must sample results of the data source[2]. By looking at several results the user may be able to find an IQ-score for the criterion to be assessed.

This sampling must only be performed once in a while, either on a regular basis or when the source undergoes relevant changes. A system should support the process by suggesting re-assessment whenever appropriate.

Continuous assessment: Just as with user sampling, users must sample the data by looking at it, reading it, or by actually doing whatever they wanted to do with the data. However, continuous assessment analyzes every data received and not only samples.

This method is by far the most time consuming and least rewarding of the three. It is applied to criteria where the score of one data allows no prediction of future scores, and where it is difficult or even impossible to find representative samples of the data.

Assessing Object-Criteria. Object-criteria scores can be assessed mostly automatically—only an occasional user or expert input may be necessary. In a Web data source setting, the scores of object-criteria can often be obtained by parsing the main page of the source.

Contract: For some criteria, scores may be assessed by considering the terms of the contract or agreement between the source and the information consumer. Usually, price and customer support are determined in some agreement. These terms can be valued by an expert who then assigns scores to the criteria.

Parsing: We distinguish structural parsing and content parsing. Structural parsing is discussed in the following section for process-criteria. Content parsing considers the actual data and other content of the data source. For instance, the presence of a documentation or customer support is gained by searching the data for help links or the like. The security of data may be assessed by analyzing the protocol, by which the data is delivered.

---

[2] Finding appropriate and representative samples is a problem of its own and not covered in this thesis.

Parsing greatly benefits from metadata that is included in the data. Section 3.2.3 discusses several metadata models that are in use today, and how their metadata can be used to assess IQ-scores.

Sampling: Some object-criteria, such as completeness, concern the entire content of the data source. To assess the precise score, the entire content would have to be considered. To avoid this time-consuming and possibly costly task, sampling techniques can be applied. Sampling techniques choose a representative subset of the data and only consider those for quality assessment.

Expert input: A human expert is needed to assess some object-criteria, such as price. The expert should follow a guideline to guarantee precision and comparability of the scores.

Expert input is a method to assess object-criteria despite the fact that an expert is a human and thus prone to assess the scores subjectively. Object-criteria are named so due to the source of their scores, i.e., the object of a user query. But also, criteria that can be assessed only by expert input are still assessed objectively—merely a human expert is needed to find the scores.

Assessing Process-Criteria. Often, process-criteria scores are measured with the help of statistics derived from previous calibration-queries to the data source. Knowledge of the technical equipment and software of the data source can also help determine the criterion scores.

Cleansing techniques: Accuracy or data quality has been subject of several research projects [56, 86, 42]. The impact of data errors on data mining methods and data warehouses gives rise to data cleansing methods. The methods identify and eliminate a variety of data errors. The identification techniques might be used to count errors and thus to assess data quality. Pierce gives a survey of counting methods for data errors [107].

Continuous assessment: Several criteria underlie frequent changes. Some changes depend on time-related aspects. For instance, latency heavily depends on net load and on the time of day. Other criteria like availability additionally depend on hardware and software aspects of the data source.

Continuous assessment measures quality scores at regular intervals. Each new score is added to the history, and statistical methods can provide accurate and timely quality scores. A simple statistical measure is the average score over the entire history. More sophisticated methods may additionally consider the aging of quality scores and add weight to more recently assessed scores.

Parsing: As explained in the previous section, we distinguish content-based and structural parsing. Structural parsing applies to process-criteria. It considers the structure of the data, such as positioning of tables, presence of graphics etc.

3.2.3 Metadata Models for IQ-assessment

Assessment of information quality scores is the process of finding and determining metadata or meta-information. Therefore, we analyze several proposals for metadata for Web sources and how they might be used for IQ-assessment. Information providers have recognized the need to describe the products they offer and provide this metadata. Obviously, this provider-metadata will not directly address IQ, and if it does, there is reason to doubt its correctness. No source admits its data to be outdated or inaccurate. Rather, metadata provided by sources covers aspects of authorship, title, etc. Such particulars can only be evaluated to indirectly find IQ-scores. For example, the creation date of a document reveals its age, the publisher may have a good or poor reputation, etc. The goal of this section is to bridge the gap between IQ-metadata requirements for IQ-assessment and actual metadata that is already provided by many sources.

Proposed Metadata Models. In the following paragraphs we review projects that attempt to set up a common metadata model for Web data and gain general acceptance in the Internet community. We cover the most important projects, and summarize the attributes of these metadata models in Table 3.4. The attribute names slightly differ from project to project and have been adapted appropriately. For a more detailed survey concerning further aspects, such as metadata for multimedia objects etc. see [30].

Dublin Core. The Dublin Core Metadata initiative with participants from many application domains developed a metadata element set, intended to facilitate the discovery of electronic resources [35]. The element set is wide spread across many types of information systems, from digital libraries to museums and many other electronic document collections. Dublin Core is especially wide-spread in HTML-documents where the META tag is used to express Dublin Core element values: `<META NAME="DC.Title" CONTENT="MyTitle">`

STARTS. In the Stanford Proposal for Internet Meta-Searching (STARTS) the authors propose a list of required metadata fields for documents [50]. It is based on the *use attributes* of Z39.50/GILS (see below). The list was developed by researchers and practitioners from large Internet companies in a number of workshops. In 1997 the Dublin Core standard was integrated.

Z39.50. Z39.50 is an ANSI and ISO standard that describes the communication between a client and a metadata server mainly with respect to searching. Originally, it was developed for the communication interoperability of libraries, but today Z39.50 is independent of any application area. A profile specifies how to use the various functions defined by Z39.50 in a specific application area. A profile also specifies which attribute set to use.

The *Attribute Set BIB-1* describes bibliographic metadata and is made up of 100 attributes [138]. The *Profile Global Information Locator Service (GILS)* is not only a means to describe books or datasets, but also to provide data about people, events, meetings, artifacts, rocks etc. [47]. The Z39.50 Profile GILS Version 2 is made up of 91 attributes. In Table 3.4 most of these attributes are summarized as description attribute.

The GILS standard to describe data and data sources is required by law for US government Web servers and is accordingly wide spread and in active use.

DIF. The Directory Interchange Format (DIF) was originally developed to make scientific, US-governmental catalogues describing data groups interoperable [34]. DIF consists of 25 data fields, 6 of them are mandatory. The DIF was designed to allow users of data to understand the contents of a data set. The DIF contains those fields that are necessary for users to decide whether a particular data set would be useful for their needs. DIF today is wide spread in many scientific areas.

Table 3.4. Metadata attribute proposals

Attribute	Dublin Core [35]	STARTS [50]	BIB-1 [138]	GILS [47]	DIF [34]
Title	✓	✓	✓	✓	✓
Author or Creator	✓	✓	✓	✓	✓
Subject and Keywords	✓		✓	✓	✓
Description	✓		✓	✓	✓
Publisher/Distributor	✓		✓	✓	✓
Other Contributor	✓				
Date	✓	✓	✓	✓	✓
Last Review Date					✓
Future Review Date					✓
Resource Type	✓		✓		
Format	✓				
Storage Medium				✓	✓
Resource Identifier	✓	✓	✓	✓	✓
Identifier Type		✓	✓	✓	
Cross References		✓	✓	✓	✓
Source	✓			✓	
Language	✓	✓	✓	✓	
Relation	✓		✓	✓	
Coverage	✓		✓	✓	✓
Rights Management	✓			✓	
Document-text		✓	✓		
Sensor name					✓
Parameter measured					✓
Quality Assurance Method					✓

Matching IQ-criteria and Metadata Models. Having introduced both a number of desired IQ-criterion sets (Section 3.1) and a number of metadata attribute sets currently in use (Table 3.4), the question arises where and how well they meet. Is it possible to derive scores for the IQ-criteria from existing metadata? The general answer is 'no', at least not in a straight-forward manner. This section discusses where and how well metadata attributes help in determining IQ-criterion scores. We do not examine each criterion in detail, but look into a few exemplary criteria—one from each class of Table 3.2. Figure 3.2 shows matches for all IQ-criteria with a selection of the metadata attributes.

Relevancy A document or piece of data is considered to be relevant to the query if the keywords of the query appear often and/or in prominent positions in the document. Thus, the metadata attributes Coverage, Title, Subject/Keywords, and Description are of help in determining relevancy. Especially Title and Subject/Keywords explicitly point out prominent representatives of the information content. The use of thesauri or ontologies can further enhance the assessment of relevancy.
Even with the help of these attributes, determining the relevancy of data is error-prone: Recall the example of querying a search engine for the term "jaguar", where some pages are relevant and some are not. A subject metadata attribute "car" or "animal" would help sort the results and guide the user to the relevant link.

Response Time The response time criterion measures the delay between submission of a query by the user and reception of the complete response from the data source. The score for this criterion depends on unknown factors, such as network traffic, server workload etc. One aspect plays an important role: the technical equipment and location of the information server. Metadata on the equipment and location can be derived from the Publisher attribute (e.g. Springer) and the Storage Medium attribute (e.g. CD). Storage Medium can directly be translated to a time factor.

Believability The main source for believability scores is the identity of the author or creator of the data. That is, the believability of authors is extended to the documents or data they create. Thus, the Author/Creator and the Contributor attributes are helpful to a user in determining a score. To some degree, the identity of the publisher (Publisher metadata) also influences the believability of the data.

Verifiability A verification process can be supported by the attributes Resource Identifier, Relation, and Cross References. Relation and cross references may point to another source, where the data can be verified. A global identifier helps identification of the object or data in that other source, where it can be verified. Thus, the content of the attributes do not directly contribute to verifiability, but their existence can help the assessment process.

3.2.4 Related Work

Several research projects have tackled the problem of assessing scores for information quality criteria. Wang et al. present an information quality as-

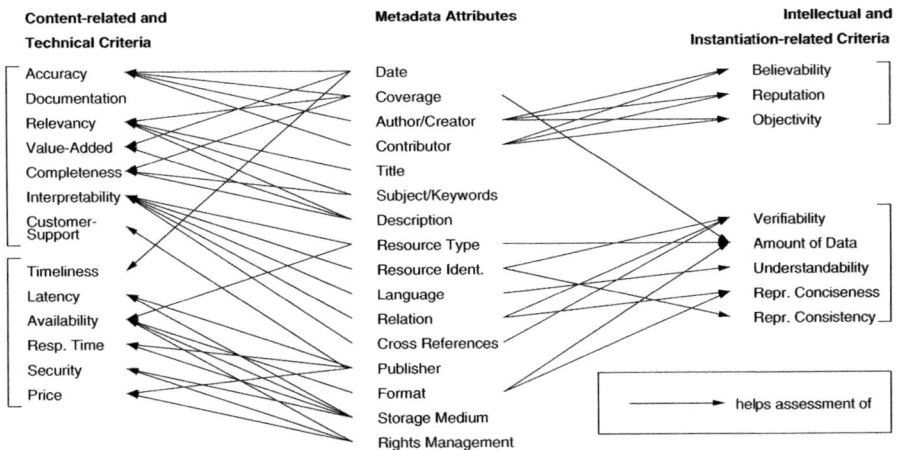

Fig. 3.2. Matching required IQ-criteria and existing general-purpose metadata attributes

sessment methodology called AIMQ, which is designed to help organizations assess the status of their organizational information quality and monitor their IQ improvements over time [129]. AIMQ consists of three components. The first component is the Product-Service-Performance model, which divides a fixed set of IQ-criteria into four classes. From this model a questionnaire— the second component—of 65 assessment items, some demographic questions, and space for comments is developed. The questionnaire should be sent to different organizations and should be answered by all respondents within an organization. The respondents are asked to focus their answers on one specific set of data that is of importance to their organization. The third component of AIMQ consists of two analysis techniques, one comparing the questionnaire results of different stakeholders of an information manufacturing system, and one comparing the questionnaire results of an organization to that of a best practices organization. Both analysis techniques are executed on each IQ-criterion class separately.

Bobrowski et al. present a methodology to measure data quality within an organization [12]. First, a list of IQ-criteria is set up. These IQ-criteria are divided into directly and indirectly assessed criteria. Scores for the indirectly assessed IQ-criteria are computed from the directly assessed IQ-criteria. To assess the latter, the authors apply traditional software metrics techniques. These techniques measure data quality following the goal-question-metric methodology: For each directly assessed criterion, a question is set up that characterizes the criterion. Then a metric is derived to answer this question, giving a precise evaluation of the quality. From these metrics a user questionnaire is set up, which is based on samples of the database.

Both AIMQ and the approach of Bobrowski et al. rely on questionnaires to find IQ-scores. Although this assessment method is inevitable for some criteria, it is by no means the only choice for all criteria. For instance, an automated method is much more precise in assessing the average response time of a source. Why should the price of some data be determined by a questionnaire? Why should we not use existing automated techniques to assess data accuracy?

Motro and Rakov address two specific criteria—soundness and completeness of data sources [88]. The authors propose automated assessment methods based on sampling of the source. Even though they are presented as an algorithm, they also rely on human input to verify whether some data is correct or not. Gruser et al. address in detail another criterion—response time [53]. The authors suggest a prediction tool that learns response times of Web data sources under several dimensions, such as time of day and quantity of data.

3.3 Summary

This chapter introduced the notion of Information Quality (IQ) to Web data sources. IQ was defined as a catalog of IQ-criteria, we presented a comprehensive set of IQ-criteria, and discussed their relation to typical Web data sources. We reviewed other projects concerned with information quality and data quality. While there exist several such projects, none apply IQ-reasoning to query planning and query processing as this thesis does.

Then, we discussed the assessment of IQ-criterion scores. We pointed out the difficulties of assessment and proposed general assessment methods for each IQ-criterion. We examined the usage of already existing metadata models and concluded that they are only partially and indirectly suitable for IQ-assessment. The assessed IQ-scores are a prerequisite to use IQ-criteria for improving the entire query answering process.

4 Quality Ranking Methods

This chapter formulates our quality model based on the set of IQ-criteria presented in Chapter 3, by assigning a quality vector to each source. To rank the sources based on these vectors, we solve the problems of scaling the IQ-scores and finding and including a user weighting. Five general ranking methods are introduced, that find a complete or partial ordering among the sources, based on the scaled and weighted IQ-scores. An analysis and evaluation of each of the methods with respect to our problem leads to a suggestion of the most suitable method.

4.1 Quality Model

Each source view receives IQ-scores for each criterion to be modelled. An IQ-vector combines these scores.

Definition 4.1.1 (IQ-Vector). *Let S_i be a data source and let d_{ij} be the score of IQ-criterion j for source S_i ($j = 1, \ldots, m$). Then $IQ(S_i) := (d_{i1}, \ldots, d_{im})$ is the IQ-vector for S_i.*

Having an IQ-vector for each source, it is not clear how to rank them. Only if a source dominates another source, i.e., if it has a better score in *each* criterion, it is clear that it should be ranked higher. Consider a source that is inexpensive but slow. It is not clear whether it is thus better than an expensive but fast source. Even if the user specifies preferences in the importance of the criteria such decisions cannot be made without ambiguity.

Given the IQ-vectors for a number of data sources, we want to find a—possibly complete—qualitative ordering of the sources to decide which ones to query. Given the IQ-vectors of a set of sources, we want to decide which set is overall preferable. Methods to solve this problem are called ranking methods or Multi-Attribute Decision-Making methods (MADM). These face three general problems:

1. The range and units of the IQ-scores of the criteria varies. For instance, understandability is measured as a user rating, while availability is a percentage. To make the scores comparable, this discrepancy must be resolved. Additionally, the range of the measured scores must be considered: While in theory the availability of a source is in $[0, 100]$, actually

F. Naumann: Quality-Driven Query Answering, LNCS 2261, pp. 51-66, 2002.
© Springer-Verlag Berlin Heidelberg 2002

scores might range only between 99% and 100%. *Scaling methods* solve these problems.

2. The importance of the criteria varies. When a user deems the completeness of a source important, its response time may be of less importance. Some of the methods to be introduced guide users in the quantification of preferences and detect inconsistencies. Apart from these methods there are special procedures to determine user preferences. *User weightings* solve this problem.

3. The IQ-scores place the data sources into a multi-dimensional space with one dimension per IQ-criterion. Because there is no natural order on a multi-dimensional space, we review several techniques or *ranking methods* that determine an ordering or that qualitatively classify the sources.

We address each of these problems in the following sections. Assuming these problems solved, we can define the IQ-score of a data source. The IQ-scores of sources define the qualitative ranking.

Definition 4.1.2 (IQ-score). *Let S_i be a data source with the scaled and weighted IQ-vector $IQ(S_i)$. The IQ-score of the source is $iq(S_i) := r(IQ(S_i))$ where r is a ranking method in $[0, 1]$.*

4.2 Scaling Methods

Scaling IQ-criterion scores solves the problems of different ranges and different units of the scores. The goal of scaling is to bring all criterion scores into non-dimensional scores within $[0, 1]$, and thus make them comparable. When scaling scores we must differentiate between positive and negative criteria:

Definition 4.2.1 (Positive and Negative Criteria). *An IQ-criterion is called* positive *if high criterion scores are considered better than low criterion scores. An IQ-criterion is called* negative *if low criterion scores are considered better than high criterion scores.*

Examples for positive criteria include accuracy, completeness, and reputation, examples for negative criteria are price and response time. We assume that all criteria have a monotonic utility function, i.e., their utility is either monotonically increasing or decreasing. Non-monotonic utility—such as for blood sugar level where the optimal utility lies in the middle of the scale—are rare in our domain of interest [59]. A goal of scaling methods is to remove this distinction so that the criteria can all be treated equally.

Example 4.2.1. Consider two search engines (S_1 and S_2) that are rated by the two criteria completeness and timeliness. Let S_1 cover a large part of the www, but have a low link update frequency (in days) and let S_2 cover only a small part of the Web but with a high update frequency. Table 4.1 shows corresponding scores.

Table 4.1. Two search engines with scores for two IQ-criteria

	completeness	timeliness
S_1	0.8	6
S_2	0.2	2

From the example, the difficulties become obvious: First, timeliness—when measured as update frequency—is a negative criterion, while completeness is positive. The unit and range of the two criteria also differ: Completeness is in $[0, 1]$ and represents a ratio while timeliness is in $[1, \infty]$ and is measured in days. Taken as absolute values, S_2 should be preferred over S_1, because S_2 is 4 points better than S_1 in timeliness but only 0.6 points worse in completeness. Taken as relative values, S_1 should be preferred over S_2, because S_1 is 4 times better in completeness and only 3 times worse in timeliness.

We describe two well-known scaling methods, linear scale transformation and normalization. Both are performed individually for each criterion across all sources.

4.2.1 Transformation

Linear scale transformation methods orientate themselves to the minimum or maximum score of a criterion, depending on whether a criterion is positive or negative. A simple scaling function is

$$v_{ij} = \frac{d_{ij}}{d_j^{\max}} \quad \text{for positive criteria} \tag{4.1}$$

$$v_{ij} = \frac{d_j^{\min}}{d_{ij}} \quad \text{for negative criteria} \tag{4.2}$$

where $d_j^{\max} := \max_i[d_{ij}]$ and $d_j^{\min} := \min_i[d_{ij}]$. This scaling approach has two deficiencies: First, the range of the actual criteria scores is not taken into account. For instance, if all availability scores of the sources are close to 100 percent, even the score of the source with the worst availability is scaled to a value close to 1, reducing discretionary power. Second, the scaling function for negative criteria is not defined for zero-values, which may well appear in the data, e.g., many search engines have a price score of zero. A scaling function without these deficiencies is

$$v_{ij} = \frac{d_{ij} - d_j^{\min}}{d_j^{\max} - d_j^{\min}} \quad \text{for positive criteria} \tag{4.3}$$

$$v_{ij} = \frac{d_j^{\max} - d_{ij}}{d_j^{\max} - d_j^{\min}} \quad \text{for negative criteria} \tag{4.4}$$

Here, the scaled scores are exactly in $[0, 1]$, i.e., the source with the best score of any criterion obtains the score 1 in that criterion, and the source with the worst score obtains the score 0. This property assures comparability of scores across criteria. A disadvantage is that the scores are not scaled proportionally, i.e., if an original score is twice as high as another, this property cannot be assured for the scaled scores.

Example 4.2.2. The scores of sources S_1 and S_2 scaled with (4.3) and (4.4) are in Table 4.2.

Table 4.2. Two search engines with scaled scores for two IQ-criteria

	completeness	timeliness
S_1	1	0
S_2	0	1

4.2.2 Normalization

The vector-normalization method divides each score by the norm of the criterion vector, i.e., the vector of all scores of one criterion across sources:

$$v_{ij} = \frac{d_{ij}}{\sqrt{\sum_{i=1}^{n} d_{ij}^2}} \tag{4.5}$$

Again, a disadvantage is that the transformed scores have different ranges and thus, a comparison across criteria is difficult. Also, the method does not distinguish positive and negative criteria, so this difference must still be resolved by the multi-attribute decision-making (MADM) method itself. An advantage is the proportional scaling of the scores.

Example 4.2.3. The scores of sources S_1 and S_2 normalized with (4.5) are in Table 4.3.

Table 4.3. Two search engines with normalized scores for two IQ-criteria

	completeness	timeliness
S_1	0.97	0.95
S_2	0.24	0.32

Concluding, there is no method without disadvantages. The MADM methods to be described in the following sections use both scaling alternatives as a basis.

4.3 User Weighting

One of the most important features of information quality reasoning across multiple criteria is the chance for users to specify their preferences concerning the importance of criteria. Varying importance has many reasons:

- The information need at hand varies: For a query for stock quotes timeliness typically is an important criterion. The same stock information system might also answer queries for news stories about a company. Here timeliness is less important, but reputation of the news sources might need a higher weighting.
- The resources available to the user might change: If the user budget rises, price may be weighted lower; if the user is in a hurry, response time will have a higher weighting.
- A user might distrust the assessed scores. For instance, if one of the criteria is reputation and it is assessed by someone other than the user, this criterion might be given a low weighting to the extreme of masking a criterion entirely, by assigning a zero-weight.

Users should be able to modify the criterion weighting for each query, depending on the situation.

Definition 4.3.1 (Weighting vector). *Let there be m IQ-criteria, then $(w_1, \ldots, w_m)$, $w_i \in \mathbb{R}^+$ is a weighting vector.*

Most MADM methods allow users to specify a weighting vector and require $\sum_{j=1}^m w_j = 1$. There are several ways of obtaining this weighting vector:

Direct Specification The user specifies weightings directly, within a given range. To achieve $\sum_{j=1}^m w_j = 1$ the weighting vector must be normalized accordingly, i.e, the final weightings are $w'_j = \frac{w_j}{\sum_{j=1}^m w_j}$.

Pair Comparison The user specifies for each pair of criteria how much more important one criterion is than the other, i.e., there are $\frac{m(m-1)}{2}$ comparisons. Result of this comparison is a matrix $A = (a_{ij})_{1 \le i,j \le m}$. The matrix is consistent if $a_{ij} = \frac{1}{a_{ji}}$ and $a_{ik} \cdot a_{kj} = a_{ij}$ for all $1 \le i, j, k \le m$. If the matrix is consistent we can determine the weighting vector unambiguously by $w_i = \frac{a_{ij}}{\sum_{j=1}^m a_{ji}}$, $i \le i \le m$. However, we cannot assume that a user specifies a consistent matrix. Either the actual inconsistencies are pointed out to the user to correct them, or a method is used to cope with the inconsistent comparisons. One of these methods is the eigenvector method.

Eigenvector Method The eigenvector method was developed by Saaty as a means to find weighting vectors and also as a component of the AHP method for multi-attribute decision-making (reviewed later) [115]. The user is asked to compare criteria within a scale from 1 to 9, where 1 means equal importance, 3 means a slightly higher importance etc., 9 meaning absolute dominance. Thus, values of the comparison matrix A are numbers from 1 to 9 and their complementary values 1 to $\frac{1}{9}$.

Such a matrix has the property that $Aw = nw$ where w is the weighting vector and n acts as an eigenvalue. In the presence of slight inconsistencies in the matrix this property does not hold, but changes of the eigenvalue are also only slight. Therefore, Saaty chooses as the weighting vector the eigenvector to the maximal eigenvalue.

4.4 Ranking Methods

The following ranking methods are taken from the literature. The contributions of this section are not the methods themselves but their adaptation to our problem of information quality ranking, the thorough analysis of their properties and suitability for our problem, and a comparison of the performance of the methods.

4.4.1 Simple Additive Weighting (Saw)

The Saw method is the simplest decision-making method. Despite its simplicity it is still effective in that its results are usually close to other methods [59]. The method involves three basic steps: Scale the scores to make them comparable, apply the user defined weighting, and sum up the scores for each source.

For scaling, the transformation functions (4.3) and (4.4) are used. The final preference score for each source is the weighted sum of the scaled scores:

$$iq(S_i) := \sum w_j v_{ij}$$

Because $\sum_{j=1}^{m} w_j = 1$, the final IQ-scores are in $[0, 1]$.

4.4.2 Technique for Order Preference by Similarity to Ideal Solution

The Technique for Order Preference by Similarity to Ideal Solution (Topsis) was developed by Hwang and Yoon [59]. Topsis ranks sources by determining their relative Euclidean distance to a virtual ideal and a virtual negative-ideal data source. Like Saw, Topsis uses (4.3) and (4.4) to scale the scores and applies the weighting vector. However, Topsis does not sum up the scores, but rather constructs a virtual ideal data source A^+ by choosing for each criterion the best score any source has reached. For positive criteria this is the maximum score, for negative criteria the minimum score. The virtual negative-ideal source A^- is defined analogously.

$$IQ(A^+) := \left(v_1^+, \ldots, v_m^+\right) \quad \text{and} \quad IQ(A^-) := \left(v_1^-, \ldots, v_m^-\right)$$

where

$$v_j^+ := \begin{cases} \max_i[v_{ij}] & \text{if criterion } j \text{ is positive} \\ \min_i[v_{ij}] & \text{if criterion } j \text{ is negative} \end{cases}$$

$$v_j^- := \begin{cases} \min_i[v_{ij}] & \text{if criterion } j \text{ is positive} \\ \max_i[v_{ij}] & \text{if criterion } j \text{ is negative} \end{cases}$$

Figure 4.1 shows some sources in two IQ-dimensions with the constructed ideal source A^+ and negative-ideal source A^-. The indifference curves show areas of equally ranked sources, i.e., sources with the same relative distance to A^+ and A^-.

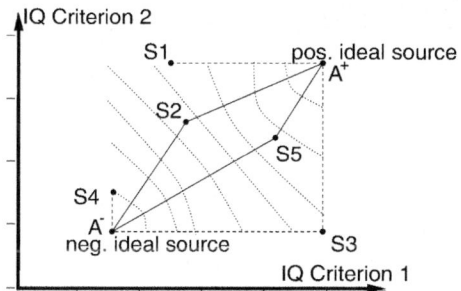

Fig. 4.1. The TOPSIS ranking method

The Euclidean distance between each source and the ideal and negative ideal solution is

$$S^{(+)}(S_i) := \sqrt{\sum_{j=1}^m (v_{ij} - v_j^{(+)})^2} \quad \text{and} \quad S^{(-)}(S_i) := \sqrt{\sum_{j=1}^m (v_{ij} - v_j^{(-)})^2}.$$

The relative closeness of a source to the ideal defines the final ranking order of TOPSIS:

$$iq(S_i) = \frac{S^-(S_i)}{S^+(S_i) + S^-(S_i)}.$$

4.4.3 Analytical Hierarchy Process (AHP)

The AHP-method was developed by Saaty [115]. It is composed of four main steps: Development of a goal hierarchy, comparison of goals in pairs, consistency check of the comparisons, and aggregation of the comparisons.

Goal hierarchies are developed individually for each application. They can range from trees spanning only one level to trees with a large number of levels. We developed an IQ-oriented hierarchy in Figure 4.2. There we show

an example with five criteria and five data sources. The main goal we want
to achieve is high information quality. We split this goal into a positive and
a negative subgoal. Each subgoal is made up of several criteria. The bottom
level consists of the data sources.

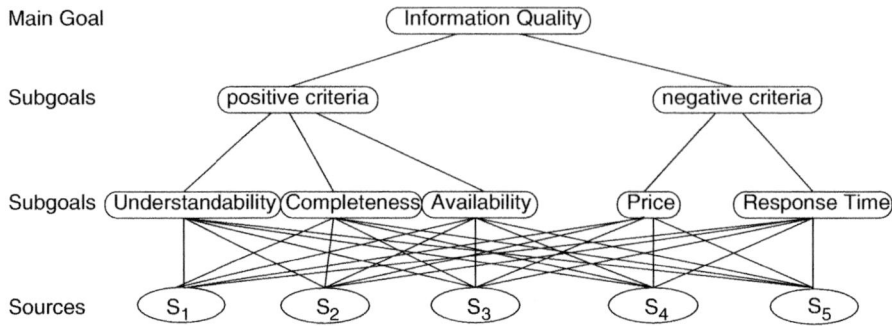

Fig. 4.2. Goal hierarchy of AHP

To represent comparisons of goals in pairs, a comparison matrix is defined
for the main goal and for each subgoal of the hierarchy. The matrix entries
for the goals information quality, and positive and negative criteria reflect
the user weighting, the matrix entries for the five criterion goals reflect the
measured IQ-scores. Matrix entries are between 1 (same importance) and 9
(absolute dominance) or their complement values. An exemplary matrix for
the positive criteria subgoal is in Figure 4.3. The entries of the table reflect
that the user considers understandability to be slightly more important than
completeness and much more important than availability.

	Understandability	Completeness	Availability
Understandability	1	2	5
Completeness	1/2	1	1/3
Availability	1/5	3	1

Fig. 4.3. Comparison matrix for the "positive criteria" subgoal of the AHP method

The next step of the AHP method checks the (transitive) consistency of
all matrices. This step would find that the matrix of Figure 4.3 is inconsistent, because the first row implies that completeness is more important than
availability, but the second row implies that this relationship is reversed. It is
left to the user to adjust the scores accordingly.

For the aggregation step, AHP calculates a weight vector for each goal
and subgoal. It is the normalized eigenvector to the maximum eigenvalue of
the matrix as described earlier in Section 4.3. Then, each arc below each
goal or subgoal is labeled with the value determined by the weight-vector of

the goal or subgoal. The final preference score of each source is calculated as the weighted sum along all paths from that source to the main goal. I.e., the weights along each path are multiplied, the results for each path from a source are summed up.

4.4.4 Elimination et Choice Translating Reality (ELECTRE)

The ELECTRE method or concordance analysis was developed by Benayoun et al. [10]. Like AHP, ELECTRE does not compare all sources at once by scaling the scores, but it undertakes a comparison of sources in pairs in each criterion. ELECTRE is based on the weighted and normalized decision scores v_{ij} according to (4.5).

By a comparison of all source pairs in each criterion, concordance and discordance sets are generated. The general concordance set C_{ij} is the set of criteria, for which source S_i is better than source S_j, i.e., for positive criteria $C_{ij} := \{k|v_{ik} \geq v_{jk}\}$ and for negative criteria $C_{ij} := \{k|v_{ik} \leq v_{jk}\}$. The notion of "better than" can be extended to non-quantifiable criteria, which are compared by the user. The discordance set D_{ij} is the complementary set of C_{ij}.

From these sets ELECTRE calculates concordance and discordance matrices. Each element of the concordance matrix $C = (c_{kl})$ is equal to the sum of weights for the criteria in the concordance set (4.6). The value of c_{kl} indicates the degree of domination of source S_k over source S_l when only considering criteria, where S_k already is better than S_l. An element of the discordance matrix $D = (d_{kl})$ is the relation of the largest difference over all discordant criteria to the largest difference over all criteria between two sources (4.7).

$$c_{kl} := \sum_{j \in C_{kl}} w_j \tag{4.6}$$

$$d_{kl} := \frac{\max_{j \in D_{kl}} |v_{kj} - v_{lj}|}{\max_{j=1,\ldots,m} |v_{kj} - v_{lj}|} \tag{4.7}$$

Based on the matrices C and D, the Boolean $n \times n$ concordance-dominance matrix $F = (f_{kl})$ and the Boolean discordance-dominance matrix $G = (g_{kl})$ are determined. The elements of F are set to $f_{kl} = 1$ if c_{kl} exceeds a certain threshold value, usually the average score of the elements of C, and to $f_{kl} = 0$ otherwise. Accordingly, $g_{kl} = 1$ if d_{kl} is below a certain threshold value, again usually the average over all d_{kl}. The two Boolean matrices are combined to the aggregated dominance matrix $E = (e_{kl})$ with $e_{kl} = f_{kl} \cdot g_{kl}$ that can be represented as a dominance graph.

The ELECTRE method does not result in a total ranking of the sources. Rather, it creates a partial ordering of sources. Depending on the threshold values chosen, more or less dominations are produced. We discuss this disadvantage and other properties of the MADM methods in Section 4.5.1.

4.4.5 Data Envelopment Analysis (DEA)

Like ELECTRE, DEA does not deliver an IQ-score for sources, but suggests which sources are better than others. It was introduced by Charnes et al. as a general method to classify a population of observations [16]. It has since been applied to many fields, for instance comparing efficiency of hospitals, airlines, or even baseball players [18].

The DEA method avoids the mentioned decision-making problems of different units and different ranges, and the problem of different importance of criteria by defining an efficiency frontier as the convex hull of the *unscaled* and *unweighted* vector space of IQ-dimensions. Figure 4.4 shows an exemplary vector space for two IQ-dimensions. Those sources on the efficiency frontier are defined as good, those below as poor. Consider the poor source S in Figure 4.4. Assuming constant returns to scale[1], a virtual but realistic source S' is constructed on the efficiency frontier. Clearly S' is better than source S, and the constant returns to scale assumption suggests that a source could realistically be as good as S'. Thus, S is deemed "poor". For sources on the frontier no such virtual source can be constructed, thus they are "good". The approach is generalized to any number of dimensions.

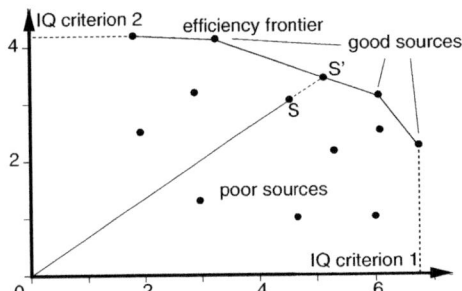

Fig. 4.4. Source classification with Data Envelopment Analysis

The DEA method determines whether a source S_{j_0} is on the frontier by solving the fractional linear program FLP-DEA (Figure 4.5). A general linear program consists of an optimization goal over one or more variables. The variables are subject to one or more conditions. A solution to a linear program is an instantiation of the variables that is optimal among all instantiations that comply with the conditions. In a *fractional* linear program the goal and the conditions are fractions. However, any fractional linear program of the DEA-form has an infinite number of optimal solutions obtained by scaling the weights in numerator and denominator. Therefore, we transform FLP-DEA into the equivalent linear program LP-DEA using a method proposed

---

[1] Constant returns to scale assume that an investment of resources like money and time into improvement of the source yields a proportional gain in quality of the source.

by Charnes and Cooper in [17]. The LP-DEA in effect maximizes quality at constant cost and has only one solution.

FLP-DEA:

$$\text{maximize} \quad \frac{\sum_{i \text{ is pos. crit.}} w_i d_{ij_0}}{\sum_{i \text{ is neg. crit.}} w_i d_{ij_0}}$$

$$\text{subject to} \quad \frac{\sum_{i \text{ is pos. crit.}} w_i d_{ij_0}}{\sum_{i \text{ is neg. crit.}} w_i d_{ij_0}} \leq 1 \text{ for all sources } S_j$$

$$w_i \geq \varepsilon > 0 \text{ for all } i$$

LP-DEA :

$$\text{maximize} \quad \sum_{i \text{ is pos. crit.}} w_i d_{ij_0} - \sum_{i \text{ is neg. crit.}} w_i d_{ij_0}$$

$$\text{subject to} \quad \sum_{i \text{ is pos. crit.}} w_i d_{ij_0} - \sum_{i \text{ is neg. crit.}} w_i d_{ij_0} \leq 1 \text{ for all } S_j$$

$$\sum_{i \text{ is neg. crit.}} w_i d_{ij_0} = 1$$

$$w_i \geq \varepsilon > 0 \text{ for all } i$$

Fig. 4.5. Two linear programs of the DEA method

With DEA, the criterion weights are not specified by the user, but rather are variables that are determined by the method. Neither a scaling nor a user weighting are necessary. The result of each LP is the optimal quality score $IQ(S_{j_0})$ of the examined source. The score for each source is either 1 (on the frontier / good) or less than 1 (below the frontier / poor).

A complete Data Envelopment Analysis involves solving n linear programs, where n is the number of sources. However, there are several ways to totally avoid or at least to accelerate computation of certain LPs. For instance, it is proven by Ali that sources, that have the single best score for a certain criterion, are always efficient [1]. LPs for those sources do not have to be solved. Inefficient sources on the other hand can easily be detected, if they are *dominated* by another source, i.e., if there is a source that is equal to or better than the dominated source in all criteria and strictly better in at least on criterion. After this preprocessing, we already have a set of efficient and a set of inefficient sources. These sets can be used to accelerate the simplex method for the remaining LPs in several ways [1].

As with ELECTRE, a shortcoming of DEA is that it only determines a set of efficient sources without ranking them by efficiency. This problem typically gets worse the more criteria are used: For each additional criterion there is a source that has the best score and is thus a candidate for being on the frontier. A solution to this problem is suggested by Dyson et al. in [38], who add individual constraints on the weights to the LP instead of the general constraint $w_i \geq \varepsilon > 0$.

4.5 Comparison and Evaluation

To decide which multi-attribute decision-making (MADM) method is the most appropriate for our problem of ranking data sources based on IQ-criteria, we analyzed decisive properties of the methods (Section 4.5.1), and implemented the methods to compare their ranking results and their sensitivity towards changes in their input (Section 4.5.2).

4.5.1 Properties of the Ranking Methods

In the following paragraphs we discuss selected properties of the decision-making methods. These properties are the amount of user interaction, the ability to detect dominance, the computational complexity, and whether the result is an IQ-score or a partial ordering. We summarize these properties in Table 4.4.

Interaction: User interaction, i.e., the necessity of the user to state preferences or compare alternatives, is undesirable, because time consuming as long as the final response to a query is fully satisfying. Interaction is undesirable, because it is slow compared to the response times of information systems and because it is tedious work for the user. It should be confined to a one-time statement of preferences between criteria and possibly between sources. The user should of course be able to change these preferences whenever this change is wanted.

This requirement is immediately met by SAW, TOPSIS, and ELECTRE. The AHP method additionally requires comparison matrices for each criterion across all sources. To some degree this comparison can be performed automatically without the user. If the number of criteria is high, this method is advantageous, because comparing two criteria can be simpler than finding an entire weighting-vector among all criteria. However, for the small number of criteria we propose, immediately finding a weighting vector is reasonable. The DEA-method demands no user interaction whatsoever. In fact, the method does not allow preferences between the criteria. Thus, the result of DEA is independent of the user.

Dominance: A data source dominates another if it is equal to or better than the other source in all criteria, and strictly better in at least one criterion. Obviously, a dominating source is always more preferable than the dominated source. Any decision-making method should be able to discover dominance, and rank a dominating source higher than the dominated one, under any given weighting. The five examined methods all discover dominance. However, AHP might miss dominance if the comparisons of the user are inconsistent. AHP discovers such inconsistencies, gives a warning, but continues nonetheless.

Computational complexity: The computational complexity of a decision-making method is of importance if the method is applied often. This is for instance the case, if criteria are query-dependent, as the method then must be applied with each query. It is also of importance, whenever not individual sources but combinations of sources are compared: For any n sources there is an exponential number of combinations[2].

The runtime of SAW, TOPSIS, and ELECTRE is polynomial in the number of criteria (m) and the number of sources (n). Computing AHP is exponential, because it determines eigenvalues and eigenvectors. For DEA several linear programs must be solved. This problem is proven to be polynomially solvable [63], but commonly the Simplex algorithm is used, which has an exponential worst-case complexity but a low average-case complexity [28].

Result type: We distinguish two result types: scalar IQ-scores of sources and a partial ordering of sources. Decision-making methods that result in IQ-scores rank the sources by that score. Typically this ranking is a complete ordering—the probability that two sources have the same IQ-score is small. Querying the top-ranked sources should result in the best query response.

SAW, TOPSIS, and AHP return a scalar IQ-score for each source. The ELECTRE and the DEA methods deliver only partial orderings of different types. DEA returns a set of good sources and a complete ordering of poor sources, while ELECTRE returns only a partial ordering, of which the maximum set can be considered as good. Thus, the usage of the latter two methods is somewhat limited.

Table 4.4. Properties of MADM methods

	SAW	TOPSIS	AHP	ELECTRE	DEA
Interaction	weighting	weighting	decisions	weighting	%
Dominance	$\checkmark$	$\checkmark$	$(\checkmark)$	$\checkmark$	$\checkmark$
Complexity	$O(n \cdot m)$	$O(n \cdot m)$	exp.	$O(n \cdot m^2)$	polynomial
Result	IQ-score	IQ-score	IQ-score	partial ord.	partial ord.

4.5.2 Evaluation of the Ranking Methods

Our analysis is made up of two main parts: (i) A comparison of the MADM methods to find if they produce similar results under different settings, and (ii) a sensitivity test of each individual method[3].

---

[2] In Chapter 5 we introduce a *query plan* as a combination of data sources.

Comparison. There is no way to determine the correctness of the methods, because there is no "true" ranking of sources. There are two possibilities to evaluate the performance of MADM methods: empirical studies and comparison. We decided to compare the methods amongst each other, because this method is independent of subjective and error prone techniques of empirical studies with many users.

For the comparison we used SAW as reference point, and measured how much the other methods deviated from the ranking of SAW. SAW suggests itself as reference point, because of its simplicity and the ability of the user to directly comprehend effects of changes in weightings and scores. Using a certain reference point only has an effect on the quantitative deviations of the methods, but not on the qualitative statements.

Because two of the five methods do not produce IQ-scores, we used the number of "good" sources of DEA as the size of the comparison set. This number of top elements of SAW were chosen, and for each other method we checked how many of these sources appear in the top set as well. In our comparisons, we varied the distribution of criterion scores (equally and Gaussian distributed), the number of criteria (5–20), the ranges of values ([0-1] – [1-1000]), the number of sources (10–90), the distribution of weightings (equally – mixed), and the type of criteria (only positive; positive and negative criteria).

We performed five extensive tests, fixing values for four of the five variables and modifying the one remaining variable. Each test was performed once for equally distributed scores and once for Gaussian distributed scores. A test results in a ranking of methods (rank 1 for the source closest to SAW, rank 4 for the method furthest from SAW), of which we computed the sum. Thus, low numbers represent results close to the reference method SAW. A summary of the results is shown in Table 4.5.

Table 4.5. Summary of MADM method comparisons

	Test 1 sources	Test 2 criteria	Test 3 range	Test 4 weighting	Test 5 positive/negative	Σ
SAW	0	0	0	0	0	0
TOPSIS	39	30	36	31	31	167
AHP	33	83	46	43	44	249
ELECTRE	39	50	24	33	45	191
DEA	105	127	60	69	64	425

We observed that throughout the tests TOPSIS was closest to SAW. We assume that this similarity is due to the same scaling function. ELECTRE performed similarly, but at the disadvantage of only a partial ordering. AHP and DEA deviated considerably more. While this is understandable for DEA

---

[3] The implementation and testing was performed in cooperation with Daniel Tonn.

because it does not regard the user weightings, it is not understandable for AHP.

Sensitivity. We performed several sensitivity tests of the methods by executing the method, changing the input data slightly, re-running the methods, and comparing the results. The results are summarized in Table 4.6.

— Add a best source: We added a source that dominates all other sources by a large amount. All algorithms discovered this source, but for AHP the range of the final ranking scores of the other sources was hardly discernible (Test a), and ELECTRE and DEA even changed the order of the remaining sources (Test b).
— Add a worst source: We added a source that was by far worse than all other sources. Again, the ranking scores of the remaining sources were hardly discernible with AHP (Test a), and again ELECTRE even changed the ranking order (Test b).
— Add a similar source: We added a source that is quite similar to an already existing (average) source. First, we tested whether it was placed correctly within the ranking, i.e., near the source it is similar to (Test a). Second, we tested whether the new source had any influence on the ranking of the remaining sources. AHP failed both tests, all other methods were not sensitive towards the new source. The failure of AHP reproduces a known and much discussed flaw of the method [37].

Additionally, we tested how the methods performed under large numbers of sources and criteria. We tested all methods for up to 50 sources and up to 50 criteria. The latter test is not as important, because one cannot expect that data sources are assessed by 50 criteria. Realistic numbers lie between 1 and 10. 50 sources does not seem like a large figure, but we know of no system that actually integrates more than 50 sources. We consider a runtime of more than 1 minute as failure. Again, AHP failed both tests, due to the complexity of finding eigenvalues. DEA failed only for many criteria, because the complexity of the problem scales only linear with the number of sources, but exponentially with the number of criteria.

Table 4.6. Summary of MADM method sensitivity analysis (+ passed, − failed)

	add best source	add worst source	add similar source	many sources	many criteria
	a / b	a / b	a / b		
SAW	+ / +	+ / +	+ / +	+	+
TOPSIS	+ / +	+ / +	+ / +	+	+
AHP	− / +	− / +	− / −	−	−
ELECTRE	+ / −	+ / −	+ / +	+	+
DEA	+ / −	+ / +	+ / +	+	−

4.6 Summary

The goal of this chapter was to establish a quality model to compare data sources based on multiple IQ-criteria. To this end, we defined the IQ-vector, showed how to scale the IQ-scores, and presented different methods to find user weightings. We presented five multi-attribute decision-making (MADM) methods to solve the problem of ranking sources based on multiple criteria and a user weighting. We undertook a thorough analysis of the methods to find out, which ones are suitable for the problem at hand.

Web data sources on a given domain typically should be assessed with only a small number of IQ-criteria. Therefore, we choose the direct specification as the user weighting method of choice. If the number of criteria were greater, one of the other methods would be advisable, because a user must only specify importance differences for two criteria at a time.

The MADM methods have quite varying properties; their suitability heavily depends on the proposed application. For the following sections we use two methods: DEA and SAW. The most distinct feature of DEA is its independence of any weighting. The method claims to find good sources *independently* of criterion preferences. This property makes DEA apt for a pre-selection of data sources. Given a set of data sources, DEA can determine in advance those sources that are "good", i.e., sources for which it is worthwhile to construct wrappers and to integrate them into the planning process. The method is not appropriate for ranking query plans, which we introduce in the following chapter, because (i) the planning process is query- and user-weighting dependent and (ii) its runtime is prohibitively high.

The method we find most appropriate for ranking query plans is SAW. It is the simplest method, it has similar results to the more complicated TOPSIS method, it produces IQ-scores unlike ELECTRE and it is stable unlike AHP. Especially the sensitivity of AHP with respect to similar sources is quite astounding and not tolerable. Note that the concepts of the next section are independent of the choice of the MADM method. We only require the possibility of a user weighting and IQ-scores as a result.

We now have the tools to deal with multiple criteria. Given a set of sources or plans, each with scores for a common set of IQ-criteria and a user weighting, we are able to determine IQ-scores of the sources or plans and thus find the best plan or best set of plans to answer a user query.

5 Quality-Driven Query Planning

Query answering on the Web can be enhanced both in effectiveness and efficiency by using IQ-criteria. The main contribution of this thesis is to bring together the concept of answering queries in mediator-based information systems and the concept of information quality. Having introduced the two in Parts I and II respectively, we combine them in this part.

First, we examine the general problem of translating a user query against the universal relation to a query against the global schema of a mediator-based information system. Next, we derive query plans from the translated query. We present a quality model that assigns IQ-scores to query plans, given IQ-scores of the individual sources in the plans. Then, we show how this IQ-reasoning can be applied to common query planning algorithms to limit the amount of queries submitted to the underlying data sources. Finally, we introduce a new algorithm that yields the same query results, but is by far more efficient than previous algorithms. We gain this efficiency by using IQ-score bounds to prune the search space.

5.1 Logical Query Planning

The data for answering a user query generally resides on more than one source. To find a response to the user, the mediator must identify the appropriate sources, collect responses from them, and combine the responses to a unified result. These instructions are represented by a query plan. Query planning is the process of finding an executable query plan for a user query. The elements of a plan are the sources themselves (or instructions to access them) and operators to combine the sources and to ensure conditions specified in the user query.

5.1.1 Query Translation

In Section 2.2.1 we defined source views as our means to describe sources. Source views are views against the global schema of the mediator restricted to a single relation. User queries on the other hand are queries against the universal relation, constructed from the global schema. User queries are merely a

F. Naumann: Quality-Driven Query Answering, LNCS 2261, pp. 69-87, 2002.
© Springer-Verlag Berlin Heidelberg 2002

set of attributes along with some conditions. To map a query to source views, we translate user queries to queries against the global relational schema. The translation ensures the requirements of *correctness* (R.1 on page 18), and intensional *completeness* (R.3), while taking into account the concession of *missing values* (C.3) from Section 2.2.2. Extensional completeness (R.2) cannot be ensured through translation. Extensional completeness depends on the sources used during plan execution and not on the query against the global schema.

Definition 5.1.1 (Translated Query). *Let $Q[A_Q] \leftarrow UR, C$ be a user query. We obtain the corresponding translated query $Q'(A_Q) \leftarrow body$ in the following way:*

1. *The body of Q' contains all relations of which A_Q contains an attribute. Conditions C are included unchanged.*
2. *The relations are only connected through joins over ID–foreign ID relationships.*
3. *The body of Q' additionally contains all necessary relations to make the graph of relations and joins connected.*

The head of the translated query ensures the intensional completeness (R.3). Even if there are no non-`null` values for an attribute in any of the sources, conforming to C.3 the attribute should be returned filled with `null` values. The first translation rule ensures safety, i.e., all attributes to be returned to the user actually appear in one of the relations in the query. The rule also ensures correctness (R.1) by including all conditions specified by the user. Rule 2 establishes the connection between the relations, and Rule 3 catches cases where users specify attributes of relations that have no ID–foreign ID relationship. Without Rule 3 cases are possible, where there is no join relationship between relations of the query, and the user would receive the cross product of the two relations, contradicting R.1.

Example 5.1.1. Table 5.1 repeats the UR-tableau with three relations, five sources, and four queries of Chapter 2 (page 17).

Queries $Q_1 - Q_4$ against the universal relation UR are translated to queries against the global schema:

$$Q'_1(a_2, a_4) \leftarrow R_1(a_1, a_2, a_3), R_2(a_3, a_4, a_5)$$
$$Q'_2(a_1, a_2, a_4, a_6) \leftarrow R_1(a_1, a_2, a_3), R_2(a_3, a_4, a_5), R_3(a_5, a_6),\ a_2 < 10$$
$$Q'_3(a_1, a_2, a_4) \leftarrow R_1(a_1, a_2, a_3), R_2(a_3, a_4, a_5),\ a_2 > 10,\ a_4 < 40$$
$$Q'_4(a_1, a_5) \leftarrow R_1(a_1, a_2, a_3), R_2(a_3, a_4, a_5), R_3(a_5, a_6)$$

For Q_4 the translation inserts R_2 even though the user specifies no attribute of the relation, to establish a relationship between R_1 and R_3 and guarantee correct tuples.

Table 5.1. Universal relation with 3 relations, 5 sources, and 3 queries

UR	a_1	a_2	a_3	a_4	a_5	a_6
$R_1:$	✓	✓	✓			
$R_2:$			✓	✓	✓	
$R_3:$					✓	✓
$S_1:$	✓	✓	✓			
$S_2:$	✓	✓				
$S_3:$			✓ > 10			
$S_4:$			✓ > 50	✓		
$S_5:$					✓	✓
$Q_1:$		✓		✓		
$Q_2:$	✓	< 10		✓		✓
$Q_3:$	✓ > 10			< 40		
$Q_4:$	✓			✓		

5.1.2 Query Planning

Given a translated query against the global schema, the mediator tries to find plans that generate answers to the query. The following definition describes how such a query against the global schema is transformed into a plan containing actual source views.

Definition 5.1.2 (Query Plan). *Let Q' be a query against the global schema. We obtain a query plan P for Q' by replacing each relation of the body of Q' with a source view corresponding to the relation it replaces.*

Such a plan is executed by accessing the sources of the plan, retrieving the results, and executing the join operations between the relations and the selection conditions on the attributes. The resulting tuples are temporarily stored in an instance of the mediator schema. Missing values are padded with null. The original query Q is computed on this instance after all results are retrieved.

For each query there is a large number of plans: Each combination of sources that provide data for the relations of the query is a plan. Each plan returns different data of different quality, because it comprises different data sources. Some plans may even return an empty result, because of contradicting selection conditions in the query and a source view, or because it implies a join operation over a foreign ID that is not exported by a source view in the plan.

Example 5.1.2. The set of all plans for user query Q_2' is

$$P_1(a_1, a_2, a_4, a_6) \leftarrow S_1, S_3, S_5, \ a_2 < 10$$
$$P_2(a_1, a_2, a_4, a_6) \leftarrow S_1, S_4, S_5, \ a_2 < 10$$
$$P_3(a_1, a_2, a_4, a_6) \leftarrow S_2, S_3, S_5, \ a_2 < 10$$
$$P_4(a_1, a_2, a_4, a_6) \leftarrow S_2, S_4, S_5, \ a_2 < 10$$

5.1.3 Top N Plans

In the presence of resource constraints it is often not possible to execute
all plans for a query. There might be technical constraints of the mediator,
such as a limited network bandwidth or limited access to the underlying data
sources. Additionally, users may have constraints, such as a limited budget or
limited time. Additionally, users might have non-technical constraints, such
as the unwillingness to browse a large result set. For instance, a meta-search
engine does not need to download all hits from all search engines it uses;
instead, integrating the top ten hits usually suffices.

   When not all plans can or should be executed, it is beneficial to restrict
execution not to arbitrary plans, but to the best plans according to a quality
model. We formulate our problem:

> Given a query against a global schema and a set of source views
> providing data for the schema, and given a set of IQ-criteria and IQ-
> scores for each source view and each criterion, our goal is to find
> the best N plans according to the information quality measure $iq(P)$
> defined in Section 4.1.

The number N can be specified by the mediator, for instance as a function
of the constraints.

Definition 5.1.3 (Search Space). *Let Q' be a query against the global
schema and let $P_{Q'}$ be the set of all plans for Q'. Then the search space for
finding the N best plans for Q' is the set of all subsets of $P_{Q'}$ of size N:*

$$\mathfrak{S}(Q') := \{P' \subseteq P_{Q'} \mid |P'| = N\}.$$

Assuming that there are s sources for each relation and assuming that Q'
includes k relations, the size of the set of all plans is $|P_{Q'}| = s^k$, and the size
of the search space is thus $|\mathfrak{S}(Q')| = \binom{s^k}{N}$. The following section shows how
to determine the quality of the different plans, so as to identify the N best
ones.

5.1.4 Merge Functions for IQ-criteria

Given IQ-vectors of sources, we aim at determining the IQ-vector of a plan
containing the sources. Following the DBMS approach of cost models for query
execution plans, we define a quality model for query plans. We describe plans
as trees (Figure 5.1.4 shows the tree for plan P_1 of the example). Leaves represent sources, which deliver the base data of one relation. Data is subsequently
processed bottom-up within the inner nodes of the tree, which represent inner
joins performed by the mediator.

   Given IQ-scores for all IQ-criteria, we must determine IQ-scores for any
inner node. The IQ-score of the root of the tree then corresponds to the
overall quality of the plan. We use merge functions to calculate these scores:

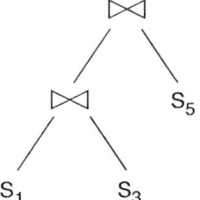

Fig. 5.1. The plan tree for P_1

Definition 5.1.4 (Merge Function). *Let D be the range of values for an* IQ-*criterion. A merge function is a commutative and associative function* $D \times D \to D$*. The general merge function is denoted* $\circ$*.*

A merge function has a different interpretation for each criterion, reflecting properties of the underlying IQ-measure. We require commutativity and associativity for merge functions, so that a change of the join execution order within a plan has no effect on its IQ-score. This property is desirable, as the user perceives the quality of the query result and not the quality of how the query result is obtained. Also, this freedom of changing the join order allows us to include binding patterns in the views, which can require a specific join order. Furthermore, a traditional post-optimization (algebraic reordering) can be performed to find the cost-based best join order of the chosen plans without influencing their quality score.

Example 5.1.3. In Table 5.2 we give exemplary merge functions for seven IQ-criteria. L represents the left child of the join operator and R the right child.

Table 5.2. Merge functions for several IQ-criteria

Criterion	Merge function "$\circ$"	Brief explanation
Availability	$d_{L1} \cdot d_{R1}$	Probability that both sites are accessible.
Price	$d_{L2} + d_{R2}$	Both sources must be payed.
Repr. Consistency	$\max[d_{L3}, d_{R3}]$	Wrapper integrates sources in parallel.
Response Time	$\max[d_{L4}, d_{R4}]$	Both children are processed in parallel.
Accuracy	$d_{L5} \cdot d_{R5}$	Probability that left and right side do not contain an error.
Coverage	$d_{L6} \cdot d_{R6}$	Probability for join match.
Density	$d_{L7} + d_{R7} - d_{L7} \cdot d_{R7}$	Probability that either left or right side has a non-**null** value.

It is not always possible to find an appropriate merge function for a criterion. Especially for subjective criteria like reputation, it is not clear how to determine the score for join results. Unfortunately, the most self-evident merge function—the average—is not associative. In the following we present a way to deal with criteria without a merge-function by considering them separately, before query planning.

In Chapter 4 we introduced IQ-vectors for individual sources consisting of IQ-scores. Now we define the IQ-vector of a join result with the help of the merge functions:

Definition 5.1.5 (Merged IQ-Vector). *Let there be m IQ-criteria and let $IQ(L) = (d_{L1}, \ldots, d_{Lm})$ and $IQ(R) = (d_{R1}, \ldots, d_{Rm})$ be the IQ-vector for the left child L and right child R of an inner join node. The IQ-vector of this node is*

$$IQ(L \bowtie R) := (d_{L1} \circ d_{R1}, \ldots, d_{Lm} \circ d_{Rm})$$

where $\circ$ are merge functions for the different criteria.

Figure 5.2 shows the plan tree of plan P_1 (page 71) with corresponding IQ-vectors. The IQ-vector of the root represents the quality of the entire plan. With this vector we can determine the scalar IQ-score $iq(P)$ for the plan using the techniques described in Chapter 4.

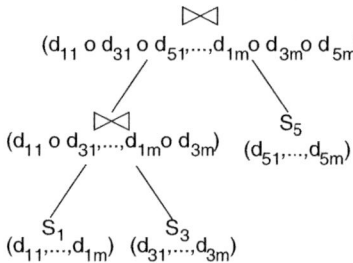

Fig. 5.2. The plan tree for P_1 with IQ-vectors and merged IQ-vectors

5.1.5 Relationship to Conventional Query Optimization

An analysis of our problem leads to a direct similarity to the problem that is attacked in a conventional query optimizer [119, 19]. Clearly, the sources providing data for a certain relation can be understood as different access paths to the relation, and a plan is a selection of one access path per relation in the query. However, we are careful not to over-stress this similarity:

– In our distributed context, it does not suffice to construct only one plan. Different plans use different sources and obtain different results. We can only be sure to compute all answers to Q if we execute all correct plans for Q'.

– The join order of a plan is not considered for two reasons. (i) A user perceives the quality of the result and not the quality of how this result is obtained. (ii) Including join order raises the complexity of the algorithm. We argue that it is better to first find the desired number of plans and then reduce their execution time through post-optimization. Information quality and execution time are orthogonal.

5.2 Attaching Quality Reasoning to Query Planning

Our first goal for the integration of IQ-reasoning and query planning is to attach IQ-selection methods to existing planning algorithms. To this end, we distinguish two classes of IQ-criteria to be used in different phases of query planning:

Source-specific criteria determine the overall quality of a data source. Criteria of this category apply to all data of the source, independently of how it is obtained. We do not need merge functions for these criteria.
   For instance, the New York Stock Exchange information system may be deemed to have a higher reputation than some obscure Web site.
Query-specific criteria determine query-dependent quality aspects of a source. Criteria of this class only apply to certain queries.
   For instance, using this finer granularity, we can model different response times for different queries to the same source. Another example is a search engine that has a high completeness for german Web sites. A query for a german Web page yields higher completeness scores for this source than for others.

Depending on the application domain and the structure of the available sources, the classification of criteria into the two classes may vary. For instance, if sources charge the same amount of money for each query, a price criterion should be only source-specific. If the price differs for different type of queries or different parts of the source, the criterion is query-specific.

   We extend existing planning algorithms with two phases: Before the actual planning, we reduce the overall number of sources in a pre-processing phase using source-specific criteria (Phase 1). Filtering sources is important, because planning algorithms in general have a computational complexity, which is exponential in the number of available sources. The remaining sources enter the query planning phase (Phase 2). Here, we create all plans for the query at hand. This phase can be performed with any algorithm generating query plans, using any kind of source description apart from ours. After creating all plans, we rank them by evaluating query-specific IQ-scores following the join-structure of a plan using merge functions (Phase 3). Eventually, we execute the top N plans. Alternatively, plans can be executed by decreasing quality until a stop criterion is reached: either the N plans have been executed or a

total quality or cost threshold is reached. Figure 5.3 shows the three phases
of the overall algorithm.

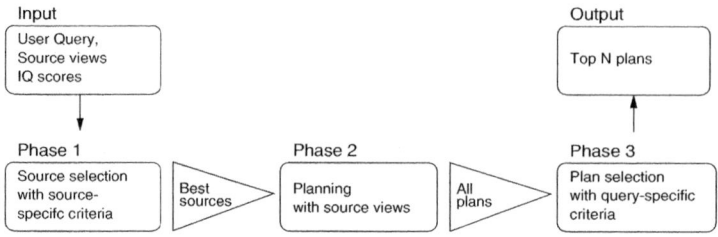

Fig. 5.3. Three-phase query planning

Example 5.2.1. Table 5.3 gives IQ-scores for each source, four source specific
criteria, and seven query-specific criteria. We use the scores to demonstrate
the three phases.

Table 5.3. IQ scores for five sources

Source-specific	S_1	S_2	S_3	S_4	S_5
Understandability(grade)	5	7	7	8	6
Reputation(grade)	5	5	7	8	7
Reliability(grade)	2	6	4	6	6
Timeliness(days)	30	30	2	1	7
View-specific					
Availability(%)	99	99	60	80	99
Price(US $)	0	0	0	0	1
Repr. Consistency(sec)	1	1	0.5	0.7	0.2
Response time(sec)	0.2	0.2	0.2	3	0.1
Accuracy(%)	99.9	99.9	99.8	99.95	99.95
Coverage(ratio)	0.6	0.8	0.9	0.8	0.8
Density(ratio)	0.89	0.2	1	0.75	1

5.2.1 Phase 1: Source Selection

The number of plans for a user query is exponential in the number of relations
in the user query and the number of sources. Any logical planning algorithm
generates this number of plans. Therefore, we thrive to decrease this number
before we start planning. To this end, we use the source-specific IQ-criteria to
"weed out" sources that are qualitatively not as good as others. Our goal is
to find a certain number or percentage of best sources independently of any
user-specific weighting or preference. The mediator performs Phase 1 only
once after start-up, and does not repeat it until a data source changes in a

source-specific criterion, or until a new data source is added to the system. A second reason for source selection is to evaluate those criteria, for which there are no associative merge functions. To evaluate a large amount of sources in a *general*, user-independent way, we use the Data Envelopment Analysis (DEA) method as introduced in Section 4.4.5.

For further planning, we completely disregard sources classified as "poor" by DEA. However, there is a danger of removing a source that has low IQ, but is the only source providing a certain attribute or relation of the global schema. Furthermore, we must retain sources that exclusively provide certain extensions of an attribute, e.g., the only source providing data on german stock quotes should be kept, even if its IQ is low and other sources provide stock quotes for other markets. Removing such sources from further consideration would "reduce" the global schema. To avoid suppressing these sources we only weed out poor sources, whose source views are all contained in views of good sources. Query containment can be checked automatically [14]. In this way, the global schema remains intact.

Example 5.2.2. For the sources of our example, the results of the DEA method using the source-specific criteria are

$$\text{DEA}(S_1) = 0.999; \ \text{DEA}(S_2) = 1; \ \text{DEA}(S_3) = 0.889;$$
$$\text{DEA}(S_4) = 1; \ \text{DEA}(S_5) = 0.998.$$

That is, we would exclude sources S_1, S_3, and S_5 from further consideration. However, all three sources exclusively provide some part of the global schema (see Table 5.1 on page 71): S_1 is the only source to provide attribute a_2, S_3 is the only source to provide attribute values of a_4 that are less than 50, and S_5 is the only source to provide data for relation R_3. Thus, in this small example we cannot dismiss a source.

5.2.2 Phase 2: Plan Creation

In our model of user queries against the universal relation and restriction of source views to one relation, plan creation is simple: For each relation R_i in the user query we create a bucket B_i. Each bucket is filled with those sources that provide data for the corresponding relation. Each combination of one source view from each bucket is a query plan. An example was shown in Section 5.1.2.

Query planning in a more general setting is more complex (see related work presented in Section 5.4). Phase 2 can be replaced by any query planning algorithm for any setting.

5.2.3 Phase 3: Plan Selection

The goal of this phase is to rank the plans of the previous phase qualitatively, and ultimately select the top N plans, or alternatively, to as many plans as necessary to meet certain cost- or quality-constraints. Plan selection proceeds in three steps:

1. Determine query-specific IQ-vectors: Unless the scores are predetermined, the scores for query-specific criteria are determined here.
2. Determine IQ-vectors of plans: Using the merge functions described in Section 5.1.4 we determine the overall IQ-vector for each plan.
3. Rank plans with SAW: Using the Simple Additive Weighting method described in Section 4.4.1 we aggregate the IQ-vector scores of a plan to a scalar IQ-score, and rank the plans accordingly.

Example 5.2.3. We continue Example 5.1.2 (page 71) with the four plans for Q_2':

$$
\begin{aligned}
P_1(a_1, a_2, a_4, a_6) &\leftarrow S_1, S_3, S_5, \ a_2 < 10 \\
P_2(a_1, a_2, a_4, a_6) &\leftarrow S_1, S_4, S_5, \ a_2 < 10 \\
P_3(a_1, a_2, a_4, a_6) &\leftarrow S_2, S_3, S_5, \ a_2 < 10 \\
P_4(a_1, a_2, a_4, a_6) &\leftarrow S_2, S_4, S_5, \ a_2 < 10
\end{aligned}
$$

For instance, plan P_1 is composed of sources S_1, S_3, and S_5, which have IQ-vectors according to the scores of Table 5.3:

$$
\begin{aligned}
IQ(S_1) &= (99, \ 0, \quad 1, \ 0.2, \ 99.9, \quad 0.6, \ 0.89) \\
IQ(S_3) &= (60, \ 0, \ 0.5, \ 0.2, \ 99.8, \quad 0.9, \ 1) \\
IQ(S_5) &= (99, \ 1, \ 0.2, \ 0.1, \ 99.95, \ 0.8, \ 1)
\end{aligned}
$$

Using the merge functions, the IQ-vectors of P_1 and of the other plans are aggregated to

$$
\begin{aligned}
IQ(P_1) &= (58.8, \ 1, \ 1, \ 0.2, \ 99.65, \ 0.432, \ 1) \\
IQ(P_2) &= (78.4, \ 1, \ 1, \quad 3, \ 99.8 \ , \ 0.384, \ 1) \\
IQ(P_3) &= (58.8, \ 1, \ 1, \ 0.2, \ 99.65, \ 0.576, \ 1) \\
IQ(P_4) &= (78.4, \ 1, \ 1, \quad 3, \ 99.8 \ , \ 0.512, \ 1)
\end{aligned}
$$

Assuming equal weighting among the criteria, SAW gives the final scores

$$
iq(P_1) = 0.3213, \quad iq(P_2) = 0.2856, \quad iq(P_3) = 0.4284, \quad iq(P_4) = 0.238,
$$

so the ranking is P_3, P_1, P_2, and P_4. P_2 and P_4 are rated low mainly due to their high price (3 compared to 0.2), and P_3 is rated better than P_1 due to its higher coverage—it includes larger sources.

5.2.4 Computational Complexity

Phase 2, the query planning phase, computationally dominates the three-phase algorithm. Source selection in Phase 1 has polynomial complexity, because we use DEA as MADM method. DEA solves n linear programs, which has been proven to be a polynomial-solvable problem. Despite this, the Simplex method developed by Dantzig is the most popular method to solve linear programs. Simplex is worst-case exponential, but has a low average-case complexity [28]. Also, Phase 1 is not executed for each query, but only once initially, and then every time a source undergoes major changes, or a new source is added to the system.

Complexity of Phase 2 depends on the query planning algorithm that is used. Query planning algorithms like the algorithm presented in Section 5.2.2 have a complexity exponential in the size of the user query $|Q|$ and the number of sources n, because the number of plans to be generated is $O(n^{|Q|})$. In our simple model all plans are sound. Current algorithms for more complex source descriptions and user queries, for instance the bucket algorithm by Levy et al. [73], implement a simple generate & test method by creating all possible combinations of views, and checking their soundness as a separate step that is exponential in the length of the plan.

In Phase 3 we calculate the IQ-score for each plan generated in Phase 2. This process is linear in the size of the user query (i.e., the length of the plan), multiplied with the number of criteria to be evaluated. Finally, the top N plans must be found, which is $O(N \cdot X)$ where X is the number of plans generated in Phase 2.

5.3 Integrating Quality Reasoning and Query Planning

Applying IQ-reasoning to query planning yields more advantages than only selecting the best sources and best plans. Instead of *attaching* source selection and plan selection phases to conventional planning algorithms, we can *integrate* these phases to a new planning algorithm that efficiently finds the top N plans for a query. This section introduces a branch & bound algorithm for query planning in our quality-enhanced framework. The High Quality Branch & Bound (HiQ B&B) algorithm intelligently enumerates plans in such a way that it usually finds the best N plans after computing only a fraction of the total number of plans. We construct upper quality bounds for partial plans and thereby prune non-promising subplans early in the search tree. The efficiency of our algorithm is shown by simulation experiments.

5.3.1 The HiQ B&B Algorithm

The HiQ B&B algorithm replaces Phases 2 and 3 of the three-phase algorithm. Source selection in Phase 1 remains unchanged. As before, the input to our algorithm is a set of buckets, each containing a set of source views. A plan is composed of exactly one source per bucket.

The main ideas of the algorithm are as follows: We incrementally construct plans by building subplans of increasing length. Because plans consist of one element per bucket, we add a new bucket to an existing subplan in each step. This step is the *branching* of branch & bound. If visualized in a search tree, each inner node of the tree represents a subplan and each leaf node represents a finished plan. After selecting a node, branching creates several child nodes, i.e., longer subplans. We use IQ-scores to prune those subplans that will provably not be part of any top N plan. This step is the *bounding* part. We calculate for each subplan the maximum IQ-score that any plan containing this subplan can ever reach. We use this score as an *upper bound.*

If we were interested in the single best plan, we could use the upper bounds in the following way: Once we have at least one complete plan P, we discard every subplan, whose upper bound is less than the IQ-score of P. As better complete plans are constructed, more and more subplans are pruned. We are finished if no promising subplan remains. Because we are interested in the top N plans, and not only in the best plan, we use the IQ-score of the Nth best plan found so far as the upper bound. The HiQ B&B algorithm is given as Algorithm 1.

Input: number N, buckets $B_1, \ldots, B_n$ filled with appropriate sources
Output: $\leq N$ best query plans

```
 1: Q1 = {}                                    {Priority queue for subplans}
 2: Q2 = {}                                {Priority queue for complete plans}
 3: for i = 1 to |B₁| do
 4:    Q1.push(Sᵢ, ub(Sᵢ));            {Initialize Q1 with subplans of length 1}
 5: end for
 6: while Q1 ≠ {} do
 7:    P = Q1.pop();                    {Get best subplan and delete it from Q1}
 8:    SP = branch(P);                         {Generate longer subplans}
 9:    for all P ∈ SP do
10:       if |P| = n then
11:          Q2.push(P, IQ(P));                   {P is a complete plan}
12:       else
13:          Q1.push(P, ub(P));                  {P is not yet complete}
14:       end if
15:       if |Q2| ≥ N then
16:          bound(Q1, IQ(Q2[N]));                   {Prune plans in Q1}
17:       end if
18:    end for
19: end while
20: return Q2;
```

Algorithm 1: The High Quality Branch & Bound Algorithm (HiQ B&B)

The algorithm takes as input the pre-calculated buckets $B_1, \ldots, B_n$ for a translated query Q' with $|Q'| = n$, and the integer N. The main data structures of the algorithm are two priority queues $Q1$ and $Q2$. The queues contain subplans and finished plans, respectively, together with their upper bound. $Q1$ contains only unfinished subplans, i.e., subplans P that contain less than n sources ($|P| < n$). These subplans are sorted decreasingly according to their upper quality bound. $Q2$ contains only complete plans, i.e., plans P with $|P| = n$. $Q2$ is ordered by the IQ-scores of the plans.

The algorithm proceeds as follows: In lines 3–5 we initialize $Q1$ by inserting all sources of bucket B_1 with their upper bound. The main loop of the algorithm successively takes and treats subplans from $Q1$ until the queue is empty, i.e., until no more promising subplan exists. In the loop, we take the most promising so-far existing subplan P from $Q1$ and branch it (line 8). The function $branch(P)$ takes as an argument a subplan with length l and returns a list SP of subplans, each with length $l+1$. These subplans are each created by adding to P one of the sources in bucket B_{l+1}.

We then consider each new subplan P of SP individually. If $|P| = n$, it is already a complete plan and is inserted into $Q2$ (Line 11). If P is not yet complete, its new upper bound is calculated and P is re-inserted into $Q1$ using the upper bound as sorting key (Line 13). Finally, we check whether we already have N complete plans in $Q2$. If this is the case, we can prune any subplan whose upper bound is lower than the IQ-score of the Nth best plan. These subplans have no chance of ever being among the N best plans. The function $bound(Q1, IQ(Q2[N]))$ takes the quality score of the Nth best plan in $Q2$ and removes from $Q1$ all subplans with a lower upper bound (Line 16). This pruning is done simply by cutting off the priority queue at the appropriate position.

We can immediately stop if $Q1$ is empty, and return $Q2$. Although probably by far not all correct plans have been constructed, the first N plans in $Q2$ are guaranteed to be the best (if N plans exist at all). Plans beyond the Nth in $Q2$ are not necessarily the next best plans.

Because the algorithm follows the standard branch & bound approach, we proceed without an example, but instead—after introducing an efficient upper bound—present a performance evaluation through simulation experiments in Section 5.3.3.

5.3.2 Information Quality Bounds

The efficiency of the branch & bound algorithm HiQ B&B relies heavily on its pruning ability. The more and the earlier branches can be pruned, the faster we reach optimal plans, and the less time is spent constructing plans that turn out to be non-optimal.

To decide correctly whether a subplan P can be pruned, we must calculate an upper bound for the best possible IQ-score of any complete plan P' containing the subplan P. Hence, we need an upper bound function $ub(P)$ such that

$$ub(P) \geq \max_{P' \supseteq P} [IQ(P')].$$

The more accurately this bound is computed, the more efficient the algorithm is. Clearly, we could calculate the *exact* bound by computing $IQ(P')$ for *each* P' with $P \subseteq P'$. This precision would require a complete enumeration of the search space *in each step*, and would hence destroy the gain of the HiQ B&B approach. Instead, we determine $ub(P)$ by forecasting plan quality. We compute $ub(P)$ as the IQ-vector of P itself combined with some IQ-vector I_i for each remaining bucket:

$$ub(P) := iq\left(IQ(P) \circ I_{i+1} \circ \cdots \circ I_n\right).$$

A first attempt for I_j, $i < j \leq n$ would be to choose the IQ-vector of the best source in B_j. But this attempt does not necessarily result in the best possible plan, because for the measure for plan quality the principle of optimality does not hold. The principle of optimality states that "the completion of an optimal sequence of decisions must be optimal" [9]. Adding a good source to a subplan does not necessarily increase plan quality more than adding a source that is not as good. Some sources complement a subplan more effectively than others do. For example, one source might provide an attribute that no source in the subplan has yet covered. This source might complement the subplan better than an otherwise good source not providing the attribute.

Choosing the best source from each B_j is therefore not safe. To compensate, we construct I_j as follows. Let $d_i^{\max}$ be the maximum score of criterion i of all sources in bucket B_j. Then $I_j := (d_1^{\max}, \ldots, d_m^{\max})$. Clearly, the IQ-vector I_j is better than that of any source of B_j. But it is now also guaranteed that the IQ-score of a plan expanded by *any* source of B_j can be bounded using I_j.

The upper bound becomes more exact, the longer the subplan gets. The upper bound of a plan of length n will finally equal its exact IQ-score. Using this observation, we can prove that $ub(P)$ actually is an upper bound, i.e., the IQ-score of any plan containing P is lower than the upper bound for P.

Theorem 5.3.1. *The upper bound for a subplan $ub(P)$, as defined previously, is an upper quality bound for complete plans P' containing this subplan, i.e.,*

$$ub(P) \geq \max_{P' \supseteq P}[IQ(P')]$$

Proof. We denote a subplan of length i with $P^{(i)}$. We show that the upper bound monotonously decreases with the length of the subplan, i.e., $ub(P^{(i-1)}) \geq ub(P^{(i)})$ for any $P^{(i)} \supset P^{(i-1)}$:

$$\begin{aligned}
ub(P^{(i-1)}) &= iq\left(IQ(P^{(i-1)}) \circ I_i \circ I_{i+1} \circ \ldots \circ I_n\right) \\
&\geq iq\left(IQ(P^{(i-1)}) \circ IQ(S_{\text{arbitrary}} \in B_i) \circ I_{i+1} \circ \ldots \circ I_n\right) \\
&= iq\left(IQ(P^{(i)}) \circ I_{i+1} \circ \ldots \circ I_n\right) \\
&= ub(P^{(i)})
\end{aligned}$$

This holds for *any* continuation of a subplan $P^{(i-1)}$. Thus,

$$ub(S_x) = ub(P^{(1)}) \geq \ldots \geq ub(P^{(i)}) \geq \ldots \geq ub(P^{(n)})$$
$$= IQ(P^{(n)}) = \max_{P' \supseteq P^{(n)}}[IQ(P')]$$

for *any* initial source S_x and *any* continuation of $P^{(j)}$ at *any* step.

We have shown that we may safely prune subplans using our upper quality estimates. The second important point of improvement of HiQ B&B as opposed to an exhaustive exploration of the search space is an intelligent branching. In our implementation of teh algorithm we added two heuristics to speed up the algorithm:

1. We sort buckets by size—decreasing in one variant, and increasing in another. As pointed out previously, the join order of a plan is of no importance, giving us some freedom for optimization: Sorting buckets by size helps to produce long subplans, and hopefully complete plans, more quickly. If small buckets are considered first, the priority queue Q does not grow as fast, giving the algorithm less subplans to choose from. If large buckets are considered first, the algorithm has a larger choice.
2. At each branch the algorithm continues with the best subplan found so far. Continuing with the best subplans is the most important heuristic of the branch & bound approach. Without it, the algorithm would be reduced to a random, though non-redundant, exploration of the search space. With it, we proceed purposefully towards best plans.

5.3.3 Evaluation

To evaluate the performance of the HiQ B&B algorithm we carried out several simulation experiments, and observed a dramatic performance increase over brute force techniques for different parameter settings, such as the size of the query, the number of sources, etc. In particular we tested three variants of the algorithm: the simple HiQ B&B algorithm, and the HiQ B&B algorithm with the additional technique of sorting buckets by size, increasingly and decreasingly.

For the experiments we used the seven query-specific IQ-criteria of the example. The scores for the criteria were distributed uniformly across given ranges. The main parameters for the simulation were the average number n of sources per bucket, the number $|Q|$ of buckets (size of the user query), and the number of best plans to be generated (N). We ran experiments varying each of these parameters and counted the number of intermediate subplans and plans created by the algorithm. The figures show the average number of subplans created in 1000 runs. The number of subplans is the main indicator for efficiency of the algorithms. The effectiveness of all algorithms is the same: All return the top N plans for a query.

Figure 5.4 shows the behavior of the algorithms for an increasing number of sources. The size of the user query was fixed at 4 and the number of top plans to be generated was 5. Since access to many sources is one of the main opportunities of the Internet, these tests are of most importance.

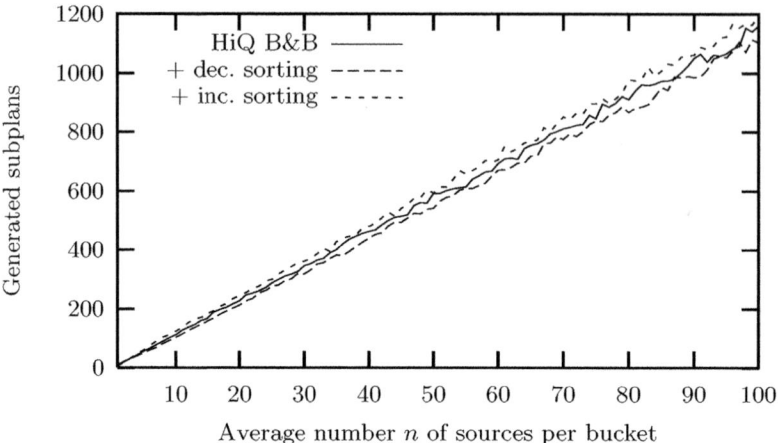

Fig. 5.4. Scalability in number of sources, $|Q| = 4$, $N = 5$

We observe a linear behavior of all variants of the algorithms. Sorting the buckets by decreasing size gives a slight advantage over the other two alternatives, as expected. The overall number of generated subplans is surprisingly low. For instance, in the case of an average of 50 sources per bucket, HiQ B&B reaches the optimal result by only generating about 550 subplans out of $50^4 + 50^3 + 50^2 + 50 = 6,387,550$ possible subplans. The reason for this efficiency is that a greedy algorithm already is a good strategy for our problem. The influence of the attributes causing the loss of the principle of optimality is not very high, i.e., long subplans usually are better than short subplans so the algorithm tends to proceed depth-first, and adding a large source to a plan is usually the best choice.

Figure 5.5 plots the number of generated subplans for different *query sizes*, i.e, for an increasing number of buckets. We chose a maximum of 10 buckets, because we do not expect global schemata to have more than 10 relations. The number of sources averaged 5 sources per bucket, and the number of top plans to be generated was 5 in all runs. Again, we observe linear scaling with the size of the user query. Therefore, the algorithm is suitable not only for many sources but also for complex global schemata where queries involve many relations.

Figure 5.6 plots the number of generated subplans for a different number N of plans to be returned. The number of sources averaged 10 per bucket and user query size was 5. With these parameters, the total number of plans

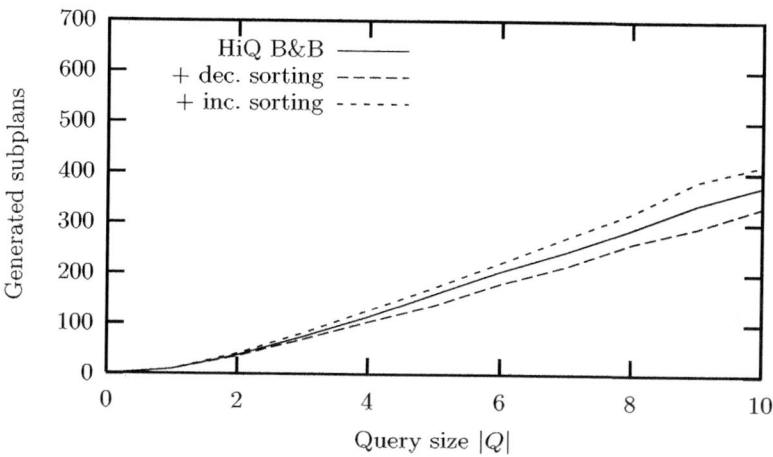

Fig. 5.5. Scalability in query size, $n = 5$, $N = 5$

is $10^5 = 100,000$ and the total number of plans and subplans is 111,110. The number of generated subplans in a run can be higher than the total number of complete plans, because construction of one final plan ensues construction of several subplans. Again, we observe linear behavior, i.e., the HiQ B&B scales well in the number of plans to be returned. For every plan in the solution approximately 10 subplans and plans were created.

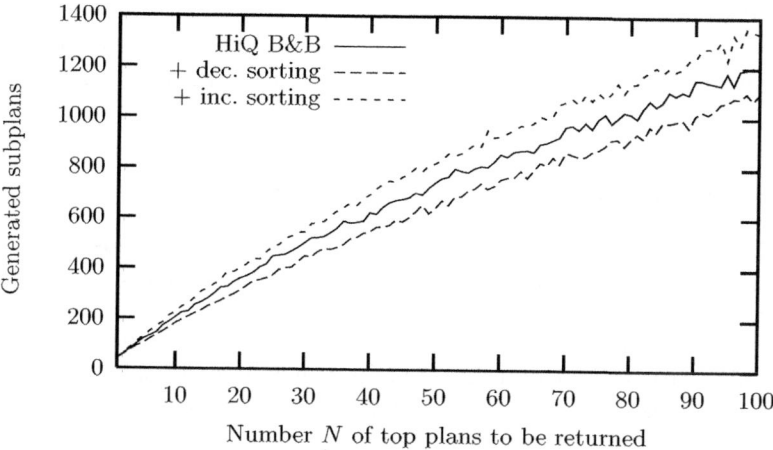

Fig. 5.6. Scalability in the number of top plans to be returned, $n = 10$, $|Q| = 5$

5.4 Related Work

Related work for this chapter draws from two areas—finding the top N results to a query and query planning algorithms. In neither research area has information quality been considered. The search for top N results is only justified by some "relevance" criterion, and no research on query planning has considered the quality of its results, despite the assumption of all projects that the underlying data sources are autonomous.

5.4.1 Top N Results

Recently, there has been some research on retrieving only the top N answers to a query [13, 21, 123]. For instance, Chaudhuri and Gravano justify the relaxed requirement with a query for houses at a certain price and with a certain number of rooms against a real estate database. Obviously, the user does not expect only houses that *exactly* match the query, rather, the N results *best* matching the query should be returned. In an earlier article the authors based the top N approach on multimedia repositories, where objects typically match conditions only to a certain degree [20]. Therefore, it does not suffice to only return exact matches, nor is it feasible to return all objects that match to even the slightest degree. In their paper, the user must specify a minimum matching degree for result objects. This research amounts to the consideration of concession C.1 for query planning (page 18).

Mihaila et al. recently suggested to use IQ-metadata for source selection [84]. To this end, the authors suggest an extension of SQL with fuzzy conditions so that the user can specify the desired quality of the result. The authors present a planning algorithm similar to our three-phase algorithm to answer the queries. However, it is left open how to determine aggregated IQ-scores for plans to rank them and select the best.

5.4.2 Query Planning

A query planner under the local-as-view paradigm effectively needs to solve the problem of "answering queries using views" [72], for which several algorithms have been proposed [110, 73, 65, 36, 68].

Levy et al. show that this problem is NP-complete for conjunctive queries and conjunctive view definitions [72]. In principle, one has to enumerate all combinations of views up to a certain length, and test for each of these, whether it is contained in the original query. In [73] and [74] the authors describe a bucket algorithm similar to ours. The algorithm constructs one bucket per relation in the query, and drops those source views into the bucket that match the relation. Then, the algorithm enumerates the cartesian product of the buckets. Because the authors do not restrict user queries to views of the universal relation like we do, many combinations in the cartesian product represent incorrect or incompatible plans. Thus, the algorithm must check whether the plan is contained in the user query, i.e., whether it returns correct tuples.

Leser presents an improved bucket algorithm that avoids redundant generation of subplans and thus redundant testing for correctness [70]. Also recently, Pottinger and Levy introduced an improved algorithm for the same problem [109]. All mentioned algorithms are suitable for Phase 2 of our 3 Phase approach in Section 5.2.2.

5.5 Summary

The contributions of this chapter are twofold: The chapter performed the integration of query planning and IQ-reasoning. It presented a quality model to determine IQ-scores for query plans, based on the IQ-scores of the sources in the plan. The quality model aggregates IQ-scores bottom up along the query tree, similar to cost models in conventional query optimization systems. Based on this quality model we justified and formulated the problem of finding the top N plans for a query.

To solve this problem optimally, the chapter presented two approaches. The first approach functions as an add-on to any given query planning algorithm—two IQ-reasoning phases are attached before and after the actual planning phase. The approach identifies the top N plans after creating all plans. The second approach is a branch & bound algorithm that also finds the top N plans, but in a more efficient manner—we use IQ-scores to prune the search space. We performed an experimental evaluation of the algorithm and observed high efficiency and scalability.

6 Query Planning Revisited

The previous chapter introduced the conventional query planning paradigm in information integration. The paradigm asks for *all* correct plans that answer a user query, i.e., all combinations of sources connected through join operations returning tuples that answer the query. Only then is an answer guaranteed that contains all available tuples matching the query. In this chapter we point out shortcomings of this paradigm, and therefore introduce a new approach. We redefine the notion of a query plan by introducing three new merge operators to combine heterogeneous data; we translate user queries against the universal relation to queries against the global schema using the new operators; and we show how to construct query plans for the translated queries. In the chapters hereafter, we revise our search for the best N plans under this new paradigm. With the new operators we are able to find a globally optimal set of plans instead of a set of locally optimal plans.

6.1 Shortcomings of Conventional Query Planning

The approach to logical query planning taken in the previous chapter and by many other research projects, has one minor and one major shortcoming with regard to our goal of finding the top N results: Data conflicts are not resolved, and the final outerjoin of plans is not modeled.

Data Conflicts. We addressed data conflicts in Section 2.3.2 (page 20). Data about a real world entity may be stored with differing attribute values at different sources. In strict, duplicate removing relational semantics, those tuples would appear individually in the result of any operator. Even in the presence of a unique ID-attribute identifying the entity—which we assume throughout the thesis to exist—a relational operator returns multiple tuples about the same entity. Integration of results is reduced to concatenation of results. It is left to the user to identify and resolve data conflicts. We propose to make use of the ID-attribute and only represent one result tuple per real world entity. To this end traditional operators must be enhanced to include resolution functions as presented earlier.

Outerjoin. Query planning as introduced in the previous chapter finds all or a set of plans answering a query. The plans form different combinations of

F. Naumann: Quality-Driven Query Answering, LNCS 2261, pp. 89-100, 2002.
© Springer-Verlag Berlin Heidelberg 2002

sources (actually source views) connected through join operators. What is not regarded is the final integration of the results of these plans; once the plans are executed, the results must be combined to a response to the user. This composition can be modeled as the outerjoin of the plans.

Example 6.1.1. Consider the four plans for query Q_2' of Example 5.1.2 (page 71):

$$P_1(a_1, a_2, a_4, a_6) \leftarrow S_1, S_3, S_5, \ a_2 < 10$$
$$P_2(a_1, a_2, a_4, a_6) \leftarrow S_1, S_4, S_5, \ a_2 < 10$$
$$P_3(a_1, a_2, a_4, a_6) \leftarrow S_2, S_3, S_5, \ a_2 < 10$$
$$P_4(a_1, a_2, a_4, a_6) \leftarrow S_2, S_4, S_5, \ a_2 < 10$$

If all plans were executed and the results integrated, we can model this process as the execution of a single larger plan, where $\sqcup$ is some operator similar to the outerjoin and yet to be defined:

$$P(a_1, a_2, a_4, a_6)$$
$$\leftarrow ((S_1, S_3, S_5) \sqcup (S_1, S_4, S_5) \sqcup (S_2, S_3, S_5) \sqcup (S_2, S_4, S_5)), \ a_2 < 10$$

By adding an outerjoin-type operator, we shift the paradigm of query planning from finding a *set* of plans to finding a single plan. With this shift we also gain the ability to obtain globally optimal solutions of our problem. By finding the set of N best plans as we did in the previous chapter, we do not consider how well the plans "fit together", i.e., how well they complement each other. By finding the best set of N plans instead, we regard the set of plans as a whole, combined through outerjoin-type operators. The quality measure for this set is the quality of the result as the user perceives it. Thus, the measure helps find the global optimum instead of several local optima.

6.2 Merge Operators

In the presence of data overlap and value conflicts between sources, standard relational operators are not useful for integration: Overlap must be recognized, conflicts must be resolved, and multiple plans must be integrated. To formalize the integration of sources and plans we define four new operators: the join-merge operator, denoted "$\sqcap$", the left outerjoin-merge operator, denoted "$\sqsupset$" (and right outerjoin-merge operator, denoted "$\sqsubset$"), and the full outerjoin-merge operator, denoted "$\sqcup$". The operators extend the relational inner join, left outerjoin, right outerjoin, and full outerjoin operators by including resolution functions in case of data conflicts. Figure 6.1 gives an intuition of the function of the operators. The figure represents the extensions of two sources corresponding to two different relations. The sources overlap intensionally in one attribute—a foreign ID of S_i which corresponds to the ID of S_j. This forms an ID–foreign ID relationship. The extensional overlap of

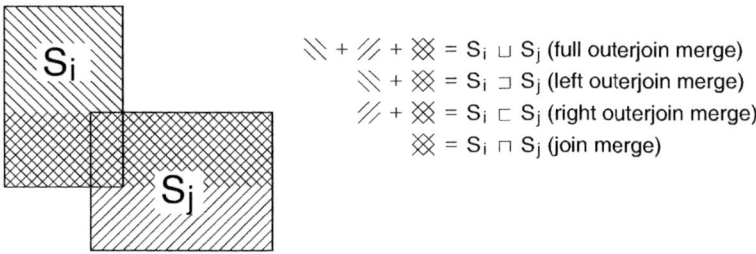

Fig. 6.1. The four merge operators

the two sources is the part shaded by a grid. The figure shows the extensions produced by the different merge-operators.

We call the operators *merge* operators, because they merge multiple results into one result. The individual results are not simply concatenated, but real world entities are represented only once in the result, possibly with attribute values from multiple sources. We define the operators between sources (i.e., source views), and not between relations, because in a plan the operator is applied to sources, not to relations. The operators naturally extend to intermediate results.

Example 6.2.1. We repeat Example 2.2.3 (page 17), combining the three relations $R_1(\underline{a_1}, a_2, a_3)$, $R_2(\underline{a_3}, a_4, a_5)$, and $R_3(\underline{a_5}, a_6)$. Primary IDs are underlined, foreign IDs have the same name as the primary ID they reference to. Table 6.1 shows the corresponding UR-tableau. We use this example to demonstrate the effect of the operators.

Table 6.1. UR-tableau with five sources.

UR	a_1	a_2	a_3	a_4	a_5	a_6
R_1 :	✓	✓	✓			
R_2 :			✓	✓	✓	
R_3 :					✓	✓
S_1 :	✓	✓	✓			
S_2 :	✓		✓			
S_3 :			✓	✓		
S_4 :			✓	✓	✓	
S_5 :					✓	✓

6.2.1 The Join-Merge Operator

We define the join-merge operator and show an example in Figure 6.2. The purpose of the join-merge operator is to perform join-like operations across sources with possibly conflicting data.

We restrict the use of the join-merge operator to two cases: Either the join attribute a_k is an ID for both sources ($S_1 \sqcap_{a_1} S_2$), or a_k is an ID for one source and a corresponding foreign ID for the other source ($S_1 \sqcap_{a_3} S_4$). We do not allow joins over other attributes than ID-attributes. Through this restriction we avoid joining over conflicting data. By definition, IDs do not conflict—if they have the same value, we assume that they represent the same entity, if they differ, we assume that they represent different entities. Wherever the join attribute is clear, we omit the operator index that specifies it.

Definition 6.2.1 (Join-Merge Operator $\sqcap$). *Let A be the set of attributes in the universal relation. Let $S_i = (A_i)$ and $S_j = (A_j)$ be two data sources with $A_i, A_j \subseteq A$, $A_i \cap A_j \neq \emptyset$, and let $a_k \in A_i \cap A_j$.*

$$
\begin{aligned}
S_i \sqcap_{a_k} S_j := \{ tuple\ t[A] \mid\ & \exists r \in S_i,\ s \in S_j\ with \\
& t[a_k] = r[a_k] = s[a_k], \\
& t[a] = r[a],\ \forall a \in A_i \setminus A_j \\
& t[a] = s[a],\ \forall a \in A_j \setminus A_i \\
& t[a] = f(r[a], s[a]),\ \forall a \in A_i \cap A_j, a \neq a_k \\
& t[a] = \bot,\ \forall a \in A \setminus (A_i \cup A_j) \},
\end{aligned}
$$

where f is a resolution function as defined in Definition 2.3.1 (Page 21).

The join-merge operator returns tuples for UR that are joined from tuples in S_i and S_j, using a_k as join attribute. For all attributes exclusively provided by S_i, the values of S_i are used, for all attributes exclusively provided by S_j, the values of S_j are used. For common attributes, the join-merge operator applies the resolution function f to determine the final value. Attributes values of all other attributes of UR are padded with `null` values.

Example 6.2.2. Assume sources S_1, S_2, and S_4 to have the content shown in Figure 6.2. Below the sources, we show the results of two join-merge operations. The two results represent the tow cases to which we restrict the join-merge operator.

The join-merge operator corresponds to a traditional inner join operation with two exceptions: (i) We allow only one attribute as join attribute, even if the two sources have more than one attribute in common. This common attribute is a_k in the definition. (ii) For all other common attributes data conflicts might arise, i.e., the sources provide different values for the attribute. Instead of creating a new tuple, resolution function f resolves these conflicts and determines which value shall appear in the result.

6.2.2 The Left Outerjoin-Merge Operator

We define the left outerjoin-merge operator and continue the example in Figure 6.3. The definition of the operator is based on the join-merge operator

$$S_1 : \underline{a_1}\ a_2\ a_3 \qquad S_2 : \underline{a_1}\ a_3 \qquad S_4 : \underline{a_3}\ a_4\ a_5$$

$$
\begin{array}{ccc}
1 & \text{`x'} & 15 \\
2 & \text{`y'} & \bot \\
3 & \bot & 15 \\
4 & \text{`z'} & 21
\end{array}
\qquad
\begin{array}{cc}
1 & 16 \\
4 & \bot \\
5 & 17
\end{array}
\qquad
\begin{array}{ccc}
15 & \text{`x'} & \text{`g'} \\
16 & \text{`y'} & \bot \\
17 & \text{`x'} & \text{`i'}
\end{array}
$$

$$S_1 \sqcap_{a_1} S_2 : \begin{array}{cccccc} a_1 & a_2 & a_3 & a_4 & a_5 & a_6 \\ 1 & \text{`x'} & f(15,16) & \bot & \bot & \bot \\ 4 & \text{`z'} & f(21,\bot) & \bot & \bot & \bot \end{array}$$

$$S_1 \sqcap_{a_3} S_4 : \begin{array}{cccccc} a_1 & a_2 & a_3 & a_4 & a_5 & a_6 \\ 1 & \text{`x'} & 15 & \text{`x'} & \text{`g'} & \bot \\ 3 & \bot & 15 & \text{`x'} & \text{`g'} & \bot \end{array}$$

Fig. 6.2. The join-merge operator

of Definition 6.2.1. We also define the right outerjoin-merge, but shall use only the left outerjoin-merge operator in the following. For the definition we use the outer-union operator $\uplus$, which performs a union over relations with differing attribute sets [26]. The attribute set of the result is the union of the attribute sets of the two relations. In our case this is the entire attribute set A because the result of a join-merge operation has A as attribute set. $[A_i]$ denotes the projection on attributes A_i.

Definition 6.2.2 (Left and Right Outerjoin-Merge Operator $\sqsupset\ /\ \sqsubset$).
Let A be the set of attributes in the universal relation. Let $S_i = (A_i)$ and $S_j = (A_j)$ be two data sources with $A_i, A_j \in A$, $A_i \cap A_j \neq \emptyset$, and let $a_k \in A_i \cap A_j$.

$$S_i \sqsupset_{a_k} S_j := (S_i \sqcap_{a_k} S_j)\ \uplus\ (S_i \setminus (S_i \sqcap_{a_k} S_j)[A_i]),$$
$$S_i \sqsubset_{a_k} S_j := S_j \sqsupset_{a_k} S_i.$$

The left outerjoin-merge corresponds to the classical left outerjoin with the same exceptions as for the join-merge operator. The left outerjoin-merge guarantees that all tuples from one source (S_1 in Figure 6.3) enter the result. Wherever possible, they are joined with tuples from the other source. If this is not possible, we pad the missing values with null ($\bot$). As for the join-merge operator, usage of the left outerjoin-merge is restricted to the two cases shown in Figure 6.3. Because the right outerjoin-merge operator is basically the same as the left outerjoin-merge, we continue the discussion only with the latter.

6.2.3 The Full Outerjoin-Merge Operator

We define the full outerjoin-merge operator and continue with the example in Figure 6.4.

S_1 : a_1 a_2 a_3
1 'x' 15
2 'y' ⊥
3 ⊥ 15
4 'z' 21

S_2 : a_1 a_3
1 16
4 ⊥
5 17

S_4 : a_3 a_4 a_5
15 'x' 'g'
16 'y' ⊥
17 'x' 'i'

$S_1 \sqsupset_{a_1} S_2$: a_1 a_2 a_3 a_4 a_5 a_6
1 'x' $f(15, 16)$ ⊥ ⊥ ⊥
2 'y' ⊥ ⊥ ⊥ ⊥
3 ⊥ 15 ⊥ ⊥ ⊥
4 'z' $f(21, \bot)$ ⊥ ⊥ ⊥

$S_1 \sqsupset_{a_3} S_4$: a_1 a_2 a_3 a_4 a_5 a_6
1 'x' 15 'x' 'g' ⊥
2 'y' ⊥ ⊥ ⊥ ⊥
3 ⊥ 15 'x' 'g' ⊥
4 'z' 21 ⊥ ⊥ ⊥

Fig. 6.3. The left outerjoin-merge operator

Definition 6.2.3 (Full Outerjoin-Merge Operator ⊔). *Let A be the set of attributes in the universal relation. Let $S_i = (A_i)$ and $S_j = (A_j)$ be two data sources with $A_i, A_j \in A$, $A_i \cap A_j \neq \emptyset$, and let $a_k \in A_i \cap A_j$.*

$$S_i \sqcup_{a_k} S_j := (S_i \sqcap_{a_k} S_j) \uplus (S_i \setminus (S_i \sqcap_{a_k} S_j)[A_i]) \uplus (S_j \setminus (S_i \sqcap_{a_k} S_j)[A_j]).$$

S_1 : a_1 a_2 a_3
1 'x' 15
2 'y' ⊥
3 ⊥ 15
4 'z' 21

S_2 : a_1 a_3
1 16
4 ⊥
5 17

S_4 : a_3 a_4 a_5
15 'x' 'g'
16 'y' ⊥
17 'x' 'i'

$S_1 \sqcup_{a_1} S_2$: a_1 a_2 a_3 a_4 a_5 a_6
1 'x' $f(15, 16)$ ⊥ ⊥ ⊥
2 'y' ⊥ ⊥ ⊥ ⊥
3 ⊥ 15 ⊥ ⊥ ⊥
4 'z' $f(21, \bot)$ ⊥ ⊥ ⊥
5 ⊥ 17 ⊥ ⊥ ⊥

$S_1 \sqcup_{a_3} S_4$: a_1 a_2 a_3 a_4 a_5 a_6
1 'x' 15 'x' 'g' ⊥
2 'y' ⊥ ⊥ ⊥ ⊥
3 ⊥ 15 'x' 'g' ⊥
4 'z' 21 ⊥ ⊥ ⊥
⊥ ⊥ 16 'y' ⊥ ⊥
⊥ ⊥ 17 'x' 'i' ⊥

Fig. 6.4. The union-merge operator

The full outerjoin-merge operator guarantees that every tuple from both sources enters the result. Missing values in attributes of tuples that do not have a matching tuple in the other source are padded with null values (⊥). Again, we restrict the operator to the two cases of Figure 6.4.

6.3 Revised Logical Query Planning

In this section we describe a revised process of query planning, i.e., establishing the search space of all correct plans answering user queries against the universal relation. As before for query planning without the new operators, we first describe how we translate user queries against the universal relation to queries against the global schema. There, we make use of the new operators. Then, we describe how we construct query plans for such translated queries.

6.3.1 Query Translation

As explained in Section 5.1, we translate queries against the universal relation UR to queries against the global schema to find source views to answer user queries. The translation here extends Definition 5.1.1 by using the three new operators:

Definition 6.3.1 (Translated Query). *Let $Q[A_Q] \leftarrow UR, C$ be a user query where A_Q is the set of requested attributes, and C the set of conditions on these attributes. We obtain the corresponding translated query $Q'(A_Q) \leftarrow body$ in the following way:*

1. *The body of Q' contains all relations of which A_Q contains an attribute. Conditions C are included unchanged.*
2. *The body of Q' additionally contains all necessary relations to make the graph of relations and joins connected.*
3. *All ID–foreign ID relationships defined for the relations contained in the body of Q' are turned into one of the three new operators:*
   - *full outerjoin-merge ($\sqcup$) if there are no selections on any attribute of either relation,*
   - *left outerjoin-merge ($\sqsupset$) if there is a selection on at least one attribute of exactly one relation. The relation with the selection condition is the "left" relation, i.e., unmatched tuples of this relation enter the the the result,*
   - *join-merge ($\sqcap$) if there are selections on attributes of both relations.*
4. *The precedence order of the operators is first $\sqcup$, then $\sqsupset$, then $\sqcap$. Parentheses are inserted accordingly.*

The roles of Rules 1 and 2 remain unchanged. Translation rule 3 combines the relations of the global schema through merge operators. The relations are combined depending on whether there are selection conditions on them or not. Intuitively, the starting point is the extensional completeness requirement R.2 of Section 2.2.2. To include all accessible data, relations should be combined with the full outerjoin-merge operator ($\sqcup$). To ensure correctness (R.1) the operator possibly must be changed to a left outerjoin-merge ($\sqsupset$) or a join-merge ($\sqcap$), depending on the distribution of the conditions.

Note that if the selection condition were applied *after* a full outerjoin-merge, those tuples would be removed from the result anyway. However, with the help of the left outerjoin-merge we allow to push selection conditions to the source. Not only does this pushing improve response time of a plan (we do not have to retrieve the entire source), but typical Web data sources also *require* some selection to be pushed. For instance, search engines require at least one keyword in the input form.

Finally, Rule 4 is necessary to ensure correctness, because a "late" outerjoin-merge could insert tuples conflicting with the conditions. The execution order can be changed later in the query plan, by repeating the selection operators that ensure the conditions.

Example 6.3.1. Recall the global schema consisting of three relations R_1, R_2, and R_3 of the previous example. Table 6.2 shows the corresponding UR-tableau. Consider user queries Q_1 requesting a_2 and a_4 without any selection conditions, Q_2 requesting a_1, a_2, a_4, and a_6 with the condition $a_2 < 10$, and Q_3 requesting a_1, a_2, and a_4 with the conditions $a_2 > 10$ and $a_4 < 40$.

Table 6.2. UR-tableau with three relations and three user queries.

UR	a_1	a_2	a_3	a_4	a_5	a_6
$R_1:$	✓	✓	✓			
$R_2:$			✓	✓	✓	
$R_3:$					✓	✓
$Q_1:$		✓		✓		
$Q_2:$	✓	< 10		✓		✓
$Q_3:$	✓	> 10		< 40		

The three queries are translated according to Definition 6.3.1:

$$Q_1'(a_2, a_4) \leftarrow R_1(a_1, a_2, a_3) \sqcup_{a_3} R_2(a_3, a_4, a_5)$$
$$Q_2'(a_1, a_2, a_4, a_6) \leftarrow R_1(a_1, a_2, a_3) \sqsupset_{a_3} (R_2(a_3, a_4, a_5)$$
$$\sqcup_{a_5} R_3(a_5, a_6)), \ a_2 < 10$$
$$Q_3'(a_1, a_2, a_4) \leftarrow R_1(a_1, a_2, a_3) \sqcap_{a_3} R_2(a_3, a_4, a_5), \ a_2 > 10, \ a_4 < 40$$

The join predicates in the index of the operators are redundant—we always use the unique common attribute of the two relations to be combined. In Q_1, the user requests two attributes from two relations without any conditions. Thus, the body of the plan contains the two relations, combined with a full outerjoin-merge. Because the user specifies no selection condition, we return any tuple that contains a value in a_2, in a_4, or in both. The result should list tuples with values in both attributes first, but we assume the user is interested in the others as well (concession C.3). Any other operator would reduce the number of the tuples in the result (contradicting requirement R.2).

With Q_2, the user requests attributes from all three relations, thus the body of the translated query contains all three. The selection on a_2 leads to the left outerjoin-merge operator. The plan returns all tuples from R_1 where the condition holds, and adds values for a_4 and a_6 from R_2 and R_3, wherever possible. A simple join-merge would remove from the result those tuples of R_1 that have no match in R_2, but we assume that the user is interested in those as well, even though they should be ranked lower in the result (C.3). A full outerjoin-merge on the other hand would add to the result tuples from $R_2 \sqcup R_3$ without matches in R_1. Those tuples have a `null` for a_2, thus, the selection condition $a_2 < 10$ does not hold (contradicting R.1).

With Q_3, the user requests attributes of two relations with selections on attributes of both relations. Thus, we combine both relations with the join-merge operator. Again, any other operator would allow tuples in the result for which not all selection conditions hold true (contradicting R.1), or retrieve unnecessary tuples that would have to be discarded later, once the selection conditions are applied.

6.3.2 Query Planning

Given a translated query against the global schema, the mediator tries to find plans that generate answers to the query. We describe how such a query against the global schema—translated from a user query—is transformed into a plan containing actual data sources.

Definition 6.3.2 (Query Plan). *Let Q' be a translated query against the global schema. We obtain a query plan P for Q' by replacing each relation of the body of Q' with a set of sources. The sources in the plan are combined by full outerjoin-merge operators. Each source in the set must correspond to the relation the set replaces.*

The set that replaces a relation can include one or more sources or can be empty. In the latter case the result of the query plan also is empty, or at least misses some attributes. Our quality model will recognize these deficiencies and assign low quality to such plans. The main difference of this definition of a query plan to Definition 5.1.2 is that not a *single* source replaces a relation, but a *set* of sources.

Example 6.3.2. Continuing the example, we give five sources $S_1, \ldots, S_5$ in the UR-tableau of Table 6.3, each providing a certain set of attributes of the universal relation UR, some having a selection condition on certain attributes. A selection indicates that the source only exports tuples to which the condition applies.

Consider the query $Q'_1(a_2, a_4) \leftarrow R_1(a_1, a_2, a_3) \sqcup_{a_3} R_2(a_3, a_4, a_5)$ translated from Q_1. The set of all possible plans for Q'_1 is

Table 6.3. UR-tableau with five sources and three user queries.

UR	a_1	a_2	a_3	a_4	a_5	a_6
$S_1:$	✓	✓	✓			
$S_2:$	✓		✓			
$S_3:$			✓	>10		
$S_4:$			✓	>50	✓	
$S_5:$					✓	✓
$Q_1:$		✓		✓		

$$P_1(a_2, a_4) \leftarrow \emptyset \qquad\qquad P_9(a_2, a_4) \leftarrow S_1 \sqcup_{a_3} S_4$$
$$P_2(a_2, a_4) \leftarrow S_1 \qquad\qquad P_{10}(a_2, a_4) \leftarrow S_2 \sqcup_{a_3} S_3$$
$$P_3(a_2, a_4) \leftarrow S_2 \qquad\qquad P_{11}(a_2, a_4) \leftarrow S_2 \sqcup_{a_3} S_4$$
$$P_4(a_2, a_4) \leftarrow S_1 \sqcup_{a_1} S_2 \qquad P_{12}(a_2, a_4) \leftarrow S_1 \sqcup_{a_3} (S_3 \sqcup_{a_3} S_4)$$
$$P_5(a_2, a_4) \leftarrow S_3 \qquad\qquad P_{13}(a_2, a_4) \leftarrow S_2 \sqcup_{a_3} (S_3 \sqcup_{a_3} S_4)$$
$$P_6(a_2, a_4) \leftarrow S_4 \qquad\qquad P_{14}(a_2, a_4) \leftarrow (S_1 \sqcup_{a_1} S_2) \sqcup_{a_3} S_3$$
$$P_7(a_2, a_4) \leftarrow S_3 \sqcup_{a_3} S_4 \qquad P_{15}(a_2, a_4) \leftarrow (S_1 \sqcup_{a_1} S_2) \sqcup_{a_3} S_4$$
$$P_8(a_2, a_4) \leftarrow S_1 \sqcup_{a_3} S_3 \qquad P_{16}(a_2, a_4) \leftarrow (S_1 \sqcup_{a_1} S_2) \sqcup_{a_3} (S_3 \sqcup_{a_3} S_4)$$

Several of these plans are useless. For instance, plans P_1 and P_3 do not return any results, because S_2 neither exports a_2 nor a_4. Many plans, such as P_5 or P_{13}, return values for only one of the two requested attributes. Only a few plans return values for both attributes and only P_{12} and P_{16} return *all* tuples given the available sources. The completeness model of the following Chapter 7 recognizes these differences by calculating the "completeness" for each of these plans. In Table 6.4, we foreclose exemplary completeness scores $C(P)$ for the 16 plans. We observe the uselessness of P_1 and P_3 (completeness 0), and we observe that P_{12} and P_{16} have the same (maximal) completeness scores, as expected. In the more general IQ-model of Chapter 4 the completeness of a plan is only one of several IQ-criteria, but the overall IQ-scores will reflect completeness to some degree.

Table 6.4. Completeness scores for translated queries

plan	P_1	P_2	P_3	P_4	P_5	P_6	P_7	P_8
$C(P)$	0	0.1	0	0.1	0.07	0.12	0.1732	0.17

plan	P_9	P_{10}	P_{11}	P_{12}	P_{13}	P_{14}	P_{15}	P_{16}
$C(P)$	0.22	0.07	0.12	0.2732	0.1732	0.17	0.22	0.2732

For a query, the search space to be considered by any query planning algorithm is the set of all possible plans for a query. The search space can be generated by determining the power set of all sources that correspond to relations of the query, and combining them with appropriate merge-operators. Assuming that there are k relations in the query and s sources for each relation, the size of the search space is 2^{ks}.

This search space differs substantially from the search space of a conventional database query optimizer. There, the search space consists of query execution plans that all return the *same* query result. They differ mainly in the order of the operators and the choice of operator algorithms. The optimizer traverses the space usually searching for the cost-optimal plan. Here, the search space consists of plans returning *different* query results, depending on which sources participate in the plan. Because the plans return different results, any optimizer should not be in search for the most efficient plan with a fixed result, but for the most effective plan—the plan with the highest quality possibly with a fixed cost limit.

6.4 Related Work

Literature describes several operators similar to the full outerjoin-merge, however none of the authors have sources in mind that possibly are mutually inconsistent. For instance, LaCroix and Pirotte define the "generalized natural join operator", denoted ⋈̇ [66]. Our full outerjoin-merge operator differs from their definition in two aspects: First, we resolve data conflicts with a resolution function f. Second, our join is not a natural join; rather, the join predicate only contains one join attribute—the ID. Other names for the full outerjoin are "two-sided outerjoin" (⋈) [43] or the "outer union" (⊐⊂ or ⊎) [39, 26]. The outer union operation is described as a union between relations that are not union compatible, i.e., that do not have identical attributes. The authors suggest to pad attributes for tuples that have no value with null values. Date offers a full discussion of outerjoins [29].

Query planning using only the join-merge operator is essentially the same as discussed in the previous chapter. We discussed related work in Section 5.4. Galindo-Legaria and Rosenthal thoroughly discuss the outerjoin operator and present optimization techniques for reordering the operators in a plan [43]. Their work addresses cost-based optimization in traditional databases, so we cannot make use of their results. We are not interested in the order of the operators but rather in the sources that are combined by the operators.

6.5 Summary

This chapter presented two main contributions: three new operators for information integration, and a revised query planning approach using the operators.

The new merge operators extend conventional operators by incorporating resolution functions to resolve data conflicts and by a special usage of IDs for integration. The left outerjoin-merge and the full outerjoin-merge operators further enhance the traditional query planning approach: There, a query result is computed by creating the set of all correct plans using only join operators. Here, we compute the same query result with only one plan. Selecting the best result can now be performed at a finer level of granularity: Selection of best plans now is refined to the selection of the top sources.

Due to this shift, the algorithms presented in Chapter 5 cannot be used for optimization. Therefore, we present algorithms for this new paradigm in Chapter 8, but first we concentrate on the completeness criterion as our main optimization goal.

7 Completeness of Data

For many data sources and many application domains, size is everything: The more tuples and the more attributes a source provides, the more attractive it is to users. For instance, users typically prefer large search engines, i.e., search engines that have indexed a large number of Web pages, over small search engines. The rationale is that the larger a search engine is, the higher the probability is, that the result the user is looking for has been indexed by the search engine (and therefore appears in the result). Also, users prefer search engines that return more attributes than others, e.g., knowing the *byte size* of a Web page before clicking on the link is advantageous. Further examples include online telephone books, where a high number of entries and a high number of additional attributes, such as *email address* or *fax number* attract users, or stock information systems, where a high coverage of world wide stock markets and a large number of attributes, such as *trade volume* for a stock quote is desirable.

In Chapter 3 we introduced the completeness criterion as one criterion among many other IQ-criteria. In this chapter we concentrate on completeness, because

- one of the main goals of information integration is to increase completeness. Many integration systems are built with the sole purpose of increasing completeness of the query results.
- the three new merge operators of the previous section were constructed to retrieve as much data as possible from the data sources to reflect that integration goal. Completeness is a measure for their efficacy.
- it is a criterion that applies to almost any application domain.

To include all facets of completeness, we divide the measure into two aspects: *Coverage* is a measure for the number of tuples a source stores; *density* is a measure for how well the attributes stored at a source are filled with actual (non-null) values. We combine the two aspects to an overall completeness measure. With the help of this measure, we are able to assess the usefulness of a source to answer a query wrt. completeness.

Queries can usually be answered better by accessing multiple sources, and often this is the only way to answer a query. Therefore, it is not enough to only regard the completeness of individual sources. To measure completeness of source combinations, we show how to measure completeness across the

F. Naumann: Quality-Driven Query Answering, LNCS 2261, pp. 101-121, 2002.
© Springer-Verlag Berlin Heidelberg 2002

new merge operators of the previous chapter. So for instance, we are able to determine the completeness of the result of a join-merge operation between two sources. These calculations are extended to determine completeness of entire query plans with different operators and sources, and different overlap situations.

7.1 A Completeness Measure for Sources

In this section we define formally the completeness criterion for data sources. Completeness is a measure for the "size" of a data source. We define it as a combination of two orthogonal criteria: coverage and density. Coverage is a measure for the relative number of tuples a source provides; density is a measure for the average amount of data a source provides for a single tuple.

7.1.1 Coverage

We define the coverage of a source as the ratio of the number of real world entities represented in the source, and the size of the universal relation UR. First, we define the extension of UR, then we define coverage of a data source.

Definition 7.1.1 (Extension of UR). *Let $S_1, \dots, S_n$ be the set of all available data sources. Then the extension of UR is $ext(UR) := S_1 \sqcup \cdots \sqcup S_n$. The size of UR is $|UR| := |S_1 \sqcup \cdots \sqcup S_n|$.*

We call the extension of UR the *world*. The world is the set of all tuples that can be obtained through the sources at hand. Thus, we make the closed world assumption. Because $|UR|$ acts only as a normalizing factor, this assumption is not necessary, but simplifies definitions and calculation of the coverage criterion.

Definition 7.1.2 (Coverage). *Let S be a data source. We define the coverage of S as*

$$c(S) := \frac{|S|}{|UR|}.$$

The coverage scores are in $[0, 1]$ due to our closed world assumption made in Definition 7.1.1. Intuitively, coverage can be regarded as the probability that an entity of the world is represented in the source.

Coverage assessment. Coverage scores may be difficult to obtain. Sometimes the sources themselves publish their size as a means for advertising their service. However, not always can these figures be trusted. A further possibility is to sample or download the source. If these assessment methods fail, coverage scores can only be estimated.

Estimating the size of the universal relation proves more difficult because of its definition as the full outerjoin of all sources. The more relations are in the global schema, the more the sizes of the individual relation extensions and the degree of overlap play a role. However as explained earlier, $|UR|$ acts only as a normalizing factor, so an exact number is not necessary. The more precise the number is, the more meaningful the absolute coverage scores are, but the coverage score of a source in relation to other sources remains unchanged.

7.1.2 Density

In our local-as-view approach of describing source schemata with respect to a global schema, the global schema is developed independently of the available sources. Once the global schema is developed, the sources are described as those parts of the global schema they contribute to. Thus, data sources do not export all attributes of the corresponding relation in the global schema. For instance, only a 4 of our sample survey of 15 search engines return the size attribute, which represents the byte size of Web pages. Also, typical sources provide attributes they do not completely cover. For instance, not all sources for company data provide a company profile text for all companies listed. Implicit null values are a common phenomenon in WWW data sources.

Missing attributes and values result in incomplete results, i.e., tuples with null values. Density is a measure for the ratio of non-null values to all values provided by a source. The term *density* is derived from the notion of dense vs. sparse matrices. Before defining density of attributes and data sources, we give a general definition.

Definition 7.1.3 (Density). *Let D be a set of values and $D^+ = D \cup \{\perp\}$ where $\perp$ denotes the null value. Let X be a multiset of values from D^+. The density of X is $|\{x \in X | x \neq \perp\}| / |X|$.*

First, we define density as an attribute specific measure, i.e., each attribute provided by a source is assigned a density score. For our purposes, we assign a density score of zero to those attributes that the source does not export. This has a decreasing effect on the overall density of the source.

Definition 7.1.4 (Attribute density). *Let A_R be the set of attributes of relation R. The density of attribute $a \in A_R$ in source S providing data for R is*

$$d_S(a) := \frac{|\{t \in S | t[a] \neq \perp\}|}{|S|},$$

where t are tuples of S, and $t[a]$ is their attribute value of a.

With Definition 7.1.4, an attribute with a non-null value for every tuple of the source has an attribute density of 1. An attribute that is not provided by a source has attribute density 0. A source that provides actual values for a certain attribute in every second tuple, has a density score of 0.5 for that attribute.

Definition 7.1.5 (Source density). *The density of a source S is the average density over all attributes of the universal relation:*

$$d(S) := \frac{1}{|A|} \sum_{a \in A} d_S(a).$$

Theorem 7.1.1. *Source density $d(S)$ is a density measure in the sense of Definition 7.1.3.*

Proof. Let the set of data items in source S be a multiset of values $x \in D^+ = D \cup \bot$, where D is a set of values (across all domains of the attributes of S). Thus, the size of the multiset is $|A| \cdot |S|$. Then

$$d(S) = \frac{1}{|A|} \sum_{a \in A} d_S(a) = \frac{\sum_{a \in A} |\{t \in S | t[a] \neq \bot\}|}{|A| \cdot |S|} = \frac{|\{x \in D\}|}{|\{x \in D^+\}|}.$$

The source density of Definition 7.1.5 is query-independent. To measure the usefulness of a source for a specific query, we introduce a query-dependent source density that takes into account the attributes of the user query.

Definition 7.1.6 (Query-Dependent Density). *The query-dependent density of a source S is the average density over all attributes of query $Q[A_Q]$:*

$$d_Q(S) := \frac{1}{|A_Q|} \sum_{a \in A_Q} d_S(a).$$

Query-dependent density is "fair", because it counts only those attributes that appear in the query. For notational brevity, we continue with the query-independent density definition, but all results hold for the query-dependent definition as well. For the examples we use query-dependent scores.

Density assessment. Like coverage scores, density scores may be assessed in several different ways, depending on the ability and willingness of the data sources to cooperate. In some cases, data sources readily provide the scores. Statements like "All search results include a page size" [48] ($d(\text{size}) = 1$) are not uncommon.

Density scores are often 0 or 1. They are 0 whenever a source does not export the corresponding attribute of the global relation. The score is 1 whenever the source always provides data for that attribute. We require a density of 1 for all ID-attributes. When direct measurement is not possible, sampling techniques can be applied.

7.1.3 Completeness

Having defined coverage and density we combine the two to the overall completeness criterion. The completeness of a data source is the ratio of its amount of data and the potential amount of data of the universal relation, i.e., the number of data items of a completely filled universal relation. This is the product of the number of tuples in the universal relation and the number of attributes of the universal relation.

Definition 7.1.7 (Completeness). *Let $S = (a_{ij})$ be a data source where a_{ij} is the value of the jth attribute of tuple t_i. Source S has completeness*

$$C(S) := \frac{|\{a_{ij} \in S | a_{ij} \neq \bot\}|}{|UR| \cdot |A|}.$$

We can calculate completeness of a data source without actually counting the number of non-`null` values, by using the coverage and density scores of the source:

Theorem 7.1.2. *Let S be a data source and let $c(S)$ and $d(S)$ be its coverage and density scores. Then*

$$C(S) = c(S) \cdot d(S).$$

Proof.

$$
\begin{aligned}
C(S) &:= \frac{|\{a_{ij} \in S | a_{ij} \neq \bot\}|}{|UR| \cdot |A|} && \text{(Definition 7.1.7)} \\
&= \frac{|S| \cdot \sum_{a \in A} d_S(a)}{|UR| \cdot |A|} && \text{(Definition 7.1.4)} \\
&= \frac{|S|}{|UR|} \cdot \frac{1}{|A|} \cdot \sum_{a \in A} d_S(a) && \\
&= c(S) \cdot d(S) && \text{(Definitions 7.1.2 and 7.1.5)}
\end{aligned}
$$

Example 7.1.1. Table 7.1 shows the five sources of our running example with fictitious coverage scores, density scores for each attribute, the overall density score, and—derived from coverage and density—the completeness score.

For instance, the completeness score of S_1 is calculated as $C(S_1) = c(S_1) \cdot d(S_1) = 0.4 \cdot \frac{1}{6}(1 + 0.5 + 1 + 0 + 0 + 0)$. Attributes a_1, a_3, and a_5 are ID or foreign ID-attributes. For the moment, we require that their density is always 1 for the corresponding sources. That is, IDs and foreign IDs do not contain `null` values in the sources. For foreign IDs, e.g., a_3 in S_1, we relax this requirement in Section 7.2.2.

Table 7.1. Sources with coverage, density, and completeness scores

	$c(S)$	$d_S(a_1)$	$d_S(a_2)$	$d_S(a_3)$	$d_S(a_4)$	$d_S(a_5)$	$d_S(a_6)$	$d(S)$	$C(S)$
S_1	0.4	1	0.5	1	0	0	0	2.5/6	1.00/6
S_2	0.8	1	0	1	0	0	0	2.0/6	1.60/6
S_3	0.7	0	0	1	0.2	0	0	1.2/6	0.84/6
S_4	0.3	0	0	1	0.8	1	0	2.8/6	0.84/6
S_5	0.2	0	0	0	0	1	0.9	1.9/6	0.38/6

7.1.4 Extensions

Several extensions to our completeness model were omitted for simplicity. We show here, which extensions are possible and how they can be included in the model.

Variable coverage scores: Until now, we assume coverage to be an unchanging global score of a source. In reality, many sources are partitioned into areas with high coverage and areas with low coverage, e.g., the Fireball search engine concentrates on german Web pages, but also indexes others. There are two approaches to such a situation: (i) The source is modeled by multiple views, one for each partition. The partitioning can be expressed as selection predicates of the view. Each partition receives an individual coverage score. (ii) Some component recognizes, which part of the source is addressed by the query and dynamically adapts coverage scores. For instance, Meng et al. present methods to estimate this number [80]. Both techniques can be combined.

Variable density scores: With the same arguments as for variable coverage scores, density scores can vary depending on the query. The same techniques as before can be employed.

Attribute weightings: We defined user queries as a subset of the attributes of UR, together with selection predicates. Situations arise where one attribute is more important to the user than others. For instance, a user might look for a stock quote with a company profile, and if possible with the address of the company. An attribute weighting in the user query can express these preferences.

If the sum of all attribute weights is equal to 1—which we can achieve through scaling—the weightings can simply be applied to the attribute-density scores. Then a source with a high density on an attribute with a high user weighting has a higher overall density score than a source with the same density on an attribute with a low user weighting. Attribute weighting seamlessly integrates into our model.

7.2 A Completeness Measure for Plans

A system that integrates multiple data sources distributes a user query to multiple data sources following a query plan. To reach our goal of finding the best query plan, we must be able to predict the coverage, density, and completeness scores of the plan. These scores depend on the degree of overlap between data sources. A full outerjoin-merge over two sources with a large overlap returns a smaller result than if the sources had only little overlap. Thus, before showing how to determine completeness of merged results, we analyze different overlap situations.

7.2.1 Overlap Situations

As discussed earlier, overlap between sources can be extensional (number of common objects) and intensional (number of common attributes). The degree of extensional overlap varies from no overlap at all to a complete overlap of two sources:

Disjointness: Two sources are disjoint if the set of tuples of UR for which both sources provide data is empty, i.e., there is no overlap. Thus, $S_i \sqcap S_j = \{\}$. Stock information systems often provide disjoint sets of data. For instance, one system provides only stock quotes from the New York Stock Exchange, another provides only quotes from the Frankfurt Stock Exchange.

Independence: Two sources are independent if there is no (known) dependency between the tuples of UR for which the sources provide data. That is, there is some coincidental overlap, determined by the size of the sources and the size of the real world they model. Whenever there is no concrete knowledge about overlap, we assume independence.

Search engine size and overlap has been analyzed by several projects. Bharat and Broder developed such a method [11]. Their technique queries search engines with sample terms and counts and compares the results. The authors observed an overlap that allows to infer independence of the search engines, i.e., the set of Web pages indexed by one search engine is statistically independent of the sets of other engines.

Quantified overlap: In some occasions the exact degree of overlap is known, i.e., $S_i \sqcap S_j = X$, where the size of X is known. The overlap can be specified by the number of tuples of UR for which both sources provide data. Quantified overlap occurs between information systems of static nature. There, the overlap can be determined once by actually performing a join operation.

Containment: One source is contained in another if every tuple of UR for which one source provides data, is also provided data from the other source. Thus, $S_i \sqcup S_j = S_i$ if S_j is contained in S_i. The actual data is not necessarily the same. For instance, one source may provide different attributes than the other. Also, the attribute values may conflict. A special case of containment is equality.

Again, stock information systems provide an example. Many stock information systems are equivalent—they cover the same stock market and their content is continuously copied from the same origin.

In the following sections we show coverage, density, and completeness calculation in depth for the case of mutually independent sources. We discuss the other cases and the case of mixed overlap situations between sources later.

Because we explicitly describe, which source exports which attribute, it is not necessary to consider different overlap situations for intensional overlap. Intensional overlap of two sources is the the set of attributes both sources export.

At a finer level of granularity—at attribute value level—we do make a simplifying assumption: We assume independence of null values between two sources, i.e., the probability that a source has a null value for an attribute of a certain tuple is independent of the probability that another source has a null value for the same attribute of the tuple representing the same real world entity. Also, we assume uniform distribution of attribute values for all attributes. If any statistics regarding distribution of attribute values or dependencies between attribute values of different sources are available, we can take them into account in our model by including selectivity factors at the proper places as we will demonstrate later.

7.2.2 Merging Coverage

For coverage calculation of merged results we are first interested in the number of tuples in a result obtained by performing one of the merge operations of Section 6.2.

Lemma 7.2.1. *Let S_i and S_j be two independent sources. Then*

$$|S_i \sqcap S_j| = \frac{|S_i| \cdot |S_j|}{|UR|} \tag{7.1}$$

$$|S_i \sqsupset S_j| = |S_i| \tag{7.2}$$

$$|S_i \sqcup S_j| = |S_i| + |S_j| - |S_i \sqcap S_j| \tag{7.3}$$

$$|S_i \sqcap S_i| = |S_i| \tag{7.4}$$

$$|S_i \sqsupset S_i| = |S_i| \tag{7.5}$$

$$|S_i \sqcup S_i| = |S_i| \tag{7.6}$$

Proof.

(7.1) According to Definition 6.2.1 of the join-merge operator, $S_i \sqcap S_j$ contains only tuples that are represented both in S_i and S_j. The other conditions in Definition 6.2.1 only concern construction of the tuple in the result and do not influence the number of tuples. For each real world entity the probability that it is represented in S_i is $\frac{|S_i|}{|UR|}$ and that it is represented in S_j is $\frac{|S_j|}{|UR|}$. Because of independence, the probability that it is represented in both is $\frac{|S_i|}{|UR|} \cdot \frac{|S_j|}{|UR|}$. Because there are $|UR|$ possible entities, we have an overall number of $|UR| \cdot \frac{|S_i|}{|UR|} \cdot \frac{|S_j|}{|UR|}$ tuples.

(7.2) follows from (7.1) and Definition 6.2.2.
(7.3) follows from (7.1) and Definition 6.2.3.
(7.4) follows from Definition 6.2.1, because $S \sqcap S = S$.
(7.5) follows from Definition 6.2.2 and (7.4).
(7.6) follows from Definition 6.2.3 and (7.4).

Notice that we require density of an ID to be 1, i.e, there are no missing values in the ID-attribute. However, because join-merge operators are performed only on ID–foreign ID relationships, the size of the result may be diminished by missing values in the foreign ID-attribute. If a_k is the foreign ID-attribute of S_i and the ID of S_j, the correct score for the result size is

$$|S_i \sqcap_{a_k} S_j| = \frac{|S_i| \cdot |S_j| \cdot d_{S_i}(a_k)}{|UR|}.$$

For simplicity, we require that density of foreign IDs is always 1. To relax this requirement, we can include the factor $d_{S_i}(a_k)$ wherever necessary without changing the properties of our measures.

Given the coverage scores of the individual data sources, we show how to determine the coverage of the merged result.

Theorem 7.2.1. *Let S_i and S_j be two independent sources. Then coverage of the merged sources is*

$$c(S_i \sqcap S_j) = c(S_i) \cdot c(S_j) \tag{7.7}$$
$$c(S_i \sqsupset S_j) = c(S_i) \tag{7.8}$$
$$c(S_i \sqcup S_j) = c(S_i) + c(S_j) - c(S_i \sqcap S_j) \tag{7.9}$$

Proof.

$$(7.7) \quad c(S_i \sqcap S_j) = \frac{|S_i \sqcap S_j|}{|UR|} \underset{\text{(Lemma 7.2.1)}}{=} \frac{|S_i| \cdot |S_j|}{|UR| \cdot |UR|} = c(S_i) \cdot c(S_j)$$

$$(7.8) \quad c(S_i \sqsupset S_j) = \frac{|S_i \sqsupset S_j|}{|UR|} \underset{\text{(Lemma 7.2.1)}}{=} \frac{|S_i|}{|UR|} = c(S_i)$$

$$(7.9) \quad c(S_i \sqcup S_j) = \frac{|S_i \sqcup S_j|}{|UR|} \underset{\text{(Lemma 7.2.1)}}{=} \frac{|S_i| + |S_j| - |S_i \sqcap S_j|}{|UR|}$$
$$= \frac{|S_i|}{|UR|} + \frac{|S_j|}{|UR|} - \frac{|S_i \sqcap S_j|}{|UR|}$$
$$= c(S_i) + c(S_j) - c(S_i \sqcap S_j)$$

Because the independence relationship is associative, Theorem 7.2.1 enables us to calculate coverage of any plan with any number of sources combined with any of the three merge operators.

Example 7.2.1. Consider query plan $P_{12}(a_2, a_4) \leftarrow S_1 \sqcup_{a_3} (S_3 \sqcup_{a_3} S_4)$ of Example 6.3.2 (page 97). With the source coverage scores of Table 7.1 (page 106) we calculate

$$
\begin{aligned}
c(P_{12}) &= c(S_1 \sqcup_{a_3} (S_3 \sqcup_{a_3} S_4)) \\
&= c(S_1) + c(S_3 \sqcup_{a_3} S_4) - c(S_1 \sqcap_{a_3} (S_3 \sqcup_{a_3} S_4)) \\
&= c(S_1) + c(S_3) + c(S_4) - c(S_3 \sqcap_{a_3} S_4) - c(S_1) \cdot c(S_3 \sqcup_{a_3} S_4) \\
&= c(S_1) + c(S_3) + c(S_4) - c(S_3) \cdot c(S_4) \\
&\quad - c(S_1) \cdot (c(S_3) + c(S_4) - c(S_3 \sqcap_{a_3} S_4)) \\
&= c(S_1) + c(S_3) + c(S_4) - c(S_3) \cdot c(S_4) \\
&\quad - c(S_1) \cdot c(S_3) - c(S_1) \cdot c(S_4) + c(S_1) \cdot c(S_3) \cdot c(S_4) \\
&= 0.4 + 0.7 + 0.3 - 0.7 \cdot 0.3 - 0.4 \cdot 0.7 - 0.4 \cdot 0.3 + 0.4 \cdot 0.7 \cdot 0.3 \\
&= 0.874
\end{aligned}
$$

The last line of the transformation corresponds to the Formula of Sylvester, which calculates the probability that at least one of n independent events occur, given their individual probability. Here we calculate the probability that a real world entity appears in at least one of the three sources.

7.2.3 Merging Density

As discussed in Section 2.3, a tuple in the combined result of two sources has a value in an attribute if either one or both sources provide some value. To compute the density of merged results we are first interested in the number of non-null values in a merged result.

Lemma 7.2.2. *Let S_i and S_j be two independent sources. We abbreviate $|\{t \in S_i | t[a] \neq \bot\}|$ with $|t_{S_i}[a] \neq \bot|$. Then for any attribute $a \in A$*

$$
|t_{S_i \sqcap S_j}[a] \neq \bot| = \frac{|t_{S_i}[a] \neq \bot| \cdot |S_j|}{|UR|} + \frac{|t_{S_j}[a] \neq \bot| \cdot |S_i|}{|UR|}
$$
$$
- \frac{|t_{S_i}[a] \neq \bot| \cdot |t_{S_j}[a] \neq \bot|}{|UR|} \tag{7.10}
$$

$$
|t_{S_i \sqsupset S_j}[a] \neq \bot| = |t_{S_i}[a] \neq \bot| + \frac{|t_{S_j}[a] \neq \bot| \cdot |S_i|}{|UR|}
$$
$$
- \frac{|t_{S_i}[a] \neq \bot| \cdot |t_{S_j}[a] \neq \bot|}{|UR|} \tag{7.11}
$$

$$
|t_{S_i \sqcup S_j}[a] \neq \bot| = |t_{S_i}[a] \neq \bot| + |t_{S_j}[a] \neq \bot|
$$
$$
- \frac{|t_{S_i}[a] \neq \bot| \cdot |t_{S_j}[a] \neq \bot|}{|UR|} \tag{7.12}
$$

Proof. (7.10) According to Lemma 7.2.1, $\frac{|S_i| \cdot |S_j|}{|UR|}$ is the number of tuples in S_j having a matching tuple in S_i. Thus, $\frac{|t_{S_i}[a] \neq \bot| \cdot |S_j|}{|UR|}$ is the number of tuples in S_j having a matching tuple in S_i with a non-null value in attribute a. Analogously, $\frac{|t_{S_j}[a] \neq \bot| \cdot |S_i|}{|UR|}$ is the number of tuples in S_i

having a matching tuple in S_j with a non-null value in attribute a. Finally we subtract the number of those tuples counted twice, i.e., those that match and have a non-null value both in S_i and S_j.

(7.11) The proof is similar to that of (7.10), only the first term is different. In (7.10) only those non-null values of S_i entered the sum whose tuple had a matching tuple in S_j. Here, all non-null values of S_i enter the sum, because with the left outerjoin-merge all tuples of S_i enter the result.

(7.12) follows from (7.10) and Definition 6.2.3.

As opposed to merging coverage scores, density scores are merged at attribute level. Theorem 7.2.2 shows how to calculate attribute density of merged attributes and Theorem 7.2.3 shows how to calculate merged source density.

Theorem 7.2.2. *Let S_i and S_j be two independent sources. Then the density of attribute a in the merged result is*

$$d_{S_i \cap S_j}(a) = d_{S_i}(a) + d_{S_j}(a) - d_{S_i}(a) \cdot d_{S_j}(a) \tag{7.13}$$

$$d_{S_i \sqsupset S_j}(a) = d_{S_i}(a) + d_{S_j}(a)c(S_j) - d_{S_i}(a)d_{S_j}(a)c(S_j) \tag{7.14}$$

$$d_{S_i \cup S_j}(a) = \frac{d_{S_i}(a) \cdot c(S_i)}{c(S_i \sqcup S_j)} + \frac{d_{S_j}(a) \cdot c(S_j)}{c(S_i \sqcup S_j)} - \frac{d_{S_i}(a) \cdot d_{S_j}(a) \cdot c(S_i \sqcap S_j)}{c(S_i \sqcup S_j)} \tag{7.15}$$

Proof.

(7.13) We apply Definition 7.1.4 and transform

$$d_{S_i \cap S_j}(a) = \frac{1}{|S_i \sqcap S_j|} \cdot |t_{S_i \cap S_j}[a] \neq \bot|$$

$$\overset{\text{(Lemma 7.2.1)}}{=} \frac{|UR|}{|S_i| \cdot |S_j|} \cdot |t_{S_i \cap S_j}[a] \neq \bot|$$

$$= \frac{|UR|}{|UR|^2 \cdot c(S_i) \cdot c(S_j)} \cdot |t_{S_i \cap S_j}[a] \neq \bot|$$

$$\overset{\text{(Lemma 7.2.2)}}{=} \frac{|t_{S_i}[a] \neq \bot| \cdot |S_j|}{|UR|^2 \cdot c(S_i) \cdot c(S_j)} + \frac{|t_{S_j}[a] \neq \bot| \cdot |S_i|}{|UR|^2 \cdot c(S_i) \cdot c(S_j)}$$

$$- \frac{|t_{S_i}[a] \neq \bot| \cdot |t_{S_j}[a] \neq \bot|}{|UR|^2 \cdot c(S_i) \cdot c(S_j)}$$

$$= \frac{|t_{S_i}[a] \neq \bot| \cdot |S_j|}{|S_i| \cdot |S_j|} + \frac{|t_{S_j}[a] \neq \bot| \cdot |S_i|}{|S_i| \cdot |S_j|}$$

$$- \frac{|t_{S_i}[a] \neq \bot| \cdot |t_{S_j}[a] \neq \bot|}{|S_i| \cdot |S_j|}$$

$$= d_{S_i}(a) + d_{S_j}(a) - d_{S_i}(a) \cdot d_{S_j}(a)$$

(7.14) We apply Definition 7.1.4 and transform

$$d_{S_i \sqsupset S_j}(a) = \frac{|t_{S_i \sqsupset S_j}[a] \neq \bot|}{|S_i \sqsupset S_j|}$$

$$\underset{\text{(Lemma 7.2.1)}}{=} \frac{|t_{S_i \sqsupset S_j}[a] \neq \bot|}{|S_i|}$$

$$\underset{\text{(Lemma 7.2.2)}}{=} \frac{|t_{S_i}[a] \neq \bot|}{|S_i|} + \frac{|t_{S_j}[a] \neq \bot||S_i|}{|UR||S_i|}$$
$$- \frac{|t_{S_i}[a] \neq \bot||t_{S_j}[a] \neq \bot|}{|UR||S_i|}$$

$$= d_{S_i}(a) + \frac{|t_{S_j}[a] \neq \bot|}{|UR|} - d_{S_i}(a) \cdot \frac{|t_{S_j}[a] \neq \bot|}{|UR|}$$

$$= d_{S_i}(a) + \frac{|t_{S_j}[a] \neq \bot|c(S_j)}{|S_j|} - d_{S_i}(a) \cdot \frac{|t_{S_j}[a] \neq \bot|c(S_j)}{|S_j|}$$

$$= d_{S_i}(a) + d_{S_j}(a)c(S_j) - d_{S_i}(a)d_{S_j}(a)c(S_j)$$

(7.15) We apply Definition 7.1.4 and transform

$$d_{S_i \sqcup S_j}(a) = \frac{|t_{S_i \sqcup S_j}[a] \neq \bot|}{|S_i \sqcup S_j|}$$

$$\underset{\text{(Lemma 7.2.1)}}{=} \frac{|t_{S_i \sqcup S_j}[a] \neq \bot|}{|S_i| + |S_j| - |S_i \sqcap S_j|}$$

$$\underset{\text{(Lemma 7.2.2)}}{=} \frac{|t_{S_i}[a] \neq \bot| + |t_{S_j}[a] \neq \bot| - \frac{1}{|UR|}|t_{S_i}[a] \neq \bot||t_{S_j}[a] \neq \bot|}{|UR| \cdot c(S_i \sqcup S_j)}$$

$$= \frac{|S_i|d_{S_i}(a) + |S_j|d_{S_j}(a) - \frac{1}{|UR|}|S_i||S_j|d_{S_i}(a)d_{S_j}(a)}{|UR| \cdot c(S_i \sqcup S_j)}$$

$$= \frac{|UR|[c(S_i)d_{S_i}(a) + c(S_j)d_{S_j}(a) - c(S_i)c(S_j)d_{S_i}(a)d_{S_j}(a)]}{|UR| \cdot c(S_i \sqcup S_j)}$$

$$= \frac{d_{S_i}(a) \cdot c(S_i)}{c(S_i \sqcup S_j)} + \frac{d_{S_j}(a) \cdot c(S_j)}{c(S_i \sqcup S_j)} - \frac{d_{S_i}(a) \cdot d_{S_j}(a) \cdot c(S_i \sqcap S_j)}{c(S_i \sqcup S_j)}$$

The density of an attribute of an outerjoin-merged result depends on coverage scores, while that of the join-merged result does not. Intuitively, this is because in join-merge operations we only regard the tuples within the overlap. For density measurements we do not care how much overlap there is. For outerjoins, we regard all tuples and coverage scores are needed to determine how much overlap there is, i.e., how many non-null values appear in both sources.

Theorem 7.2.3. *Let S_i and S_j be two independent sources. Given the density scores for all attributes of a merged result, the density of the entire result is*

$$d(S_i \sqcap S_j) = \frac{1}{|A|} \sum_{a \in A} d_{S_i \sqcap S_j}(a) \tag{7.16}$$

$$d(S_i \sqsupset S_j) = \frac{1}{|A|} \sum_{a \in A} d_{S_i \sqsupset S_j}(a) \tag{7.17}$$

$$d(S_i \sqcup S_j) = \frac{1}{|A|} \sum_{a \in A} d_{S_i \sqcup S_j}(a) \tag{7.18}$$

Proof. The proof is analog to that of Theorem 7.1.1.

Because the independence relationship is associative, Theorem 7.2.3 enables us to calculate the density of any plan with any number of sources combined with any of the three merge operators.

7.2.4 Merging Completeness

As before for single sources, we calculate completeness of a plan using the coverage and density scores of the plan:

Theorem 7.2.4. *Let P be a query plan. Then completeness of P is $C(P) = c(P) \cdot d(P)$.*

Proof. The proof follows from Theorem 7.1.2, because a plan P represents a set of tuples, just as a source S does.

So, to determine completeness of a plan, we determine coverage and density scores of the plan using Theorems 7.2.1 and 7.2.3 and multiply the two. Our ultimate goal in the following chapter is to find the most complete plan under a cost constraint.

Example 7.2.2. Recall the 16 alternative plans for the translated user query

$$Q'_1(a_2, a_4) \leftarrow R_1(a_1, a_2, a_3) \sqcup_{a_3} R_2(a_3, a_4, a_5)$$

of Example 6.3.2 (page 97). Table 7.2 shows these plans with their merged coverage, attribute density, density, and completeness scores. We used the previous theorems to calculate the scores. To answer a user query with maximal completeness, an integrated system can construct all plans, calculate their completeness, and choose a plan with maximal completeness for execution.

A first observation is that source S_2 does not contribute to plan completeness in any way, because it does not export a_2. Compare plans P_7 and P_{13}: P_{13} corresponds to P_7 with S_2 added. P_{13} has a higher coverage, because it involves more sources, but it has a lower density, because the additional source only contributes null values. Their overall completeness is the same, which is what we expected, because the actual number of non-null values is the same for both plans.

Table 7.2. Plans for Q_1 with merged coverage, density, and completeness scores

Plan P	$c(P)$	$d_P(a_2)$	$d_P(a_4)$	$d_{Q'_1}(P)$	$C(P)$
$P_1(a_2, a_4) \leftarrow \emptyset$	0	0	0	0	0
$P_2(a_2, a_4) \leftarrow S_1$	0.4	0.5	0	0.25	0.1
$P_3(a_2, a_4) \leftarrow S_2$	0.8	0	0	0	0
$P_4(a_2, a_4) \leftarrow S_1 \sqcup_{a_1} S_2$	0.88	0.2$\overline{27}$	0	0.113$\overline{6}$	0.1
$P_5(a_2, a_4) \leftarrow S_3$	0.7	0	0.2	0.1	0.07
$P_6(a_2, a_4) \leftarrow S_4$	0.3	0	0.8	0.4	0.12
$P_7(a_2, a_4) \leftarrow S_3 \sqcup_{a_3} S_4$	0.79	0	0.4385	0.2192	0.1732
$P_8(a_2, a_4) \leftarrow S_1 \sqcup_{a_3} S_3$	0.82	0.2439	0.1707	0.2073	0.17
$P_9(a_2, a_4) \leftarrow S_1 \sqcup_{a_3} S_4$	0.58	0.3448	0.4138	0.3793	0.22
$P_{10}(a_2, a_4) \leftarrow S_2 \sqcup_{a_3} S_3$	0.94	0	0.1489	0.0745	0.07
$P_{11}(a_2, a_4) \leftarrow S_2 \sqcup_{a_3} S_4$	0.86	0	0.2791	0.1396	0.12
$P_{12}(a_2, a_4) \leftarrow S_1 \sqcup_{a_3} (S_3 \sqcup_{a_3} S_4)$	0.874	0.2288	0.3964	0.3126	0.2732
$P_{13}(a_2, a_4) \leftarrow S_2 \sqcup_{a_3} (S_3 \sqcup_{a_3} S_4)$	0.958	0	0.3616	0.1808	0.1732
$P_{14}(a_2, a_4) \leftarrow (S_1 \sqcup_{a_1} S_2) \sqcup_{a_3} S_3$	0.964	0.2075	0.1452	0.1764	0.17
$P_{15}(a_2, a_4) \leftarrow (S_1 \sqcup_{a_1} S_2) \sqcup_{a_3} S_4$	0.916	0.2183	0.262	0.2402	0.22
$P_{16}(a_2, a_4) \leftarrow (S_1 \sqcup_{a_1} S_2)$ $\sqcup_{a_3} (S_3 \sqcup_{a_3} S_4)$	0.9748	0.2052	0.3554	0.2803	0.2732

Another observation is that completeness increases monotonously with the number of sources for the full outerjoin-merge, i.e., if a source is added to a plan, the plans completeness does not decrease. Consequently, plan P_{16} is the most complete, but potentially the most expensive, because it accesses the most sources. Coverage scores are also monotonous, however, density scores are not: Consider again plan P_7. If we add S_2 to the plan, we arrive at plan P_{13}, which has a lower density score.

If the user query had additional weightings for the attributes, we would multiply the attribute density scores with these weights and possibly arrive at different overall scores.

We now have a comprehensive model for source and plan completeness. We are able to compare sources with one another, and we are able to compare plans with one another. Completeness is a measure for the amount of data to expect from a source or from a plan. We can use the completeness model to assess completeness of each plan in the search space of a query.

7.3 Properties of the Measures

Algebraic reorderings within plans are performed to reduce response time or network traffic. The following properties show which reorderings are possible without changing the overall coverage, density, and thus completeness of a plan. We propose to perform such a reordering *after* finding a plan with good completeness (see Section 8.4).

The findings of this section also prove correctness of our completeness calculation. Whenever our operators are commutative, associative or distributive, we expect our measures to have the same properties. Because an algebraic reordering does not change the result, it should also not change the completeness of the result.

Theorem 7.3.1. *Coverage is commutative, associative, and distributive for $\sqcap$ and $\sqcup$, and associative for $\sqsupset$ for independent sources:*

$$c(S_i \sqcap S_j) = c(S_j \sqcap S_i) \tag{7.19}$$

$$c(S_i \sqcup S_j) = c(S_j \sqcup S_i) \tag{7.20}$$

$$c(S_i \sqcap S_i) = c(S_i) \tag{7.21}$$

$$c(S_i \sqsupset S_i) = c(S_i) \tag{7.22}$$

$$c(S_i \sqcup S_i) = c(S_i) \tag{7.23}$$

$$c((S_i \sqcap S_j) \sqcap S_k) = c(S_i \sqcap (S_j \sqcap S_k)) \tag{7.24}$$

$$c((S_i \sqsupset S_j) \sqsupset S_k) = c(S_i \sqsupset (S_j \sqsupset S_k)) \tag{7.25}$$

$$c((S_i \sqcup S_j) \sqcup S_k) = c(S_i \sqcup (S_j \sqcup S_k)) \tag{7.26}$$

$$c(S_i \sqcap (S_j \sqcup S_k)) = c((S_i \sqcap S_j) \sqcup (S_i \sqcap S_k)) \tag{7.27}$$

$$c(S_i \sqcup (S_j \sqcap S_k)) = c((S_i \sqcup S_j) \sqcap (S_i \sqcup S_k)) \tag{7.28}$$

Proof. The proofs of (7.19) – (7.23) are trivial with Lemma 7.2.1. For the rest, we apply the definitions and algebraic transformations:

(7.24)
$$\begin{aligned}
c((S_i \sqcap S_j) \sqcap S_k) &= (c(S_i) \cdot c(S_j)) \cdot c(S_k) \\
&= c(S_i) \cdot (c(S_j) \cdot c(S_k)) \\
&= c(S_i \sqcap (S_j \sqcap S_k))
\end{aligned}$$

(7.25)
$$\begin{aligned}
c((S_i \sqsupset S_j) \sqsupset S_k) &= c(S_i \sqsupset S_j) \\
&= c(S_i) \\
&= c(S_i \sqsupset (S_j \sqsupset S_k))
\end{aligned}$$

(7.26)
$$\begin{aligned}
c((S_i \sqcup S_j) \sqcup S_k) &= c(S_i) + c(S_j) + c(S_k) - c(S_j)c(S_k) - c(S_i)c(S_k) \\
&\quad - c(S_i)c(S_j) + c(S_i)c(S_j)c(S_k) \\
&= c(S_i \sqcup (S_j \sqcup S_k))
\end{aligned}$$

(7.27)
$$\begin{aligned}
c(S_i \sqcap (S_j \sqcup S_k)) &= c(S_i) \cdot (c(S_j) + c(S_k) - c(S_j)c(S_k)) \\
&= c(S_i)c(S_j) + c(S_i)c(S_k) - c(S_i)c(S_j)c(S_k) \\
&= c(S_i)c(S_j) + c(S_i)c(S_k) - c(S_i \sqcap S_i)c(S_j)c(S_k) \\
&= c(S_i)c(S_j) + c(S_i)c(S_k) - c((S_i \sqcap S_j) \sqcap (S_i \sqcap S_k)) \\
&= c((S_i \sqcap S_j) \sqcup (S_i \sqcap S_k))
\end{aligned}$$

(7.28)
$$\begin{aligned}
c(S_i \sqcup (S_j \sqcap S_k)) &= c(S_i) + c(S_j \sqcap S_k) - c(S_i \sqcap (S_j \sqcap S_k)) \\
&= c(S_i \sqcap (S_i \sqcup S_j \sqcup S_k)) + c(S_j)c(S_k) \\
&\quad - c(S_i)c(S_j)c(S_k) \\
&= c(S_i)\big(c(S_i) + c(S_k) - c(S_i)c(S_k) + c(S_j) \\
&\quad - c(S_i)c(S_j) - c(S_j)c(S_k) + c(S_j)c(S_j)c(S_k)\big) \\
&\quad + c(S_j)c(S_k) - c(S_i)c(S_j)c(S_k) \\
&= c(S_i)c(S_i) + c(S_i)c(S_k) - c(S_i)c(S_i)c(S_k) \\
&\quad + c(S_j)c(S_i) + c(S_j)c(S_k) - c(S_j)c(S_i)c(S_k) \\
&\quad - c(S_i)c(S_j)c(S_i) - c(S_i)c(S_j)c(S_k) \\
&\quad + c(S_i)c(S_j)c(S_i)c(S_k) \\
&= (c(S_i) + c(S_j) - c(S_i)c(S_j)) \cdot (c(S_i) + c(S_k) \\
&\quad - c(S_i)c(S_k)) \\
&= c(S_i \sqcup S_j) \cdot c(S_i \sqcup S_k) \\
&= c((S_i \sqcup S_j) \sqcap (S_i \sqcup S_k))
\end{aligned}$$

Results similar to (7.24)–(7.28) are shown by Galindo-Legaria and Rosenthal in [43] for the relational operators themselves. Coverage for the left outerjoin-merge operator is not commutative, because the operator itself is not commutative.

Lemma 7.3.1. *Attribute density is commutative, associative and distributive for* $\sqcap$ *and* $\sqcup$ *for independent sources.*

$$d_{S_i \sqcap S_j}(a) = d_{S_j \sqcap S_i}(a) \tag{7.29}$$

$$d_{S_i \sqcup S_j}(a) = d_{S_j \sqcup S_i}(a) \tag{7.30}$$

$$d_{(S_i \sqcap S_j) \sqcap S_k}(a) = d_{S_i \sqcap (S_j \sqcap S_k)}(a) \tag{7.31}$$

$$d_{(S_i \sqcup S_j) \sqcup S_k}(a) = d_{S_i \sqcup (S_j \sqcup S_k)}(a) \tag{7.32}$$

$$d_{S_i \sqcap (S_j \sqcup S_k)}(a) = d_{(S_i \sqcap S_j) \sqcup (S_i \sqcap S_k)}(a) \tag{7.33}$$

$$d_{S_i \sqcup (S_j \sqcap S_k)}(a) = d_{(S_i \sqcup S_j) \sqcap (S_i \sqcup S_k)}(a) \tag{7.34}$$

Proof. The proofs of (7.29) and (7.30) are trivial. The proof of (7.31) is analog to that of (7.26) in Theorem 7.3.1. Due to the length of the following expressions, we use a shorthand notation to prove (7.32) and abbreviate $c(S_i)$ with c_i and $d_{S_i}(a)$ with d_i. Also, we treat numerator and denominator separately. The denominator is transformed with Theorem 7.3.1. We transform the numerator:

$$d_{(S_i \sqcup S_j) \sqcup S_k}(a) = \frac{1}{c((S_i \sqcup S_j) \sqcup S_k)} \cdot \left(d_{S_i \sqcup S_j}(a) \cdot c(S_i \sqcup S_j) + d_{S_k}(a) \cdot c(S_k) \right.$$

$$\left. - d_{(S_i \sqcup S_j) \sqcap S_k}(a) \cdot c((S_i \sqcup S_j) \sqcap S_k) \right)$$

$$\text{(only numerator)} = d_i c_i + d_j c_j - d_{i \sqcap j} c_{i \sqcap j} + d_k c_k - ((d_{i \sqcup j} + d_k - d_{i \sqcap j} d_k) c_{i \sqcup j} c_k)$$

$$= d_i c_i + d_j c_j + d_k c_k - (d_i + d_j - d_i d_j) c_i c_j - d_{i \sqcup j} c_{i \sqcup j} c_k$$

$$- d_k c_{i \sqcup j} c_k + d_{i \sqcap j} d_k c_{i \sqcup j} c_k$$

$$= d_i c_i + d_j c_j + d_k c_k - d_i c_i c_j - d_j c_i c_j + d_i d_j c_i c_j$$

$$- (d_i c_i + d_j c_j - d_{i \sqcap j} c_{i \sqcap j}) c_k - d_k (c_i + c_j - c_i c_j) c_k$$

$$+ (d_i + d_j - d_i d_j) d_k (c_i + c_j - c_i c_j) c_k$$

$$= d_i c_i + d_j c_j + d_k c_k - d_i c_i c_j - d_j c_i c_j + d_i d_j c_i c_j - d_i c_i c_k$$

$$- d_j c_j c_k + (d_i + d_j - d_i d_j) c_i c_j c_k - d_k c_i c_k - d_k c_j c_k$$

$$+ d_k c_i c_j c_k + (d_i d_k + d_j d_k - d_i d_j d_k)(c_i c_k + c_j c_k - c_i c_j c_k)$$

$$= d_i c_i + d_j c_j + d_k c_k - d_i c_i c_j - d_j c_i c_j + d_i d_j c_i c_j - d_i c_i c_k$$

$$- d_j c_j c_k + d_i c_i c_j c_k + d_j c_i c_j c_k - d_i d_j c_i c_j c_k - d_k c_i c_k$$

$$- d_k c_j c_k + d_k c_i c_j c_k + d_i d_k c_i c_k + d_j d_k c_i c_k - d_i d_j d_k c_i c_k$$

$$+ d_i d_k c_j c_k + d_j d_k c_j c_k - d_i d_j d_k c_j c_k - d_i d_k c_i c_j c_k$$

$$- d_j d_k c_i c_j c_k + d_i d_j d_k c_i c_j c_k$$

$$= d_i c_i + d_j c_j + d_k c_k - d_i c_i c_j - d_i c_i c_k - d_j c_i c_j - d_j c_j c_k$$

$$- d_k c_i c_k - d_k c_j c_k + d_i c_i c_j c_k + d_j c_i c_j c_k + d_k c_i c_j c_k$$

$$+ d_i d_j c_i c_j + d_i d_k c_j c_k + d_i d_k c_i c_k + d_j d_k c_j c_k + d_j d_k c_i c_k$$

$$- d_i d_j c_i c_j c_k - d_i d_k c_i c_j c_k - d_j d_k c_i c_j c_k$$

$$- d_i d_j d_k c_i c_k - d_i d_j d_k c_j c_k + d_i d_j d_k c_i c_j c_k$$

The final expression is symmetric with respect to j, i.e., wherever j appears in combination with i, it also appears in combination with k in the same manner. Hence, we can deduce associativity.

For brevity we omit the tedious proofs of (7.33) and (7.34). Their structure is similar to the proof of (7.32).

Theorem 7.3.2. *Source density is commutative, associative, and distributive for $\sqcap$ and $\sqcup$ for independent sources.*

$$d(S_i \sqcap S_j) = d(S_j \sqcap S_i) \tag{7.35}$$

$$d(S_i \sqcup S_j) = d(S_j \sqcup S_i) \tag{7.36}$$

$$d((S_i \sqcap S_j) \sqcap S_k) = d(S_i \sqcap (S_j \sqcap S_k)) \tag{7.37}$$

$$d((S_i \sqcup S_j) \sqcup S_k) = d(S_i \sqcup (S_j \sqcup S_k)) \tag{7.38}$$

$$d(S_i \sqcap (S_j \sqcup S_k)) = d((S_i \sqcap S_j) \sqcup (S_i \sqcap S_k)) \tag{7.39}$$

$$d(S_i \sqcup (S_j \sqcap S_k)) = d((S_i \sqcup S_j) \sqcap (S_i \sqcup S_k)) \tag{7.40}$$

Proof. All properties follow trivially from Theorem 7.1.1 with Lemma 7.3.1.

Theorem 7.3.3. *Completeness is commutative, associative, and distributive for $\sqcap$ and $\sqcup$ and independent sources.*

Proof. The proof follows from Theorems 7.2.4, 7.3.1, and 7.3.2.

7.4 Other Overlap Situations

The completeness measure assumes mutual independence of sources. Here, we show the consequences of relaxing this assumption. Recall the different overlap profiles: Sources may be disjoint, i.e., $S_i \sqcap S_j = \{\}$, contained, i.e., $S_i \sqcup S_j = S_i$, or there can be quantified overlap between sources, i.e., $S_i \sqcap S_j = X$. Tables 7.3 and 7.4 summarize coverage and density calculation for two merged sources.

Table 7.3. Coverage and density measures for different overlap situations

	$S_i \sqcap S_j = \{\}$	$S_i \sqcap S_j = X$
$c(S_i \sqcap S_j)$	0	$|X|/|UR|$
$c(S_i \sqsupseteq S_j)$	$c(S_i)$	$c(S_i)$
$c(S_i \sqcup S_j)$	$c(S_i) + c(S_j)$	$c(S_i) + c(S_j) - |X|/|UR|$
$d_{S_i \sqcap S_j}(a)$	undefined	$d_{S_i}(a)c(S_i) + d_{S_j}(a)c(S_j)$ $- \dfrac{d_{S_i}(a)c(S_i)d_{S_j}(a)c(S_j)}{c(S_i \sqcap S_j)}$
$d_{S_i \sqsupseteq S_j}(a)$	$d_{S_i}(a)$	$d_{S_i}(a) + \dfrac{d_{S_j}(a)c(S_j)c(S_i \sqcap S_j)}{c(S_i \sqsupseteq S_j)}$ $- d_{S_i}(a)d_{S_j}(a)c(S_i \sqcap S_j)$
$d_{S_i \sqcup S_j}(a)$	$\dfrac{d_{S_i}(a)c(S_i) + d_{S_j}(a)c(S_j)}{c(S_i \sqcup S_j)}$	$\dfrac{d_{S_i}(a) \cdot c(S_i)}{c(S_i \sqcup S_j)} + \dfrac{d_{S_j}(a) \cdot c(S_j)}{c(S_i \sqcup S_j)}$ $- \dfrac{d_{S_i}(a) \cdot d_{S_j}(a) \cdot c(S_i \sqcap S_j)}{c(S_i \sqcup S_j)}$

Calculating completeness for more than two sources is more difficult. We distinguish two situations: uniform overlap situations and mixed overlap situations.

Uniform Overlap   We call an overlap situation uniform, if only one type of overlap exists between sources, i.e., all sources are mutually independent, mutually disjoint, etc. The previous sections covered the case of all mutually independent sources. Completeness calculation is similar in the case of mutually disjoint sources, because the disjointness property is associative: If all sources are mutually disjoint, the content of any source is also disjoint with the combinations of any other sources. Calculation of completeness, when all sources are contained in one another is also straight forward.

Table 7.4. Coverage and density measures for different overlap situations

	$S_i \sqcup S_j = S_i$	$S_i \sqcup S_j = S_j$
$c(S_i \sqcap S_j)$	$c(S_j)$	$c(S_i)$
$c(S_i \sqsupset S_j)$	$c(S_i)$	$c(S_i)$
$c(S_i \sqcup S_j)$	$c(S_i)$	$c(S_j)$
$d_{S_i \sqcap S_j}(a)$	$c(S_i)d_{S_i}(a) + d_{S_j}(a)$ $-c(S_i)d_{S_i}(a)d_{S_j}(a)$	$d_{S_i}(a) + c(S_j)d_{S_j}(a)$ $-c(S_j)d_{S_i}(a)d_{S_j}(a)$
$d_{S_i \sqsupset S_j}(a)$	$d_{S_i}(a) + d_{S_j}(a)$ $-c(S_i)d_{S_i}(a)d_{S_j}(a)$	$d_{S_i}(a) + c(S_j)d_{S_j}(a)$ $-c(S_j)d_{S_i}(a)d_{S_j}(a)$
$d_{S_i \sqcup S_j}(a)$	$d_{S_i}(a) + d_{S_j}(a)$ $-c(S_i)d_{S_i}(a)d_{S_j}(a)$	$d_{S_i}(a) + d_{S_j}(a)$ $-c(S_j)d_{S_i}(a)d_{S_j}(a)$

Mixed Overlap Situations We call an overlap situation mixed when either independence relationships and disjointness relationships occur simultaneously within a plan, or if any quantified overlap occurs within a plan. In these cases, the relationships are no longer associative. Consider for example three sources S_1, S_2, and S_3, where S_1 and S_2 are independent of each other, S_1 and S_3 are also independent, and S_2 and S_3 are disjoint. Determining completeness of plan $P \leftarrow (S_1 \sqcap S_2) \sqcap S_3$ is not possible with the current calculation rules, because the relationship between S_3 and the intermediate result of $S_1 \sqcap S_2$ is not defined.

We do not cover such situations in this thesis. Solutions similar to those of join size estimation in conventional DBMS might help and are discussed in the related work section.

7.5 Related Work

Related work on our completeness measure draws from two areas: Determining the completeness of single data sources, and determining the completeness of combined sources, in particular, join size estimation.

7.5.1 Completeness of Single Sources

Determining the "size" of a data source has only recently become a problem, when such metadata was desired for autonomous sources of unknown size, such as typical WWW information sources. There are yet few projects striving to model or determine the size of Web data sources. Chen et al., who address query processing in the WWW, mention the quality criteria "size of result" and "number of documents accessed", but they neither define them, nor point out the difference between the two [23]. Also, the authors do not integrate the two criteria into a general value model as we do. Motro and Rakov define a "completeness" criterion, which matches our coverage criterion [88]. Motro suggests to add "completeness assertions" as accompanying information in the query result, adding more meaning to the result [87]. Completeness assertions are statements, such as "the data contains *all* recordings on the CBS label". These assertions are aggregated along query plans in a similar fashion to our coverage and density scores. Thus, the author can give qualitative statements about the completeness of results, but no quantitative statements as we do. To the best of our knowledge, the density criterion as we define it, has never been addressed in literature before, even though missing attribute values are all too common.

In the GlOSS system [51], the authors assume that each participating source provides data on the total number of documents in the source and for each word the number of documents it appears in. These values are used to calculate the estimated percentage of query-matching documents in a source. The source with the highest percentage is selected for querying. Several methods on how to evaluate these estimations are discussed.

As already mentioned, the set of Web pages indexed by search engines is independent of the set of other search engines [11]. Notess performs a comprehensive and continuously updated analysis of current search engine sizes, overlaps, etc. [101]. However, to the best of our knowledge, no project has examined the size of a set of integrated search engines, i.e., the "virtual size" of a meta-search engine, let alone of integrated systems of other application domains. We performed this completeness estimation under different overlap profiles using coverage and density scores of the individual sources.

7.5.2 Completeness of Merged Sources

Calculation or prediction of join result sizes is an important technique for cost-based query optimization in DBMS. In general terms, join result size is the size of the cross-product of the two relations in the join, multiplied with a *selectivity factor*. Selectivity factors are statistical values stored in the data dictionary of the DBMS. Many research efforts tackled the problem of join size estimation [113, 45, 122]; Mannino et al. give a survey on the suggested statistical values to store, how to maintain them, and how to use them to predict the result sizes of various database operations [79]. Most projects make the same simplifying assumptions as we do: uniformity of attribute values and independence of attribute values [25].

Our completeness model is an extension to the notion of join size: Coverage is a measure for the number of tuples in an intermediate result like a join. In our setting however, sources do not export all attributes of a relation and often return null values. So we introduced density to extend coverage, to gain a comprehensive completeness model. As we pointed out, we can use techniques for join size estimation, but must keep in mind that the statistics on which such estimations are based, are unstable due to the autonomy of sources.

Florescu et al. attempt to describe quantitatively the content of distributed autonomous document sources using probabilistic measures [41]. In their model, the authors calculate two values: "Coverage" of data sources, determining the probability that a matching document is found in the source, and "overlap" between two data sources, determining the probability that an arbitrary document is found in both sources. These probabilities are calculated with the help of word-count statistics. Their coverage measure is similar to the *precision* measure of the information retrieval field and determines the query dependent usefulness of a source. Their overlap measure expresses ideas similar to ours, but the authors do not consider different types of overlap, such as independence or disjointness. Rather, it is a measure solely based on probability.

In the SCAM project, Shivakumar and Garcia-Molina discover similar documents by analyzing word sequences in the text. That is, the authors calculate the overlap between different pieces of text [121]. This technique was extended by Cho et al. to discover replicated web pages and sites [24].

7.6 Summary

This chapter presented two main contributions: a completeness model to measure the amount of data provided by data sources, and a model to calculate the completeness of query results obtained by combining sources through merge operators.

We argued that the completeness criterion is one of the most important aspects of Web integration. Completeness measures the portion of the real world entities that is represented in a source, and how much data per entity is stored. Sources with a high completeness contain more data about the real world and are thus more attractive to users.

In integrated information systems, results are usually obtained by integrating data from multiple sources. In Chapter 6 we presented operators to perform this integration, and here we extended the completeness model to determine completeness across those operators. The case of mutually independent sources was considered in depth, but also various other overlap situations were considered. Finally, we proved several properties of the completeness measure that allow certain algebraic reorderings within query plans.

Having defined a data model, a search space of query plans, and a measure to value the plans, we turn to search algorithms to find the most complete plan under a cost constraint.

8 Completeness-Driven Query Optimization

Completeness measures the usefulness of a source or of a plan to answer a user query. Therefore, completeness is a valuable tool to guide query planning in the same way as a cost model guides query optimization in centralized DBMS.

To reflect reality, we additionally assign a cost to each source. Depending on the application domain, this could be monetary cost, response time, or any other punishment function for accessing sources and retrieving data from sources. In most projects for information integration, cost is not considered and it is implicitly assumed that the mediator should always compute the extensionally and intensionally complete answer. We have argued already that from the point of view of a typical user, the intensionally complete answer is neither always necessary nor always possible (concession C.2 on page 17).

Also, we have argued that the extensionally complete answer is not always necessary. In the presence of cost constraints it is also not always possible: Computing the complete answer may be too expensive, if querying data sources costs money; it may take too long if the user has little time. Thus, the mediator should instead aim at retrieving the best result possible within a cost limit.

In the following sections, we formalize the problem of finding an optimal query plan under cost constraints by introducing a cost model, defining the optimization problem, and analyzing its complexity. First, we concentrate on a special case of the problem, for which we develop and test several algorithms with different properties. Then, we introduce an algorithm for the general problem and again evaluate its performance. Finally, we show how algebraic reordering of plans can improve response time of query plans, without changing completeness of the result.

The problem and the algorithms in this chapter differ from those in Chapter 5. There, the algorithms optimized toward finding the best N plans with only join-operators. Here, we are searching for the single best plan under the new query planning paradigm introduced in Chapter 6. There, the algorithms maximized information quality in general, using multiple criteria. Here, the problem is to maximize only one criterion: completeness.

F. Naumann: Quality-Driven Query Answering, LNCS 2261, pp. 123-149, 2002.
© Springer-Verlag Berlin Heidelberg 2002

8.1 Completeness Maximization

This section formally introduces the *completeness maximization problem*. We introduce a cost model for autonomous sources; the cost model leads to the optimization problem, for which we prove NP-hardness.

8.1.1 Cost Model

Chapter 3 introduced the IQ-criteria response time and price as regular IQ-criteria among many others. However, there are real world applications, where such cost criteria play a more prominent role. In the real world, there is a certain limit on both response time and price. Response time experiences a limit, because users are not willing to wait indefinitely for the desired information. Especially in Web data sources users tend to hit the "stop" button if the data does not appear fast enough. Price experiences an even stricter limit: Users will not submit a query to a system if the price is not known in advance or if the price is too high. The limit is the amount of money a user is willing to spend for an answer to a query.

In general, there are two variations to compute cost: a sequential and a parallel cost model. If only monetary cost is regarded, the cost model is sequential, i.e., the merged cost is the sum of the individual costs. Such a model applies to molecular biology systems, where many queries are connected with fees, but response time is not as important. A cost model solely based on response time applies to search engines, where queries typically are free, but some search engines are faster than others. The merged cost then is the maximum response time of all participating sources, assuming that all sources can be accessed in parallel. A mixture of both types for example applies to stock information services, which typically charge money, but where a low response time is also of great importance. The merged cost is then some—possibly weighted—function of both factors.

Obtaining the actual costs of the sources is simple for the monetary case: Fees for queries do not change frequently, thus they can be determined by hand. Obtaining a good response time model is more difficult: Response time depends on many factors, such as time of day, network congestion, hardware, etc. Gruser et al. recently presented a prediction tool that learns a response time model for Web data sources [53], and Naacke et al. describe how to integrate such a cost model into the architecture and query process of mediator-based information systems [89].

For simplicity we concentrate on the sequential cost model. For some applications a parallel cost model might be more realistic, but using such a model does not forward the ideas of this thesis. For an overview of parallel cost models and how to adapt algorithms to them, see for instance [44, 49].

We assume a cost $Cost(S)$ to be assigned to each source. The cost may be fixed or query dependent. If it is query-dependent, we require that it can be determined at query planning time.

Definition 8.1.1 (Cost). *The cost of a plan P is defined as the sum of all source-costs of the sources in the plan*

$$Cost(P) := \sum_{S_i \in P} Cost(S_i).$$

8.1.2 Problem Definition

Given a set of source views, their coverage and density scores, their cost, a user query, and a cost limit, it is our goal to find the query plan with a maximal merged completeness, whose cost does not exceed the limit. The dual problem is to minimize cost, while achieving (or exceeding) a certain completeness threshold. Both variants are sensible in certain applications; here, we consider only the former.

Without the cost limit, an optimal solution would always be to access *all* data sources. Only if the number of participating sources is low and if they are all free, is this solution acceptable.

Definition 8.1.2 (Completeness Maximization Problem). *Given a translated query Q' against the global schema obtained from user query Q, given a cost limit L, and given data sources $S_1, \ldots, S_n$ with coverage scores, density scores, and cost, find plan P for Q' with maximal completeness $C(P)$ such that $Cost(P) \leq L$.*

8.1.3 Complexity Analysis

The completeness maximization problem is similar to the well-known *knapsack* problem [46]. In the knapsack problem, there are given a number of items (here: sources) with different fixed costs and different fixed benefits (here: completeness scores), a limit, and the goal of optimizing the overall benefit. The knapsack problem is a special case of our problem, because in our problem the completeness benefit of a source to a query plan is not fixed. It varies non-monotonically, depending on the sources already in the plan. Considering the exponential nature of the knapsack problem, we cannot hope to efficiently guarantee an optimal solution for any reasonable number of sources.

Theorem 8.1.1. *The Completeness Maximization Problem is NP-hard.*

Proof. The Completeness Maximization Problem is in NP, because we can check in polynomial time the cost and completeness score of a given plan.

The proof of NP-hardness is by reducing the NP-hard knapsack optimization problem to our problem. In the knapsack optimization problem, we are given a set of items with benefits and costs and a cost limit. The problem is to find the subset that has the largest sum of benefits with a total sum of costs that is under the limit. We polynomially reduce this problem to our problem as follows:

First, we create a global schema with one relation and one attribute. We model each source as a view on the one relation. The query to be answered asks for this attribute. For each item of the knapsack problem, we create a source and populate it with as many unique objects as the benefit of the item. That is, we create a set of mutually disjoint sources, whose completeness scores are in the same proportion as the benefits of the corresponding knapsack items. The costs of the source queries are the same as the costs of the corresponding items in the knapsack problem. Finally, the cost limit for the query in our problem is equal to the cost limit specified in the knapsack problem. Thus, we have polynomially transformed an instance of the knapsack problem to an instance of our problem.

Adding to the difficulty of our problem is the nature of the completeness measure: As for the general quality model, the principle of optimality does not hold. In our case, merging some source with a more complete source does not necessarily yield a higher completeness score than merging it with a less complete source, i.e.,

$$C(S_i) \leq C(S_j) \nRightarrow C(S_i \sqcap S_k) \leq C(S_j \sqcap S_k)$$
$$C(S_i) \leq C(S_j) \nRightarrow C(S_i \sqsupset S_k) \leq C(S_j \sqsupset S_k)$$
$$C(S_i) \leq C(S_j) \nRightarrow C(S_i \sqcup S_k) \leq C(S_j \sqcup S_k)$$

This property is in the nature of information integration, and not a flaw of the completeness measure, as we can see from the following example.

Example 8.1.1. Consider the simplified example of three independent sources each with the same two attributes a_1 and a_2 and each with coverage 1, i.e., all sources cover the entire world. Assume that coverage, density, and completeness scores are as follows:

	$c(S)$	$d_S(a_1)$	$d_S(a_2)$	$d(S)$	$C(S)$
S_1	1	1	0	0.5	0.5
S_2	1	0	1	0.5	0.5
S_3	1	0.6	0.6	0.6	0.6

Here $C(S_3) > C(S_2)$, but combining each with S_1 yields $C(S_1 \sqcap S_3) < C(S_1 \sqcap S_2)$, i.e, source S_2 complements source S_1 better than S_3 does, even though S_3 has a higher overall completeness score. Similar examples can be given for $\sqsupset$ and $\sqcup$.

8.2 Maximizing Coverage

This section specializes the general problem of maximizing completeness: Of the completeness measure we consider only the coverage aspect, i.e., we present and examine algorithms to maximize coverage of the result. In Section 8.3 we shall deal with the general problem.

Regarding coverage alone suffices when all sources export the same attributes of UR and all attributes have the same density, or when the mediator only exports those attributes to the user that are common in all data sources. For instance, this is the case for existing meta-search engines, that only integrate URL, title, and description of a Web page. Because all search engines export at least those attributes with density 1, the density aspect of our completeness measure can be dropped.

The restriction substantially simplifies the optimization problem: We regain the principle of optimality—the larger the source, the more it contributes to the result, at least for simple overlap profiles. Without loss of generality we make another simplification: We assume that selection conditions in user queries are migrated toward the output of the plan, i.e., plans only contain full outerjoin merge operators. Any selection conditions that motivated the use of the join-merge and left outerjoin-merge operators are applied later to the optimized plan, and full outerjoins can be replaced later by one of the other operators.

First, we consider simple overlap profiles, then turn to complex profiles, and add a further complication to reflect real life situations: We review the proposed algorithms when sources unexpectedly fail. Finally we present a performance evaluation of the algorithms.

8.2.1 Algorithms for Simple Overlap Profiles

In a simple overlap profile all sources are mutually disjoint or mutually independent. For example, this is the case for stock information systems of different stock exchanges (disjointness) or for search engines (independence). The three algorithms presented in this section pursue greedy strategies in different variants.

Algorithm SIMPLE. Algorithm SIMPLE implements a greedy strategy, choosing sources in descending coverage order. As long as the budget is not used up, it continues issuing queries (see Algorithm 2). SIMPLE does not consider source costs when choosing the next source to query. If the source costs vary, SIMPLE may fail arbitrarily poor, as we show when discussing optimality results.

Algorithm RATIO. Algorithm RATIO is a cost-aware extension of algorithm SIMPLE. Instead of choosing sources solely by their coverage scores, RATIO chooses sources with the highest coverage-cost ratios first. Even though RATIO is cost-aware we do not achieve bounded optimality, as we show in a counter-example.

Algorithms SIMPLE and RATIO are presented formally as Algorithm 2. Lines 5 present the alternatives for the two algorithms. The function *max-Coverage(R)* returns the source with the highest coverage score among the remaining sources R. Function $maxCoverageCostRatio(R)$ returns the source from R with the highest coverage-cost ratio.

Input: Query Q, sources $S = \{S_1, S_2, \ldots S_n\}$; costs $\{c_1, c_2, \ldots c_n\}$; limit L
Output: Result of executing Q at S

```
 1:  P ← {};                                              {Plan}
 2:  R ← S;                                  {Remaining sources}
 3:  U ← 0;                                         {Used cost}
 4:  while (R is not empty) do
 5:      Next ← maxCoverage(R);            {For algorithm SIMPLE}
 5:      Next ← maxCoverageCostRatio(R);    {For algorithm RATIO}
 6:      U ← U + c_Next;
 7:      if (U > L) then
 8:          break;
 9:      end if
10:      R ← R − {Next};
11:      P ← P + Next;
12:  end while
13:  Execute P;
```

Algorithm 2: Algorithms SIMPLE and RATIO

Theorem 8.2.1. *Algorithms* SIMPLE *and* RATIO *run in* $O(n^2)$ *time, where n is the number of sources.*

Proof. Each iteration of the *while* loop in both algorithms takes $O(n)$ time as it involves finding the next best source. It is also clear that the number of iterations of the *while* loop is $O(n)$ as in each iteration a source is removed from the remaining list of sources to be considered.

We can reduce the runtime of the algorithms to $O(n \log n)$ by precalculating the query order. To this end, we sort all sources by coverage or by their coverage-cost ratio respectively in $O(n \log n)$, and in the loop simply fetch the next source from the sorted list in $O(n)$. Note that in Theorem 8.2.1, we do not take into consideration the actual time to query the sources when computing the running time of the algorithm.

Algorithm DOMINATING. Algorithm DOMINATING first considers a sequence of sources greedily based on the coverage-cost ratio as does algorithm RATIO. However, we add an optimization step: Before sending queries to the selected sources, the overall coverage of the greedy sequence is compared with the coverage of the largest source. If the largest source has a higher coverage than the total greedy sequence, the greedy sequence is discarded, and only the largest source is queried. This technique of choosing a *dominating* single source, in preference to a greedy sequence of sources, protects algorithm

DOMINATING against notorious worst-cases as we show later. This technique is well-known for solving the knapsack problem [46].

DOMINATING computes the coverage of the greedy sequence in Line 5 and the coverage of the single largest source in Line 6 (see Algorithm 3). Line 8 chooses the source with the largest coverage-cost ratio from those chosen for the greedy sequence.

Input: Query Q; sources $S = \{s_1, s_2, \ldots s_n\}$; costs $\{c_1, c_2, \ldots c_n\}$; limit L
Output: Result for Q

```
 1: P ← {};                                              {Plan}
 2: R ← S;                                  {remaining sources}
 3: U ← 0;                                          {used cost}
 4: while (R is not empty) do
 5:    greedy ← greedySequenceCoverage(R);
 6:    single ← singleLargestCoverage(R);
 7:    if (greedy > single) then
 8:       Next ← maxCoverageCostRatio(greedy);
 9:    else
10:       Next ← single;
11:    end if
12:    U ← U + c_Next;
13:    if (U > L) then
14:       break;
15:    end if
16:    R ← R − {Next};
17:    P ← P + Next;
18: end while
19: Execute P;
```

Algorithm 3: DOMINATING

Theorem 8.2.2. *Algorithm* DOMINATING *runs in* $O(n^2)$ *time, where* n *is the number of sources.*

Proof. We first note that, in algorithm DOMINATING, the number of iterations of the *while* loop is $O(n)$ as in each iteration one source is removed from the remaining list of sources to be considered. Even though it appears that in each iteration the algorithm needs to find the best greedy sequence, it can be implemented with a preprocessing step of constructing a global greedy sequence at the beginning and then efficiently deriving the best possible greedy sequence in each iteration. The construction of the global greedy sequence can be accomplished in $O(n \log n)$ time (sorting by coverage-cost ratio) and the derivation of the best possible greedy sequence in each iteration takes $O(n)$ time. In summary, each iteration of the *while* loop takes $O(n)$ time, there are $O(n)$ iterations and there is an $O(n \log n)$ preprocessing step involved. Therefore, DOMINATING requires $O(n^2)$ time.

We analyze the algorithms with regard to two overlap profiles—a simple profile allowing only mutually disjoint sources or mutually independent sources, and a complex profile allowing mixed overlap relationships. The three algorithms were designed for the first case, and we can prove optimality. For the second case we show how our algorithms may fail to produce optimal results. This failure leads to the development of overlap-aware algorithms in the next section.

Theorem 8.2.3. *If the sources are all mutually disjoint or all mutually independent of each other, and if all sources have the same cost, algorithms* SIMPLE, RATIO, *and* DOMINATING *access the optimal set of sources.*

Proof. Let N be the number of sources we can access. If C is the cost of each source and L is the given limit then $N = \lfloor L/C \rfloor$. We prove the theorem by induction over N.

$N = 1$: All three algorithms choose the source with the maximal coverage. This is the optimal solution.

$N \to N + 1$: Let P be the set of N sources already accessed. All three algorithms choose the same source S next: The functions $maxCoverage(R)$ and $maxCoverageCostRatio(R)$ of SIMPLE and RATIO always return the same source if all costs are the same. DOMINATING also chooses the same source next, because the single largest source is always also the first source of the greedy sequence. If all sources are disjoint, $c(P \sqcup S) = c(P) + c(S)$, which is optimal, because $c(S)$ is the maximum among the remaining sources. If all sources are mutually independent, $c(P \sqcup S) = c(P) + c(S) - c(P) \cdot c(S)$, which is optimal, because $c(P) \cdot c(S) < c(S)$ for any S.

If we drop the uniform cost assumption, optimality is more difficult to achieve. In fact, when source costs vary we are not able to come up with efficient algorithms that guarantee optimal solutions (Theorem 8.1.1). A first solution addressing different source costs is the RATIO algorithm. Even though this algorithm—based on the coverage-cost ratio—seems to be more careful than algorithm SIMPLE, it may still produce plans that are arbitrarily poor, as shown in the following notorious example:

Example 8.2.1. Consider two sources S_1 and S_2. Let S_1 have a coverage of 0.99 and a cost of 100 units. Let S_2 have a coverage of 0.1 and a cost of 10 units. Let the sources be mutually disjoint and let the overall cost limit be 100 units. Because the coverage-cost ratio of the smaller source S_2 is slightly higher (0.01) than that of the larger source S_1 (0.0099), algorithm RATIO queries S_2 first. Having used up 10 units of cost, the larger source cannot be queried any more without violating the cost limit. That is, algorithm RATIO is "stuck" with a plan that is almost 10 times worse than the optimal plan that queries only the larger source S_1.

The example illustrates that we can trick algorithm RATIO to not only miss the optimal solutions, but even to miss it by arbitrarily large margins.

Algorithm DOMINATING explicitly avoids such situations and we can show an optimality guarantee of 50%, i.e., the result of DOMINATING has *at least* 50% coverage of an optimal result:

Theorem 8.2.4. *If the sources are all mutually disjoint or all mutually independent, algorithm* DOMINATING *is guaranteed to achieve 50% optimality.*

Proof. Let RA be the coverage result of RATIO, let Do be the coverage result of DOMINATING, let $S_{\max}$ be the single source with maximum coverage, and let OPT be an optimal solution. Let FR be the fractional solution, obtained by adding to RA a fraction of the next source S_{Next} to be chosen. This fraction of a source has the size to exactly use up the cost limit. Note that FR is *not* a valid solution of the problem, because in reality we cannot query a fraction of a source. We use FR only within the proof. Trivially FR $\geq$ OPT, i.e., the coverage of plan FR is greater than or equal to the coverage of an optimal plan. We distinguish the two cases of the algorithm choosing either the greedy sequence or the single largest source.

$$\text{RA} \geq S_{\max} : \quad 2\text{Do} = 2\text{RA} \geq \text{RA} + S_{\max} \geq \text{RA} + S_{\text{Next}} \geq \text{FR} \geq \text{OPT}$$
$$\text{RA} < S_{\max} : \quad 2\text{Do} = 2S_{\max} \geq \text{RA} + S_{\max} \geq \text{RA} + S_{\text{Next}} \geq \text{FR} \geq \text{OPT}$$

Theorems 8.2.3 and 8.2.4 establish optimality results as long as the sources are mutually disjoint or mutually independent. In the general case, we need to consider more complex overlaps. Specifically, when the pairwise-overlap relationships are heterogeneous—a mix of disjointness, independence, and containment—the algorithms may no longer be optimal, even if all sources cost the same. This behavior is illustrated for algorithm SIMPLE by the following example.

Example 8.2.2. Consider three sources S_1, S_2, and S_3, with coverage scores 0.3, 0.2, and 0.1 respectively. Assume that S_2 is a subset of S_1, while S_3 is disjoint from S_1 (and S_2). Let each source cost 1 unit and let the overall cost limit be 2 units. That is, the mediator can query at most two 2 sources.

Algorithm SIMPLE yields an execution that includes S_1 and S_2, the two largest sources. The overall coverage of this execution is 0.3 (S_2 does not contribute anything). Another set of sources, namely S_1 and S_3, has a coverage of 0.4. Thus, algorithm SIMPLE may miss the optimal solution when some sources are subsets of others.

Algorithms RATIO and DOMINATING stumble over such cases in similar ways. Therefore, we introduce overlap-aware algorithms for complex overlap profiles.

8.2.2 Algorithms for Complex Overlap Profiles

In this section we develop two overlap-aware algorithms that efficiently find good and in special cases optimal solutions.

Algorithm CAREFUL. Algorithm CAREFUL is shown as Algorithm 4; it is an enhanced version of algorithm SIMPLE. CAREFUL refrains from querying a source if it is a subset of an already queried source. This technique is reflected in Line 8 and is the main difference to algorithm SIMPLE. To illustrate this difference, recall that in Example 8.2.2 there were three sources S_1, S_2, and S_3, with S_2 being a subset of S_1, and S_3 being disjoint from S_1 and S_2. In this scenario, algorithm SIMPLE made a suboptimal choice. However, algorithm CAREFUL correctly chooses the optimal set of sources to query (i.e., S_1 and S_3). We cannot remove all contained sources in advance because there are situations, where querying a source that is contained in another is advantageous, because it has lower cost.

Input: Query Q; sources $S = \{S_1, S_2, \ldots S_n\}$; costs $\{c_1, c_2, \ldots c_n\}$; limit L
Output: Result for Q

```
 1: P ← {};                                              {Plan}
 2: R ← S;                                   {Remaining sources}
 3: CHOSEN ← {};                         {Already chosen sources}
 4: U ← 0;                                          {Used cost}
 5: while (R is not empty) do
 6:    Next ← maxCoverage(R);
 7:    R ← R − {Next};
 8:    if (Next is not a subset of some source in CHOSEN) then
 9:       if (U > L) then
10:          break;
11:       end if
12:       U ← U + c_Next;
13:       P ← P + Next;
14:       CHOSEN ← CHOSEN ∪ {Next};
15:    end if
16: end while
17: Execute P;
```

Algorithm 4: Algorithm CAREFUL

Theorem 8.2.5. *Algorithm* CAREFUL *runs in* $O(n^2)$ *time, where n is the number of sources.*

Proof. Each iteration of the *while* loop takes $O(n)$ time as it involves finding the next best source and checking if it is superfluous. It is also clear that the number of iterations of the *while* loop is $O(n)$ as in each iteration a source is removed from the remaining list of sources to be considered.

Algorithm SUPER. Algorithm SUPER is an enhancement of algorithm DOMINATING. In the same way as CAREFUL evolved from SIMPLE, the only difference between algorithm SUPER and algorithm DOMINATING is that when looking for a greedy sequence, algorithm SUPER eliminates sources from consideration if they are subsets of other sources already visited. Moreover, we assume that SUPER uses the CAREFUL variant to determine the coverage of the best greedy sequence.

Theorem 8.2.6. *Algorithm* SUPER *runs in $O(n^3)$ time, where n is the number of sources.*

Proof. We first note that, in algorithm SUPER, the number of iterations of the *while* loop is $O(n)$ as in each iteration a source is removed from the remaining list of sources to be considered. In each iteration, we find the best greedy sequence in $O(n^2)$ time, at the same time eliminating the appropriate subset sources. Thus, the total running time of the algorithm is $O(n^3)$.

We prove optimality of CAREFUL if a disjointness relationship and an independence relationship are not simultaneously within a profile.

Theorem 8.2.7. *If the source overlaps are limited to equivalence, containment, and disjointness relationships or to equivalence, containment, and independence relationships and if all sources have the same cost, algorithm* CAREFUL *accesses the optimal set of sources.*

Proof. If all sources have the same cost, CAREFUL behaves the same as algorithm RATIO if we remove all contained sources and all equivalent sources in advance. What remains are only mutually disjoint or only mutually independent sources. Then with Theorem 8.2.3, CAREFUL is optimal.

The following example illustrates that, when the source overlaps include a mix of independence and disjointness relationships, algorithm CAREFUL may not generate an optimal execution.

Example 8.2.3. Consider three sources S_1, S_2, and S_3, with coverage scores 0.5, 0.5, and 0.4 respectively. Assume that S_1 and S_2 are independent, while S_3 is disjoint from S_1 and S_2. Let each source-query cost 1 unit and let the overall cost limit be 2 units. That is, the mediator can access two sources.
Algorithm CAREFUL yields a plan that includes S_1 and S_2, the two largest sources, with an overall coverage of 0.75. However, there are plans involving S_1 (or S_2) and S_3 that yield a coverage of 0.9. Thus, CAREFUL may miss the optimal plan when there is a mix of independent and disjoint overlaps.

Theorem 8.2.8. *If the sources are all mutually disjoint or all mutually independent, algorithm* SUPER *is guaranteed to achieve 50% optimality.*

Proof. If the sources are all mutually disjoint or all mutually independent, algorithm SUPER is equivalent to DOMINATING. Thus, with Theorem 8.2.4, SUPER achieves 50% optimality.

Theorem 8.2.9. *If the source overlaps are limited to equivalence, containment, and disjointness relationships or to equivalence, containment, and independence relationships and if all sources have the same cost, algorithm* SUPER *accesses the optimal set of sources.*

Proof. When all sources have the same cost, SUPER is equivalent to CARE-FUL. Thus, with Theorem 8.2.7 SUPER is optimal.

Table 8.1 summarizes the complexity and optimality results of this section. To show the performance of the algorithms in cases where the theoretically can achieve arbitrarily poor results, we provide a performance evaluation in the following section.

Table 8.1. Overview of completeness-optimization algorithms

	runtime	uniform cost		varying cost
		simple overlap	complex overlap	simple overlap
SIMPLE	$O(n^2)$	optimal	arb. poor	arb. poor
RATIO	$O(n^2)$	optimal	arb. poor	arb. poor
DOMINATING	$O(n^2)$	optimal	arb. poor	50%
CAREFUL	$O(n^2)$	optimal	optimal	arb. poor
SUPER	$O(n^3)$	optimal	optimal	50%

8.2.3 Performance Evaluation

For our experiments, we implemented all five algorithms; created a simulation testbed with synthetic data; ran the algorithms on the testbed; and documented the performance of the algorithms. In each experiment we ran 1000 trials and computed the average behavior of the various algorithms. Coverage scores were uniformly distributed between 0 and 0.25 to reflect coverage scores of search engines.

In our first experiment we varied the number of sources from 1 to 50 to study how the algorithms scaled (see Figure 8.1). The maximum number of 50 is sufficiently high—we know of no system integrating more than 50 data sources. Source costs varied between 1 and 10, the cost limit was 20, so an average of 4 sources could be chosen. An average of 75 percent of the sources was independent, the rest were subsets or supersets of one another.

We observed the greatest difference between the two families of algorithms in the range between 15 and 35 sources. With less than 15 sources, even the simple algorithms have no chance to make "mistakes", and with more than 35 sources, options of selecting sources are so many that even simple algorithms perform well. As expected, DOMINATING performs almost identically to RA-TIO. The special cases for which DOMINATING was designed rarely occur.

In our second experiment we fixed the number of sources to 15 and varied the overlap profile (see Figure 8.2). We implemented a parameter giving the percentage on independent source pairs. This percentage ranged from 100 to 25. The remaining overlap relationships are evenly and consistently distributed between subset and equivalence relationships. The other parameters remained the same. With mutual independence of all sources, algorithms

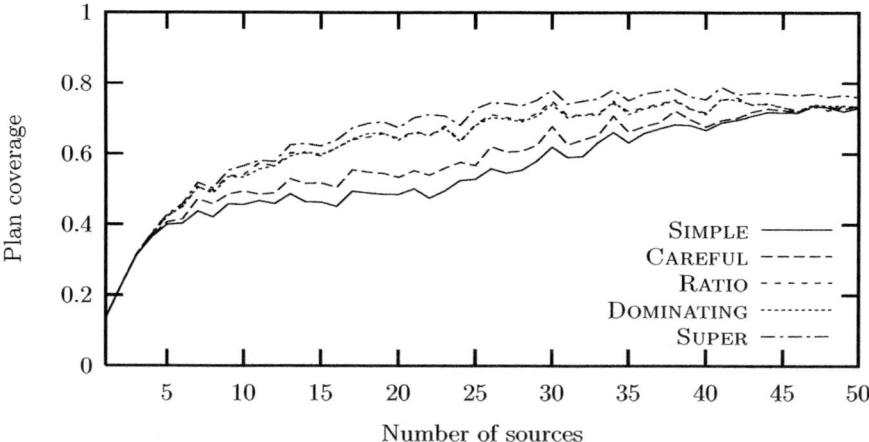

Fig. 8.1. Scalability in the number of sources

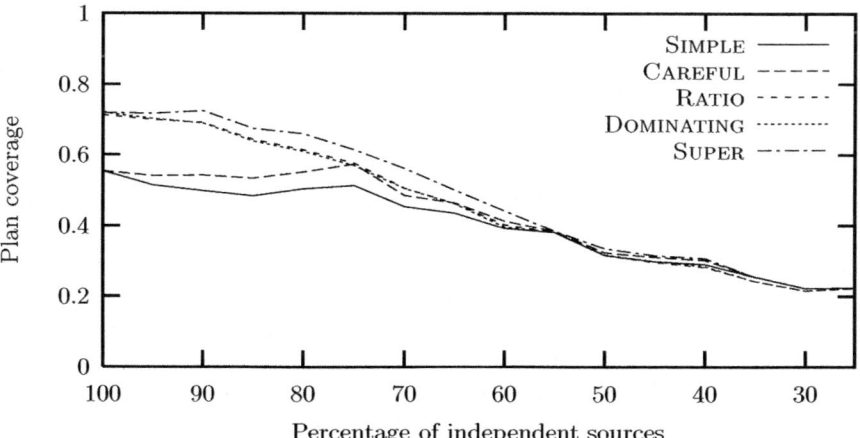

Fig. 8.2. Varying percentage of independent sources

SIMPLE and CAREFUL perform identically, and algorithms RATIO, DOMI-NATING, and SUPER also have the same performance at a higher level. The latter three perform better due to their cost-awareness. This gap closes at 75 percent independent sources, i.e., from that parameter on, the advantage of being overlap-aware is equal to the advantage of being cost-aware. The overall trend is decreasing, because the optimum decreases as well. With more and more sources being subsets of one another, the overall number of available objects decreases.

Our third experiment varied the cost range of the sources (see Figure 8.3). The minimal cost is always 1 and we increased the maximal cost to 50. This experiment shows the large difference of the cost-aware algorithms vs. the other two algorithms. Again the overall tendency is decreasing, because the average cost of a source rises while the cost limit remains the same.

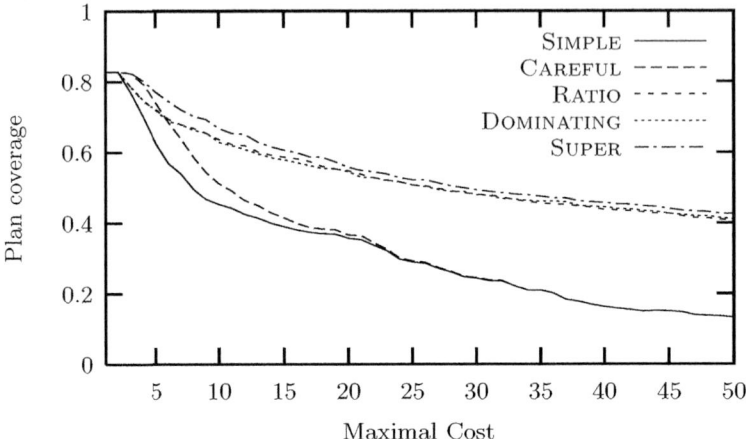

Fig. 8.3. Varying maximal cost

Our final experiment varied the cost limit from 1 to 100 while source costs averaged 5 (see Figure 8.4). From this experiment we observe two findings: First, we see again the difference of the algorithms. The cost-aware algorithms RATIO, DOMINATING, and SUPER perform much better than the other two, while the overlap-aware algorithms have a slight advantage over their counterparts. The second observation is the asymptotic behavior towards a coverage of 0.82. This is the maximum coverage that any algorithm can achieve given the cost limit. The best benefit to cost ratio lies at a cost limit of about 10, increasing the cost limit above 40 only returns a marginal increase in coverage.

8.2.4 Adding Availability Constraints

To better reflect data sources on the Web, we now examine an additional complication: Sources may unexpectedly be temporarily unavailable during query processing, e.g., due to network congestion or source overload. Mediators have no *a priori* availability knowledge. The only way a mediator can find out if a source is available is by sending it the query at hand. Note that mediators may not be able to find out, which sources are unavailable by simply "pinging" the sources. A Web source can time out in answering a query, not because its machine is down, but because it has too much backlog of work.

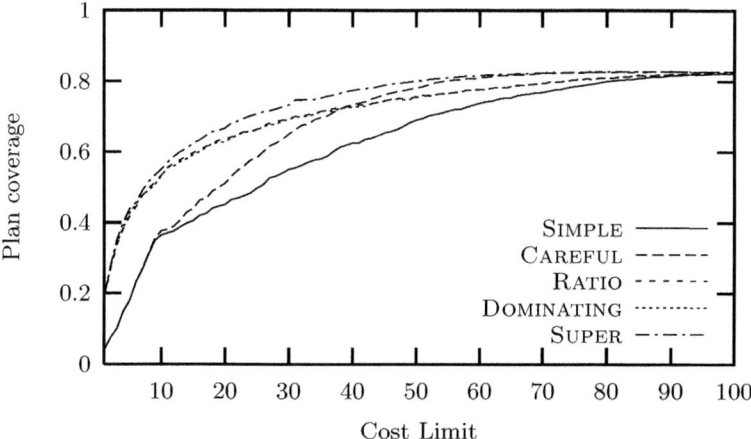

Fig. 8.4. Varying cost limit

To simplify our model, we assume that if a mediator observes an unavailable source, then that source is not available for the rest of the time, in which the user query is processed. That is, the mediator can eliminate a source from consideration (for the given query) once the mediator notices that the source is unavailable. Also, we assume there is no cost involved in sending a query to an unavailable source.

When sources are unavailable, we must redefine optimality of a solution, because an otherwise optimal solution might try to access unavailable sources, rendering the solution suboptimal in the new situation. At query time, we assume that the set S of sources can be partitioned into a set A of available sources and a set U of unavailable sources. Of course, we do not know in advance, which source is in which set. In the presence of unavailable sources, a set of sources is called an optimal selection if it is an optimal selection for the sources in A in retrospect.

Adaptations to the Algorithms. The main change to our algorithms in the presence of source unavailability is that all algorithms proceed dynamically: If an algorithm encounters an unavailable source, it simply proceeds to the next best source without having to start a new strategy from scratch. In this manner, we dynamically deal with the problem by finding an alternative source to an unavailable one, instead of pre-selecting sources possibly using scores for the availability criterion. The availability-aware versions of the algorithms are indexed with an "a", i.e., SIMPLE[a], RATION[a], etc.

If a source is discovered to be unavailable, algorithms SIMPLE[a] and RATIO[a] simply choose the next available source in the descending order of coverage or coverage-cost ratios. Thus, Lines 10-13 change to

```
10: Send query to Next;
11: if Next is available then
12:    R ← R − {Next};
13:    Collect result of Next into Answer;
14: end if
```

Algorithm CAREFUL is changed in a similar manner to CAREFUL^a, i.e., Lines 12–17 are changed to

```
12: Send query to Next;
13: if Next is available then
14:    Collect result of Next into Answer;
15:    U ← U + c_{Next};
16:    CHOSEN ← CHOSEN ∪ {Next};
17: end if
```

Optimality results. Even in the presence of unexpectedly unavailable source, we are able to achieve optimality in some cases. We prove optimality where possible and show experimental results where we cannot guarantee optimality.

Theorem 8.2.10. *If the sources are all mutually disjoint or all mutually independent, and if all sources have the same cost, algorithms* SIMPLE^a, RATIO^a, *and* DOMINATING^a *access the optimal set of sources in the presence of unavailability.*

Proof. We prove the theorem for the case where all sources are mutually disjoint. The proof for the other case is similar.

Due to uniform cost, all three algorithms produce the same result. Let ALG be the set of sources that are available in the execution produced by the algorithms. We show that there is an optimal execution, whose set of available sources is the same as ALG. That is, the execution produced by the algorithms is optimal.

Let an optimal set of sources be OPT. First, we note that ALG has $\lfloor L/C \rfloor$ sources and we can assume that OPT also has $\lfloor L/C \rfloor$ sources. Obviously, OPT cannot have more than $\lfloor L/C \rfloor$ sources, and if it has fewer than $\lfloor L/C \rfloor$ sources, we can extend OPT by querying additional sources, without compromising the optimality of the execution and without exceeding the cost limit.

We show that if OPT and ALG differ in the specific sources they contain, we can construct another optimal set that is closer to ALG.

Let S be a source in ALG that is not in OPT. There must exist a source S' in OPT that is not in ALG (because they have the same number of sources). Moreover, S' cannot be larger than S (because otherwise S' would have been chosen by algorithm SIMPLE^a ahead of S). Consequently, if we replace S' by S in OPT, we end up with a set that is at least as good. The reason why the replacement is guaranteed to produce a set that cannot be worse, is that all the sources are mutually disjoint and we are bringing in a source that is at least as large as the replaced source. Thus, we have produced a new optimal set that is closer to ALG. Continuing in this manner, we can construct an optimal set set of available sources that is identical to ALG.

If we drop the assumption of uniform cost, we cannot carry over solutions of Theorem 8.2.4 for algorithm DOMINATING[a], i.e, the use of this technique no longer guarantees 50 percent optimality, as illustrated by the following example.

Example 8.2.4. Consider three sources S_1, S_2, and S_3. Suppose that S_1 has a coverage of 0.9 and a cost of 100 units, S_2 has a coverage of 0.1 and a cost of 5 units, and S_3 has a coverage of 0.9 and a cost of 90 units. Let the overall cost limit be 100 units and let the three sources be mutually disjoint. Finally, let S_1 and S_2 be available, while S_3 is unavailable.

Algorithm DOMINATING[a] first considers the greedy sequence $\langle S_2, S_3 \rangle$. Then, it compares the combined coverage of this sequence with the coverage of the largest source S_1. Consequently, it decides to go with the greedy sequence. After executing the S_2 query, the algorithm attempts the S_3 query, but discovers that S_3 is unavailable. Unfortunately, algorithm DOMINATING is "stuck" with the small source S_2, as the larger source S_1 can no longer be queried (its cost exceeds the current budget). Algorithm DOMINATING[a] finishes with a coverage of 0.1, albeit the optimal solution achieves a coverage of 0.9.

To avoid such situation, we add two optimization techniques to algorithms DOMINATING[a] and SUPER[a]:

1. Large sources first, within a sequence of high coverage-cost ratios: Whenever algorithm DOMINATING[a] chooses a greedy sequence of sources over a single large source, it executes the queries at the sources in descending order of their coverage scores. The idea is that if all sources in the greedy sequence are available, it does not matter in what order these sources are queried. If some of these sources are not available, it may be better if sources queried are as large as possible before the greedy sequence must be reconsidered due to unavailable sources.

2. Dynamic adaptation by recalculation after each source failure: Whenever algorithms DOMINATING[a] or SUPER[a] encounter an unavailable source, while executing the query from a greedy sequence of sources, they reassess the continuation of the previously chosen greedy sequence. Specifically, they allow the possibility of abandoning the suffix of the greedy sequence, and instead querying a single large source that is larger than all the sources in the suffix put together.

Lemma 8.2.1. *If the sources are all mutually disjoint or all mutually independent and if algorithm DOMINATING[a] selects the single-largest source in its first iteration and this source is available, then DOMINATING[a] is guaranteed to achieve 50% optimality.*

Proof. The proof is similar to the proof of the second case of Theorem 8.2.4. Let the coverage of the single-largest source be S_{max}. Because algorithm DOMINATING^a picked the single-largest source in its first iteration, we know that S_{max} is at least as large as the combined coverage of the greedy sequence, say GR. The greedy sequence chooses sources that have the highest coverage-cost ratio. Let FRA be the fractional solution, i.e., the greedy sequence plus a fraction of the source with the next best ratio. Then

$$2 \cdot S_{\mathrm{max}} \geq \mathrm{GR} + S_{\mathrm{max}} \geq \mathrm{FRA} \geq \mathrm{OPT}.$$

Theorem 8.2.11. *If the sources are all mutually disjoint or all mutually independent, and in the presence of unavailability, algorithms* DOMINATING^a *and* SUPER^a *guarantee solutions that are within a factor of $\frac{1}{n-1}$ of the optimal solutions, for $n > 1$, where n is the number of sources.*

Proof. We prove the theorem inductively for DOMINATING^a. If all sources are mutually disjoint or mutually independent, SUPER^a is equivalent to DOMINATING^a.

$n = 2$. There are three cases to consider. In the first case, both sources are unavailable. In this case, algorithm DOMINATING^a produces the optimal solution, albeit not returning any results to the user query. In the second case, exactly one source is available. If the source has a cost that is under the limit for the query, algorithm DOMINATING^a correctly chooses the source and produces the optimal result. Otherwise, the optimal result is empty and DOMINATING^a returns the empty result. In the third case, both sources are available. If both sources can be queried (their combined cost is lower than the limit), DOMINATING^a queries both sources and obtains the optimal result. If neither source can be queried, DOMINATING^a yields the optimal result containing no answer objects. If either source but not both can be queried, DOMINATING^a picks the larger source and so obtains the optimal result. If one of the two sources has a cost under the limit, while the other has a cost over the limit, DOMINATING^a once again obtains the optimal result by executing the query at that source. Thus, in all cases, for $n = 2$, DOMINATING^a is guaranteed to produce optimal solutions. In other words, its solutions are guaranteed to be within a factor of $\frac{1}{n-1} = 1$ of the optimal solution.

$n \to n + 1$. Based on Lemma 8.2.1, whenever DOMINATING^a decides on the single largest source and that source is available, it achieves a result that is within a factor of $1/2$ of the optimum. If the single-largest source is unavailable or if the greedy sequence is chosen in the first place, we examine the largest source of this greedy sequence. By the technique of executing the query at the largest source of the greedy sequence first, DOMINATING^a is guaranteed a solution that achieves at least $1/(n-1)$ of the optimal coverage. If this source is available, our goal is reached, if it is not available, the problem is reduced to one with $n - 1$ sources, for which we can inductively guarantee $1/(n-2)$ optimality.

The bound of Theorem 8.2.11 is tight: We can construct examples where algorithm DOMINATING^a only reaches $1/(n-1)$ optimality. However, in many practical situations, DOMINATING^a yields solutions that are optimal or near-optimal. This fact is demonstrated by the excellent performance of algorithm DOMINATING^a in our experimental study.

Theorem 8.2.12. *If the source overlaps are limited to equivalence, containment, and disjointness relationships or to equivalence, containment, and independence relationships and if all sources have the same cost, algorithms* CAREFUL^a *and* SUPER^a *access the optimal set of sources in the presence of unavailability.*

Proof. For CAREFUL^a the proof is the same as for Theorem 8.2.7, only let CA be the set of *available* sources CAREFUL^a accesses. With uniform source costs SUPER^a is equivalent to CAREFUL^a.

Table 8.2 summarizes the optimality results of the adapted algorithms of this section. To show the performance of the algorithms in cases where the theoretically can achieve arbitrarily poor results, we provide a performance evaluation in the following section.

Table 8.2. Overview of adapted algorithms in the presence of unavailability

	uniform cost		varying cost
	simple overlap	complex overlap	simple overlap
SIMPLE^a	optimal	arb. poor	arb. poor
RATIO^a	optimal	arb. poor	arb. poor
DOMINATING^a	optimal	arb. poor	$\frac{1}{n-1}$
CAREFUL^a	optimal	optimal	arb. poor
SUPER^a	optimal	optimal	$\frac{1}{n-1}$

Performance Evaluation. We study the performance of the revised algorithms in the same testbed as before, but add an availability parameter. We chose the default value of 80 percent of the sources being available, i.e., on average every fifth source fails unexpectedly.

In Figure 8.5 we repeat the experiment of Figure 8.1, i.e., we vary the number of sources from 1 to 50. The general behavior of the algorithms in the presence of unavailability is the same as the original algorithms, i.e., close coverage scores from 1 to 10 sources and with more than 40 sources and a larger difference in between. We conclude that all algorithms react to unavailability in a similar way. Also, we see that the absolute coverage scores are close to the original ones. Our next experiment examines this difference under different availability situations.

In Figure 8.6 we show the behavior of the algorithms as source availability is varied for 20 sources. On the horizontal axis, the availability is plotted

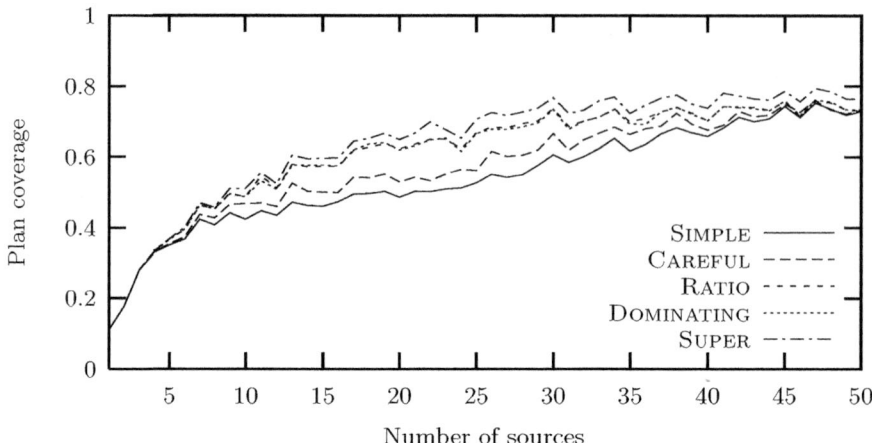

Fig. 8.5. Varying availability of sources

decreasing from 100 percent availability to 10 percent availability, where availability is treated as the probability that a source does not fail. Thus, with each experiment different sources and a different number of sources failed. The vertical axis represents the difference between the original version of the algorithms and the adapted dynamic version in percent, as the average over 1,000 runs.

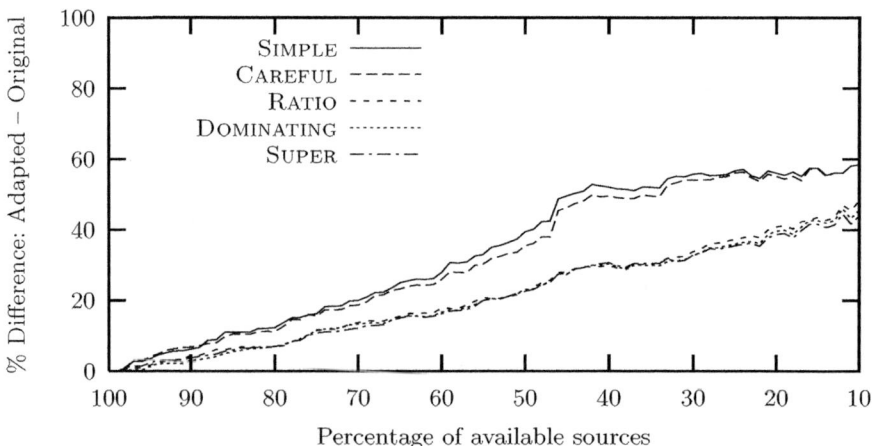

Fig. 8.6. Varying availability of sources

We observed a linearly growing error of the original versions if the algorithms. Algorithms $SIMPLE^a$ and $CAREFUL^a$ are most sensitive with errors up to 60 percent, i.e., adapting them to deal with unavailability is quite rewarding.

On the whole, we note that all the algorithms performed well over a wide range of scenarios. In particular, CAREFUL^a and SUPER^a did consistently well, with SUPER^a being the best performer among all algorithms, and in all the experiments involving variations in source unavailability, cost range, and source overlaps.

8.3 Maximizing Completeness

When moving from coverage maximization to completeness maximization we lose the principle of optimality. Recall that completeness is the product of coverage and density. With density in the maximization goal, the benefit of including a source in a plan depends on the sources already in the plan. Therefore, simple greedy strategies are bound to fail, even when all sources cost the same. Simply including the remaining most complete source in a plan does not guarantee the plan completeness to increase by the largest possible amount.

To cope with this problem, we devise a greedy strategy with a "look-ahead" technique. When deciding, which source to access next, this technique does not regard the completeness score of the remaining sources, but determines the new completeness of the plan if the source were accessed—the technique "looks ahead" to what would happen if the source were accessed. The look-ahead strategy is not new for conventional query optimization. For instance, Chang proposed this technique as an addition to the SDD-1 query optimizer [15]. Theorem 8.3.1 shows that looking ahead indeed yields the best choice of sources regarding our completeness measure:

Theorem 8.3.1. *Let P be a plan, let R be a set of sources not in the plan, and let source $S \in R$. If $C(P\,\theta\,S) \geq C(P\,\theta\,S_i)$ for all $S_i \in R$, then $C(P\,\theta\,S\,\theta\,P') \geq C(P\,\theta\,S_i\,\theta\,P')$ for all plans P' containing sources only from $R \setminus S$, where $\theta \in \{\sqcap, \sqsupset, \sqcup\}$.*

Proof. We prove the theorem only for $\theta = \sqcap$, the proofs for the other cases are similar. We use

$$C(P \sqcap S) \geq C(P \sqcap S_i)$$
$$\Rightarrow c(P \sqcap S) \cdot d(P \sqcap S) \geq c(P \sqcap S_i) \cdot d(P \sqcap S_i) \tag{8.1}$$
$$C(P) = c(P) \cdot d(P) \text{ and } d(P) \in [0,1] \Rightarrow c(P) \geq C(P) \tag{8.2}$$

and consider two cases:

Case 1: $c(P \sqcap S) \geq c(P \sqcap S_i)$

$$
\begin{aligned}
C(P \sqcap S \sqcap P') &= c(P \sqcap S \sqcap P') \cdot d(P \sqcap S \sqcap P') \\
&= c(P \sqcap S)c(P') \cdot (d(P \sqcap S) + d(P') - d(P \sqcap S)d(P')) \\
&= c(P \sqcap S)c(P') \cdot d(P \sqcap S) + c(P \sqcap S)c(P') \cdot d(P') \\
&\quad - c(P \sqcap S)c(P') \cdot d(P \sqcap S)d(P') \\
&= C(P \sqcap S)c(P') + c(P \sqcap S)C(P') - C(P \sqcap S)C(P') \\
&\overset{\text{(because (8.2))}}{\geq} C(P \sqcap S_i)c(P') + c(P \sqcap S)C(P') - C(P \sqcap S_i)C(P') \\
&\overset{\text{(case 1)}}{\geq} C(P \sqcap S_i)c(P') + c(P \sqcap S_i)C(P') - C(P \sqcap S_i)C(P') \\
&= c(P \sqcap S_i)c(P')d(P \sqcap S_i) + c(P \sqcap S_i)c(P')d(P') \\
&\quad - c(P \sqcap S_i)c(P')d(P \sqcap S_i)d(P') \\
&= c(P \sqcap S_i)c(P') \cdot (d(P \sqcap S_i) + d(P') - d(P \sqcap S_i)d(P')) \\
&= C(P \sqcap S_i \sqcap P')
\end{aligned}
$$

Case 2: $c(P \sqcap S) < c(P \sqcap S_i) \Rightarrow d(P \sqcap S) > d(P \sqcap S_i)$

$$
\begin{aligned}
C(P \sqcap S \sqcap P') &= c(P \sqcap S \sqcap P') \cdot d(P \sqcap S \sqcap P') \\
&= c(P \sqcap S)c(P') \cdot (d(P \sqcap S) + d(P') - d(P \sqcap S)d(P')) \\
&\geq c(P \sqcap S)c(P') \cdot (d(P \sqcap S_i)\frac{c(P \sqcap S_i)}{c(P \sqcap S)} + d(P') \\
&\quad - d(P \sqcap S_i)\frac{c(P \sqcap S_i)}{c(P \sqcap S)}d(P')) \\
&= c(P')d(P \sqcap S_i)c(P \sqcap S_i) + c(P \sqcap S)c(P')d(P') \\
&\quad - c(P')d(P \sqcap S_i)c(P \sqcap S_i)d(P') \\
&= c(P')(d(P \sqcap S_i)c(P \sqcap S_i) + c(P \sqcap S)d(P') \\
&\quad - d(P \sqcap S_i)c(P \sqcap S_i)d(P')) \\
&= c(P')(d(P \sqcap S_i)c(P \sqcap S_i) + c(P \sqcap S_i)\frac{d(P \sqcap S_i)}{d(P \sqcap S)}d(P') \\
&\quad - d(P \sqcap S_i)c(P \sqcap S_i)d(P')) \\
&= c(P')c(P \sqcap S_i)(d(P \sqcap S_i) + \frac{d(P \sqcap S_i)}{d(P \sqcap S)}d(P') \\
&\quad - d(P \sqcap S_i)d(P')) \\
&\overset{\text{(case 2)}}{\geq} c(P')c(P \sqcap S_i)(d(P \sqcap S_i) + d(P') - d(P \sqcap S_i)d(P')) \\
&= C(P \sqcap S_i \sqcap P')
\end{aligned}
$$

We generalize this technique to different look-ahead distances. The technique just described looks ahead one step (one source). To look ahead two steps an algorithm would consider the completeness of the plan for all pairs of remaining sources to be added. A look-ahead of n steps where n is the number of sources is equivalent to an exhaustive search of the search space. A look-ahead of zero is equivalent to the greedy algorithms SIMPLE or RATIO. Thus, we have a natural transition from a simple greedy algorithm to an exhaustive search algorithm. The higher the look-ahead, the higher the run time of the algorithm, but also the better the result.

8.3.1 The Greedy Look-Ahead Algorithm

Algorithm 5 shows the Greedy Look-Ahead algorithm (GLA). The main body is similar to that of the previous algorithms. GLA differs only in the selection of the next sources to enter the plan. This selection is performed in Lines 7–12, where the algorithm regards of the remaining sources all subsets B of size less than or equal to the look-ahead la, determines their added value to plan P, and their combined cost. If there is still enough budget to execute all sources of the subset and if it is indeed the best subset, it is added to the plan (Lines 16–18). The algorithm terminates when there is no more subset that can be executed within the remaining budget.

Input: Query Q, sources $S = \{S_1, S_2, \ldots S_n\}$; costs $\{c_1, c_2, \ldots c_n\}$; limit L; look-ahead la
Output: Result of executing Q at S

```
 1:  P ← {};                                              {Plan}
 2:  R ← S;                               {Remaining sources}
 3:  U ← 0;                                      {Used cost}
 4:  while (R is not empty) do
 5:    max ← 0;
 6:    MAX ← {};
 7:    for each B ⊆ R, |B| ≤ la do
 8:      if C(P + B) > max and Cost(B) ≤ L − U then
 9:        max ← C(P + B);
10:        MAX ← B;
11:      end if
12:    end for
13:    if (MAX = {}) then
14:      break;
15:    end if
16:    U ← U + Cost(MAX);
17:    P ← P + MAX;
18:    R ← R − MAX;
19:  end while
20:  Execute P;
```

Algorithm 5: The Greedy Look-Ahead Algorithm (GLA)

8.3.2 Performance Evaluation

The look-ahead parameter la adjusts performance and efficiency of GLA. We discuss runtime complexity, optimality results, and experimental results of the algorithm for different look-ahead values.

The worst-case complexity of GLA occurs, if in each step GLA chooses subsets of size 1. The outer *while* loop (Line 4) is performed n times, because in each pass at least one element is removed from R (Line 18). The inner *for* loop (Line 7) is performed $\sum_{i=0}^{la} \binom{n-j}{i}$ times where j is the number of sources removed. I.e., the overall worst-case complexity is $\sum_{j=0}^{n} \sum_{i=0}^{la} \binom{n-j}{i} = O(n2^n)$. There is no closed form for this series, so we show the complexity graph in Figure 8.7 for 20 sources ($n = 20$).

The average-case complexity of GLA is lower, because typically more than one source is chosen in each step. In fact, we observed in our simulation testbed that usually subsets of size la are chosen and the average size is $la - 1$ for $la > 3$. Thus, each step reduces the set of remaining sources by $la - 1$ on average. The overall average-case complexity is thus $\sum_{j=0}^{\lceil n/(la-1)\rceil} \sum_{i=0}^{la} \binom{n-j\cdot(la-1)}{i}$. Again, we show the complexity graph in Figure 8.7.

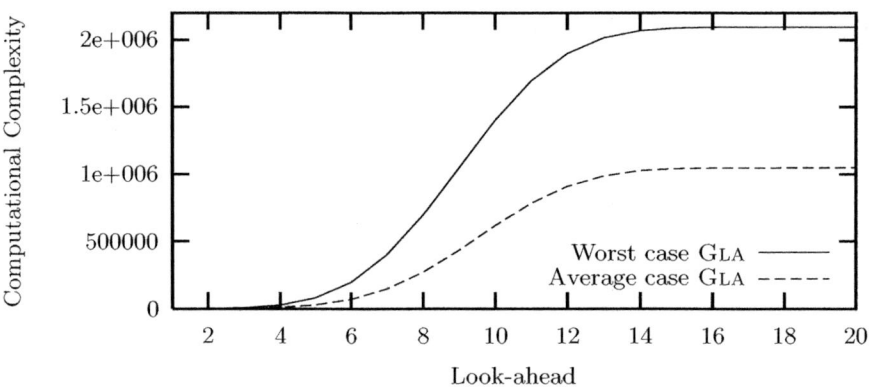

Fig. 8.7. Runtime complexity of GLA

It is clear that a look-ahead of more than one-half of the number of sources is neither feasible nor necessary. In the transition to an exhaustive search, runtime becomes prohibitively high, while the additional gain in performance decreases. After studying complexity of the algorithms we turn to their performance.

Theorem 8.3.2. *If all sources have the same cost, GLA yields optimal results for a look-ahead of 1 ($la = 1$).*

Proof. If all sources cost the same, say c, GLA accesses $\lfloor L/c \rfloor$ sources. Theorem 8.3.1 guarantees that the choice in each step is optimal.

Theorem 8.3.2 shows that a look ahead of 1 already takes care of the difficulties of our completeness measure. The only remaining detriment to optimality is the non-uniform cost of sources. If costs vary, we cannot guarantee optimal results. To show the performance of GLA, we implemented and tested the algorithm for different look-ahead distances. Figure 8.8 shows the results of our simulation experiments. The algorithm could choose from 20 sources, with cost distributed uniformly between 1 and 10, a cost limit of 25, and coverage scores and density scores for 10 attributes uniformly distributed between 0 and 1. For each look-ahead distance we ran 1,000 experiments and plotted the average performance.

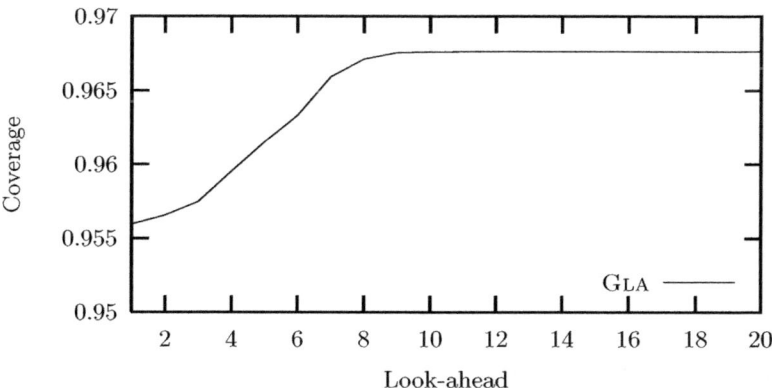

Fig. 8.8. Varying look-ahead distance

We observed a curve similar to the complexity curve of Figure 8.7, i.e., a small look-ahead yields low complexity but also slightly lower performance. Note however, that performance is plotted in the range [0.95; 0.97], i.e., all results are at a very high level of performance. A look-ahead of 1 already yields results that are only marginally lower than with higher look-ahead distances. In fact, in many of the 1,000 runs a look-ahead distance of 1 already found the optimal solution. We observed this tendency in many experiments not shown here. We conclude that a look-ahead of 1 is already sufficient in most situations.

8.4 Algebraic Reordering

After finding the optimal subset of sources to query we now move to the conventional paradigm of optimizing a plan: Using traditional optimization techniques we can perform algebraic transformations of the plan to improve response time without changing the result. For instance, the execution plan for the set of sources may be optimized towards response time or some other criterion.

Because the result of query plans remains the same after reordering, we require the completeness score of a plan to remain the same as well. Completeness is a measure for the plan result and not for how the result is obtained. The properties of $\sqcap$ and $\sqcup$ proven in Theorems 7.3.1 and 7.3.2 guarantee unchanging plan completeness under a number of reorderings. The properties for $\sqsupset$ are more limited; Galindo-Legaria and Rosenthal discuss outerjoin reordering in greater detail [43].

Example 8.4.1. Post-optimizing a plan may have great effect on plan cost. Consider plan P_{30} for query Q'_3 of Example 6.3.1 (page 96):

$$P_{30}(a_1, a_2, a_4) \leftarrow (S_1 \sqcup_{a_1} S_2) \sqcap_{a_3} S_3, \ a_2 > 10, \ a_4 < 40.$$

Assume that all selections can be pushed to the sources, i.e., we can retrieve from S_3 only those tuples where $a_4 < 40$, etc. Assume further, that the selection condition $a_2 > 10$ is not very selective and that the selection condition $a_4 < 40$ is very selective. If the plan were executed as is, a huge intermediate result of $(S_1 \sqcup_{a_1} S_2)$ would be created, of which only few tuples enter the final result after the join-merge with the small intermediate result of S_3. Using Theorem 7.3.1 we can transform plan P_{30} to

$$P'_{30}(a_1, a_2, a_4) \leftarrow (S_3 \sqcap_{a_3} S_1) \sqcup_{a_1} (S_3 \sqcap_{a_3} S_2), \ a_2 > 10, \ a_4 < 40.$$

Using this plan, we can first retrieve from S_3 only those tuples where $a_4 < 40$ and then push their IDs (attribute a_3) as an additional selection condition to sources S_1 and S_2. The overall number of tuples retrieved over the net decreases dramatically, saving time and possibly money. Of course, there are many other possibilities to transform the plan. An optimizer should consider all and find the best.

8.5 Summary

This chapter formally defined the problem of maximizing completeness under cost constraints and analyzed its complexity. In particular, we showed its NP-hardness and also showed that the principle of optimality does not hold for the completeness measure.

Therefore, we initially concentrated on solving the special case of all density scores being 1. For this subproblem we presented several algorithms to maximize coverage under cost constraints, and carefully examined the optimality properties under different parameters, including cost distribution and different overlap profiles. Also, we analyzed the adaptability of the algorithms to an environment where sources unexpectedly fail to response. We evaluated all algorithms in simulation experiments.

Then, we turned to the general problem and presented the greedy look-ahead algorithm, which is especially suited for solving problems where the principle of optimality does not hold. Again, we were able to show optimality in some cases, and evaluated the algorithm with simulation experiments, showing its overall effectiveness for the other cases.

9 Conclusion

In this thesis we gave convincing arguments that quality-driven query answering in integrated information systems is both useful and feasible. After a summary of the main contributions of this work, we suggest further applications for IQ-reasoning, and conclude with an appeal for the pervasion of IQ-reasoning in modern integrated information systems.

9.1 Summary

The main contribution of this thesis is the integration of two important concepts of information systems: *query answering* in integrated information systems and *information quality*. We solved the general problem of generating the qualitative best query response given a set of autonomous information sources and a cost limit. We take up on the subproblems formulated in the introduction and review their solutions as they were presented in this work.

Description of data sources and user query. We used the mediator-wrapper architecture as the foundation of our model. We mapped the given relational global schema of the mediator to the universal relation, and modeled both sources and user queries as views against the universal relation. These mappings and models were represented in the newly introduced UR-tableau. This approach relieved us of the difficulties of the more general problem of answering any query against any relational schema using views or against the Web itself, without compromising expressiveness too much.

Information integration. Autonomous data sources providing data for the same global schema might overlap in the information they provide. We identified extensional overlap as the set of common real world entities represented in the sources, and intensional overlap as the common attributes exported by the sources. When integrating information, extensional overlap must be identified and intensional overlap may cause data conflicts. We required IDs to identify overlap and presented a general resolution function to resolve data conflicts.

For the actual integration we presented three new merge operators: the join-merge, the left outerjoin-merge, and the full outerjoin-merge. These

F. Naumann: Quality-Driven Query Answering, LNCS 2261, pp. 153-157, 2002.
© Springer-Verlag Berlin Heidelberg 2002

operators use the IDs and resolution functions to perform the integration of data returned by the sources.

Definition of information quality. We characterized information quality (IQ) of Web data sources by providing a comprehensive list of IQ-criteria, each with a definition and a discussion about their importance for Web sources. Our list is a compilation of many related research efforts and some new criteria.

Assessment of IQ-criteria. To apply IQ-reasoning to query answering, one must numerically assess scores for the IQ-criteria. To this end, we identified three sources for IQ-scores: the user, the data source, and the query process. We presented general methods for determining the scores from each of the three sources, and paid special attention to existing metadata models, which already provide some IQ-scores indirectly.

Multiple criterion ranking. To find an ordering among sources or query plans based on multiple criteria, one must solve the problem of multi-attribute decision-making. We presented methods for scaling and weighting quality vectors of sources and five ranking methods that find partial or complete orderings among the sources. We compared the methods with regard to our problem and evaluated their sensitivity in experiments. The DEA method was chosen as a user independent source selection method and the SAW method to rank query plans.

Definition of query plan and result. Conventional query planning using views tries to find all correct query plans for a given user query, where a query plan is a collection of source views connected with join operators. The final result is the union of all plan results. We argued that in many situations it is not necessary or even possible to generate the complete result by executing all plans. Rather, we search for the top N plans, whose results already generate a satisfying response to the user.

In this new paradigm of finding only top plans, we showed shortcomings of the conventional query planning approach. Instead of generating a set of conjunctive plans, we represent the entire process of distributing the query and merging the result in a single plan, using the new merge operators. Thus, the search for top plans is reduced to finding the single best plan. Hence, we are able to find the globally optimal result and not just a combination of locally optimal plans.

Merging IQ-criteria. To determine the overall quality of a query plan, one must aggregate the quality scores of the sources in the plan. We developed merge functions for IQ-criteria. A merge function for a criterion takes the quality scores of two sources or intermediate results and determines the IQ-score of the combination of the two. The scores were aggregated along the query plans to finally find the IQ-vector of the root node, in a fashion similar to cost models for conventional query optimizers. This IQ-vector represents the overall quality of the plan. The SAW ranking method then aggregates the vector to a scalar IQ-score for the plan.

Apart from simple merge functions for several IQ-criteria, we dealt in detail with the completeness criterion. Assuming a closed world, completeness was defined as a combination of coverage (number of tuples) and density (number of non-null values). We showed how to calculate completeness across all three merge operators and proved several properties that allow algebraic reorderings of a query plan.

Efficient and effective planning. We developed algorithms for both the problem of finding the top N conjunctive plans and of finding the best plan using the new merge operators.

For the first problem two approaches were presented. One attaches a source selection phase before and a plan selection phase after an existing query planning algorithm; the other integrates these phases in a branch & bound algorithm. The branch & bound approach not only finds the qualitatively best plans, but also uses IQ-based bounds to dramatically increase efficiency, which was demonstrated with simulation experiments. For the second problem, we concentrated on maximizing completeness under some cost constraints. A first family of algorithms maximizes only coverage. In many situations they achieve optimal results or at least guarantee optimality bounds. Their general efficiency and scalability was shown through experiments. Even after adding the difficulty of unexpected failure of sources, we were able to show the good performance of the algorithms. For the general problem of maximizing completeness we suggested a look-ahead algorithm and again showed an optimality result and its performance through experiments.

Put together, the solutions to these problems allow quality-driven query answering in integrated information systems. The thesis covers all necessary stages from the definition of information quality, to the assessment of quality scores, to a model to describe sources and queries; and to algorithms that find qualitative best answers under different paradigms and in different situations. With these solutions we have addressed the pressing problem of integrating information sources that are autonomous and therefore display varying quality. Even though the problem has been identified by many, no comprehensive solution has been presented before. This thesis is the first research approach to define quality and put quality scores to use, to find high quality answers to user queries against integrated information systems.

9.2 Further Applications for IQ-reasoning

Apart from the information integration scenario, which was the basis of this thesis, information quality reasoning is helpful for further applications. All scenarios in which the underlying data stems from multiple, autonomous sources can profit from reasoning about information quality.

9.2.1 Data Warehouses

A data warehouse is a repository of integrated data from distributed, autonomous, and possibly heterogeneous sources. Data warehouses are typically used to aggregate data, for instance, the sales of distributed retail stores. The same issues and problems apply as for the information integration scenario, the only difference is the materialization of the data in a repository rather than at the data sources in our approach. The mediator-wrapper architecture may be viewed to some degree as a virtual data warehouse. The problems and solutions of this thesis regarding IQ-reasoning can be applied directly to the data warehouse scenario.

The effect of poor information quality in data warehouses has been pointed out by many authors [61, 112, 127]. Incorrect data leads to incorrect aggregation and possibly to poor management decisions. Furthermore, to save space, data warehouses often only store the aggregated values, thus loosing the ability to identify and correct inaccurate data.

9.2.2 Data Mining

Data warehouses are often the basis for data mining techniques; in fact some data warehouses are used solely to apply data mining techniques. Data mining techniques are especially sensitive towards poor data quality [67]. For instance, outliers, i.e., data points that lie far from the average, severely skew the results of data mining algorithms. Outliers are usually produced where the data itself is generated: Sensors give incorrect output, a human accidentally adds a decimal to a number, etc. Therefore, any data mining method is preceded by a data cleaning technique to improve data quality, before applying the actual mining algorithms.

Also, other aspects of information quality play an important role for data mining. The completeness of the data is of importance so as not to mine on a subset of the available data. If the data, such as consumer behavior data, is obtained from a third party, the reputation and objectivity of the source are an important factor. The techniques of quality assessment and quality improvement presented in this thesis are well applicable to data mining.

9.2.3 Quality-Driven Integration of Query Results

IQ-reasoning can enhance the integration of incoming query results in two ways: Conflict resolution may benefit from IQ-reasoning and result tuples may be ranked by their quality.

The general resolution function introduced in Section 2.3.2 resolves conflicts between non-null values by mapping the two values to a single value of the same domain. This mapping can be specified in a quality-dependent way. If the resolution function must decide between one of the two values, it can favor the value from the qualitatively better source. For instance, when deciding, which address to include in a result for a person search, the address of the source with the higher update frequency can be chosen. Another example are search engines that export a date attribute specifying the last update of the page index. In this case, the more recent data about the Web page should be chosen. Quality-dependent resolution functions enhance the query result by favoring high quality information over low quality information.

This thesis dealt with the problem of gathering the best response to a user query, but has not addressed the problem of presenting the information to the user. Again, the presentation profits from IQ-reasoning. The quality determined for a source, a part of a plan, or an entire plan represents the quality of the data generated by the plan. Instead of dropping this information once the data is received, it can be used to rank the query results. If the user does not specify another order, high quality tuples should be ranked first. High quality tuples contain many attribute values (little null values) and contain attribute values from high quality sources.

9.3 An Appeal

Data integrated from autonomous data sources, especially on the Web, is of poor quality. Discussions with many researchers from different fields have made it clear that poor information quality has been identified as a pressing problem, both on a personal and a professional level. With more and more publicly available data and more and more autonomous sources, the problem will increase in the future. To make full use of the opportunity to integrate large amounts of data from various sources, IQ-reasoning methods must be applied.

For our approach of quality-driven query answering, we assume a closed world consisting of wrapped data sources. Each source is described with respect to a given global, relational schema. This thesis has shown that IQ-reasoning under these reasonable assumptions is feasible: Many IQ-criteria can be assessed automatically, existing query planning algorithms can be enhanced using IQ-scores, and optimizing towards information quality follows principles that are similar to well-known cost-based optimization techniques. The thesis has also shown that IQ-reasoning is useful: Query planning is made efficient and executing only top plans saves valuable resources while still satisfying the user.

We hope that our findings about information quality and our IQ-reasoning techniques will find their way into integrated information systems, thereby regaining the ability to deliver high quality query results to users, once lost in the transition from centralized database management systems to systems integrating autonomous information sources.

References

1. Agha Iqbal Ali. Streamlined computation for data envelopment analysis. *European Journal of Operational Research*, 64:61–67, 1993.
2. The AltaVista search engine. `www.altavista.com`.
3. The AltaVista Money stock quote service. `money.altavista.com`.
4. S.F. Altschul, W. Gish, W. Miller, E.W. Myers, and D.J. Lipman. Basic local alignment search tool. *Journal of Molecular Biology*, 215:403–410, 1990.
5. Y. Arens, R. Hull, and R. King. Reference architecture for the intelligent integration of information; version 2.0 (draft). Technical report, DARPA - Defense Advanced Research Project Agency, August 1995.
6. Yigal Arens, Chung-Nan Hsu, and Craig A. Knoblock. Query processing in the SIMS information mediator. In Austin Tate, editor, *Advanced Planning Technology*, pages 61–69. AAAI Press, Menlo Park, California, 1996.
7. Reva Basch. Measuring the quality of the data: Report on the fourth annual SCOUG retreat. *Database Searcher*, 6(8):18–24, October 1990.
8. C. Batini, M. Lenzerini, and Shamkant B. Navathe. A comparative analysis of methodologies for database schema integration. *ACM Computing Surveys*, 18(4):323–364, 1986.
9. Richard E. Bellman. Dynamic programming and stochastic control processes. *Information and Control*, 1(3):228–239, 1958.
10. R. Benayoun, B. Roy, and N. Sussman. Manual de reference du programme ELECTRE. In *Note de Synthese et Formation*, volume 17, Paris, 1966. Direction Scientifique SEMA.
11. Krishna Bharat and Andrei Broder. A technique for measuring the relative size and overlap of public web search engines. In *Proceedings of the International World Wide Web Conference*, Brisbane, Australia, April 1998.
12. Mónica Bobrowski, Martina Marré, and Daniel Yankelevich. A homogeneous framework to measure data quality. In *Proceedings of the International Conference on Information Quality (IQ)*, pages 115–124, Cambridge, MA, 1999.
13. Michael J. Carey and Donald Kossmann. On saying "Enough already!" in SQL. In *Proceedings of the ACM International Conference on Management of Data (SIGMOD)*, pages 219–230, Tucson, AZ, 1997.
14. Ashok K. Chandra and Philip M. Merlin. Optimal implementation of conjunctive queries in relational databases. In *Proceedings of the ACM Symposium on Theory of Computing*, pages 77–90, 1977.
15. Jo-Mei Chang. A heuristic approach to distributed query processing. In *Proceedings of the International Conference on Very Large Databases (VLDB)*, pages 54–61, Mexico City, Mexico, 1982.
16. A. Charnes, W.W. Cooper, and E. Rhodes. Measuring the efficiency of decision making units. *European Journal of Operational Research*, 2:429–444, 1978.
17. Abraham Charnes and William Cooper. Programming with linear fractional functionals. *Naval Research Logistics Quarterly*, 9:181–185, 1962.

F. Naumann: Quality-Driven Query Answering, LNCS 2261, pp. 159-166, 2002.
© Springer-Verlag Berlin Heidelberg 2002

18. Abraham Charnes, William Cooper, Arie Y. Lewin, and Lawrence M. Seiford. *Data Envelopment Analysis: Theory, Methodology and Applications.* Kluwer Academic, Boston, 1994.
19. Surajit Chaudhuri. An overview of query optimisation in relational systems. In *Proceedings of the Symposium on Principles of Database Systems (PODS)*, pages 34–43, Seattle, Washington, 1998.
20. Surajit Chaudhuri and Luis Gravano. Optimizing queries over multimedia repositories. In *Proceedings of the ACM International Conference on Management of Data (SIGMOD)*, pages 91–102, Montreal, Canada, 1996.
21. Surajit Chaudhuri and Luis Gravano. Evaluating top-k selection queries. In *Proceedings of the International Conference on Very Large Databases (VLDB)*, pages 397–410, Edinburgh, Scotland, 1999.
22. S. Chawathe, H. Garcia-Molina, J. Hammer, K. Ireland, Y. Papakonstantinou, J. Ullman, and J. Widom. The TSIMMIS project: Integration of heterogeneous information sources. In *Proceedings of IPSJ Conference*, pages 7–18, Tokyo, Japan, 1994.
23. Ying Chen, Qiang Zhu, and Nengbin Wang. Query processing with quality control in the World Wide Web. *World Wide Web*, 1(4):241–255, 1998.
24. Junghoo Cho, Narayanan Shivakumar, and Hector Garcia-Molina. Finding replicated web collections. In *Proceedings of the ACM International Conference on Management of Data (SIGMOD)*, pages 355–366, Dallas, Texas, 2000.
25. Stavros Christodoulakis. Implications of certain assumptions in database performance evaluation. *ACM Transactions on Database Systems (TODS)*, 9(2):163–186, 1984.
26. E.F. Codd. Extending the relational database model to capture more meaning. *ACM Transactions on Database Systems (TODS)*, 4(4):397–434, December 1979.
27. Francis S. Collins, Ari Patrinos, Elke Jordan, Aravinda Chakravarti, Raymond Gesteland, LeRoy Walters, the members of the DOE, and NIH planning groups. New goals for the US Human Genome Project: 1998-2003. *Science*, 282:682–689, 1998.
28. G.B. Dantzig. *Linear Programming and Extensions.* Princeton University Press, Princeton, NJ, 1963.
29. C.J. Date. *Relational Database (selected writings).* Addison-Wesley, Reading, MA, USA, 1986.
30. Ana Maria de Carvalho Moura, Maria Luiza Machado Campos, and Cassia Maria Barreto. A survey on metadata for describing and retrieving internet resources. *World Wide Web*, pages 222–240, 1998.
31. Stefan Decker, Dieter Fensel, Frank van Harmelen, Ian Horrocks, Sergey Melnik, Michel R. Klein, and Jeen Broekstra. Knowledge representation on the web. In *Proceedings of the International Workshop on Description Logics (DL)*, pages 89–97, Aachen, Germany, 2000.
32. W.H. Delone and E.R. McLean. Informaton systems success: the quest for the dependent variable. *Information Systems Research*, 3(1):60–95, 1992.
33. Rajiv M. Dewan, Marshall L. Freimer, and Abraham Seidmann. Internet service providers, proprietary content, and the battle for users' dollars. *Communications of the ACM*, 41(8):43–48, 1998.
34. Directory Interchange Format (DIF). `http://gcmd.gsfc.nasa.gov/difguide/`.
35. Dublin Core Metadata Initiative. `http://purl.org/dc/index.htm`.
36. Oliver M. Duschka and Michael R. Genesereth. Answering recursive queries using views. In *Proceedings of the Symposium on Principles of Database Systems (PODS)*, pages 109–116, Tucson, Arizona, 1997.

37. James S. Dyer. Remarks on the analytical hierarchy process. *Management Science*, 36(3):249–258, 1990.
38. R.G. Dyson, E. Thanassoulis, and A. Boussofiane. *Tutorial Papers in Operational Research*, chapter Data Envelopement Analysis. Operational Research Society, 1990.
39. Ramez Elmasri and Shamkant B. Navathe. *Fundamentals of Database Systems*. Benjamin/Cummings Publishing Company, Redwood City, 2. edition, 1994.
40. The e*trade stock trade service. www.etrade.com.
41. Daniela Florescu, Daphne Koller, and Alon Levy. Using probabilistic information in data integration. In *Proceedings of the International Conference on Very Large Databases (VLDB)*, pages 216–225, Athens, Greece, 1997.
42. Helena Galhardas, Daniela Florescu, Dennis Shasha, and Eric Simon. An extensible framework for data cleaning. In *Proceedings of the International Conference on Data Engineering (ICDE)*, page 312, San Diego, CA, 2000.
43. César Galindo-Legaria and Arnon Rosenthal. Outerjoin simplification and reordering for query optimization. *ACM Transactions on Database Systems (TODS)*, 22(1):43–74, March 1997.
44. Sumit Ganguly, Waqar Hasan, and Ravi Krishnamurthy. Query optimization for parallel execution. In *Proceedings of the ACM International Conference on Management of Data (SIGMOD)*, pages 9–18, San Diego, CA, 1992.
45. Danièle Gardy and Claude Puech. On the effects of join operations on relation sizes. *ACM Transactions on Database Systems (TODS)*, 14(4):574–603, 1989.
46. Michael R. Garey and David S. Johnson. *Computers and Intractability*. W.H. Freeman and Company, New York, 1979.
47. Global information locator service (GILS). http://www.gils.net.
48. The Google search engine. www.google.com.
49. Goetz Graefe. Query evaluation techniques for large databases. *ACM Computing Surveys*, 25(2):73–170, 1993.
50. Luis Gravano, Chen-Chuan K. Chang, and Hector Garcia-Molina. STARTS: Stanford proposal for internet meta-searching. In *Proceedings of the ACM International Conference on Management of Data (SIGMOD)*, pages 207–218, Tucson, Arizona, 1997.
51. Luis Gravano, Hector Garcia-Molina, and Anthony Tomasic. The effectiveness of GlOSS for the text database recovery problem. In *Proceedings of the ACM International Conference on Management of Data (SIGMOD)*, pages 126–137, Minneapolis, Minnesota, 1994.
52. Luis Gravano, Héctor Garcia-Molina, and Anthony Tomasic. GlOSS: Textsource discovery over the internet. *ACM Transactions on Database Systems (TODS)*, 1999.
53. Jean-Robert Gruser, Louiqa Raschid, Vladimir Zadorozhny, and Tao Zhan. Learning response time for websources using query feedback and application in query optimization. *VLDB Journal*, 9(1):18–37, 2000.
54. Ashish Gupta. Some data integration and database issues in e-commerce (and world peace). Invited talk at the International Conference on Extending Database Technology (EDBT), 2000.
55. Theo Härder, Günter Sauter, and Joachim Thomas. The intrinsic problems of structural heterogeneity and an approach to their solution. *VLDB Journal*, 8(1):25–43, 1999.
56. Mauricio A. Hernández and Salvatore J. Stolfo. Real-world data is dirty: Data cleansing and the merge/purge problem. *Data Mining and Knowledge Discovery*, 2(1):9–37, 1998.
57. The Hoovers Online company profile service. www.hoovers.com.

58. Richard Hull. Managing semantic heterogeneity in databases: A theoretical perspective. In *Proceedings of the Symposium on Principles of Database Systems (PODS)*, pages 51–61, Tuscon, Arizona, 1997.

59. Ching-Lai Hwang and Kwangsun Yoon. *Multiple Attribute Decision Making*. Number 186 in Lecture Notes in Economics and Mathematical Systems. Springer-Verlag, Berlin – Heidelberg – New York, 1981.

60. M. Jarke and Y. Vassiliou. Data warehouse quality design: A review of the DWQ project. In *Proceedings of the International Conference on Information Quality (IQ)*, Cambridge, MA, 1997.

61. M.A. Jeusfeld, C. Quix, and M. Jarke. Design and analysis of quality information for data warehouses. In *Proceedings of the International Conference on Conceptual Modeling (ER)*, pages 349–362, Singapore, November 1998.

62. William Kent. The breakdown of the information model in multi-database systems. *SIGMOD Record*, 20(4):10–15, 1991.

63. L.G. Khachian. A polynomial algorithm for linear programming. *Soviet Math. Doklady*, 20:191–194, 1979.

64. W. Kim, I. Choi, S. Gala, and M. Scheevel. On resolving schematic heterogeneity in multidatabase systems. In W. Kim, editor, *Modern Database Systems*, chapter 26, pages 521–550. ACM Press, New York, NY, USA, 1995.

65. Chung T. Kwok and Daniel S. Weld. Planning to gather information. In *AAAI National Conference on Artificial Intelligence*, pages 32–39, Portland, Oregon, 1996.

66. M. LaCroix and A. Pirotte. Generalized joins. *SIGMOD Record*, 8(3):14–15, September 1976.

67. Mong-Li Lee, Tok Wang Ling, Hongjun Lu, and Yee Teng Ko. Cleansing data for mining and warehousing. In *Proceedings of the International Conference on Database and Expert Systems Applications (DEXA)*, volume 1677 of *LNCS*, pages 751–760, Florence, Italy, 1999. Springer.

68. Ulf Leser. Combining heterogeneous data sources through query correspondence assertions. In *Workshop on Web Information and Data Management, in conjunction with CIKM'98*, pages 29–32, Washington, D.C., 1998.

69. Ulf Leser. Designing a global information resource for molecular biology. In *Proceedings of the Conference Datenbanksysteme in Büro, Technik und Wissenschaft (BTW)*, pages 362–369, Freiburg, Germany, 1999.

70. Ulf Leser. *Query Planning in Mediator Based Information Systems*. PhD thesis, University of Technology, Berlin, 2000.

71. Ulf Leser and Felix Naumann. Query planning with information quality bounds. In *Proceedings of the International Conference on Flexible Query Answering Systems (FQAS)*, Advances in Soft Computing, Warsaw, Poland, 2000. Springer.

72. Alon Y. Levy, Alberto O. Mendelzon, Yehoshua Sagiv, and Divesh Srivastava. Answering queries using views. In *Proceedings of the Symposium on Principles of Database Systems (PODS)*, pages 95–104, San Jose, CA, 1995.

73. Alon Y. Levy, Anand Rajaraman, and Joann J. Ordille. Query-answering algorithms for information agents. In *AAAI National Conf. on Artificial Intelligence*, pages 40–47, Portland, Oregon, 1996.

74. Alon Y. Levy, Anand Rajaraman, and Joann J. Ordille. Querying heterogeneous information sources using source descriptions. In *Proceedings of the International Conference on Very Large Databases (VLDB)*, pages 251–262, Bombay, India, 1996.

75. Alon Y. Levy, Divesh Srivastava, and Thomas Kirk. Data model and query evaluation in global information systems. *Journal of Intelligent Information*

Systems - Special Issue on Networked Information Discovery and Retrieval,
5(2):121–143, 1995.
76. Menchi Liu and Tok Wang Ling. A data model for semistructured data with
partial and inconsistent information. In *Proceedings of the International Conference on Extending Database Technology (EDBT)*, pages 317–331, Konstanz,
Germany, 2000.
77. The London Stock Exchange stock quote server. www.londonstockexchange.
com.
78. David Maier, Jeffrey D. Ullman, and Moshe Y. Vardi. On the foundations of
the universal relation model. *ACM Transactions on Database Systems (TODS)*,
9(2):283–308, 1984.
79. Michael V. Mannino, Paicheng Chu, and Thomas Sager. Statistical profile
estimation in database systems. *ACM Computing Surveys*, 20(3):191–221, 1988.
80. Weiyi Meng, King-Lup Liu, Clement T. Yu, Wensheng Wu, and Naphtali Rishe.
Estimating the usefulness of search engines. In *Proceedings of the International
Conference on Data Engineering (ICDE)*, pages 146–153, Sydney, Australia,
1999.
81. The Merrill Lynch company profile service. www.ml.com.
82. The MetaCrawler meta-search engine. www.metacrawler.com.
83. MetaSpy, a search engine spying utility. www.metaspy.com.
84. George A. Mihaila, Louiqa Raschid, and Maria-Esther Vidal. Using quality
of data metadata for source selection and ranking. In *Proceedings of the ACM
SIGMOD Workshop on The Web and Databases (WebDB)*, pages 93–98, Dallas,
Texas, 2000.
85. Steve Mohan and Mary Jane Willshire. DataBryte: A data warehouse cleansing framework. In *Proceedings of the International Conference on Information
Quality (IQ)*, pages 77–88, Cambridge, MA, 1999.
86. Steve Mohan, Mary Jane Willshire, and Charles Schroeder. DataBryte: A proposed data warehouse cleansing framework. In *Proceedings of the International
Conference on Information Quality (IQ)*, pages 283–291, Cambridge, MA, 1998.
87. Amihai Motro. Completeness information and its application to query processing. In *Proceedings of the International Conference on Very Large Databases
(VLDB)*, pages 170–178, Kyoto, August 1986.
88. Amihai Motro and Igor Rakov. Estimating the quality of databases. In *Proceedings of the International Conference on Flexible Query Answering Systems
(FQAS)*, pages 298–307, Roskilde, Denmark, May 1998. Springer Verlag.
89. Hubert Naacke, Georges Gardarin, and Anthony Tomasic. Leveraging mediator
cost models with heterogeneous data sources. In *Proceedings of the International
Conference on Data Engineering (ICDE)*, pages 351–360, February 1998.
90. Felix Naumann. Data fusion and data quality. In *Proceedings of the New Techniques & Technologies for Statistics Seminar (NTTS)*, pages 147–154, Sorrento,
Italy, 1998.
91. Felix Naumann and Johann Christoph Freytag. Completeness of information
sources. Technical Report 135, Humboldt-Universität zu Berlin, Institut für
Informatik, 2000.
92. Felix Naumann, Johann Christoph Freytag, and Myra Spiliopoulou. Quality-
driven source selection using Data Envelopment Analysis. In *Proceedings of the
International Conference on Information Quality (IQ)*, pages 137–152, Cambridge, MA, 1998.
93. Felix Naumann and Ulf Leser. Density scores for cooperative query answering.
In *Proceedings of the Workshop Föderierte Datenbanken*, pages 103–116, Berlin,
1999.

94. Felix Naumann and Ulf Leser. Cooperative query answering with density scores. In *Proceedings of the International Conference on Management of Data (CO-MAD)*, Pune, India, 2000.

95. Felix Naumann, Ulf Leser, and Johann Christoph Freytag. Quality-driven integration of heterogenous information systems. In *Proceedings of the International Conference on Very Large Databases (VLDB)*, pages 447–458, Edinburgh, 1999.

96. Felix Naumann and Claudia Rolker. Do metadata models meet IQ requirements? In *Proceedings of the International Conference on Information Quality (IQ)*, pages 99–114, Cambridge, MA, 1999.

97. Felix Naumann and Claudia Rolker. Assessment methods for information quality criteria. In *Proceedings of the International Conference on Information Quality (IQ)*, Boston, MA, 2000.

98. Mattis Neiling and Hans-Joachim Lenz. Data integration by means of object identification in information systems. In *Proceedings of European Conference on Information Systems*, Vienna, Austria, 2000.

99. The New York Stock Exchange stock quote server. www.nyse.com.

100. H.B. Newcombe. *Handbook of Record Linkage*. Oxford University Press, Oxford, UK, 1988.

101. Greg R. Notess. Search engine showdown, 2000. www.notess.com/search/.

102. Frank Olken and Doron Rotem. Random sampling from database files: A survey. In *Proceedings of the International Conference on Scientific and Statistical Database Management (SSDBM)*, pages 92–111, Charlotte, NC, 1990.

103. Ken Orr. Data quality and systems theory. *Communications of the ACM*, February 1998.

104. Tamer Özsu and Patrick Valduriez. *Principles of Distributed Database Systems*. Prentice Hall International Editions, 1991.

105. Yannis Papakonstantinou, Serge Abiteboul, and Hector Garcia-Molina. Object fusion in mediator systems. In *Proceedings of the International Conference on Very Large Databases (VLDB)*, pages 413–424, Bombay, India, 1996.

106. Yannis Papakonstantinou, Hector Garcia-Molina, and Jeffrey D. Ullman. MedMaker: A mediation system based on declarative specifications. In *Proceedings of the International Conference on Data Engineering (ICDE)*, pages 132–141, New Orleans, Louisiana, 1996.

107. Elizabeth M. Pierce. Enumerating data errors - a survey of the counting literature. In *Proceedings of the International Conference on Information Quality (IQ)*, Cambridge, MA, 1998.

108. Robert Pirsig. *Zen and the Art of Motocycle Maintenance*. Bantam Books, New York, 1974.

109. Rachel A. Pottinger and Alon Levy. A scalable algorithm for answering queries using views. In *Proceedings of the International Conference on Very Large Databases (VLDB)*, pages 484–495, Cairo, Egypt, 2000.

110. Xiaolei Qian. Query folding. In *Proceedings of the International Conference on Data Engineering (ICDE)*, pages 48–55, New Orleans, LA, 1996.

111. Thomas C. Redman. *Data Quality for the Information Age*. Artech House, Boston, London, 1996.

112. Thomas C. Redman. The impact of poor data quality in the typical enterprise. *Communications of the ACM*, 41(2):79–82, 1998.

113. Arnon Rosenthal. Note on the expected size of a join. *SIGMOD Record*, 11(4):19–25, 1981.

114. Mary Tork Roth and Peter M. Schwarz. Don't scrap it, wrap it! A wrapper architecture for legacy data sources. In *Proceedings of the International Conference on Very Large Databases (VLDB)*, pages 266–275, 1997.

115. Thomas Lorie Saaty. *The Analytic Hierarchy Process*. McGraw-Hill, Inc., New York, NY, 1980.

116. Arnaud Sahuguet and Fabien Azavant. Building light-weight wrappers for legacy web data-sources using W4F. In *Proceedings of the International Conference on Very Large Databases (VLDB)*, pages 738–741, 1999.

117. Gerard Salton and Michael J. McGill. *Introduction to Modern Information Retrieval*. McGraw-Hill, Inc., New York, NY, 1983.

118. The SavvySearch meta-search engine. www.savvysearch.com.

119. P.G. Selinger, M.M. Astrahan, D.D. Chamberlin, R.A. Lorie, and T.G. Price. Access path selection in a relational database management system. In *Proceedings of the ACM International Conference on Management of Data (SIGMOD)*, pages 23–34, Boston, MA, 1979.

120. Amit P. Sheth and James A. Larson. Federated database systems for managing distributed, heterogeneous, and autonomous databases. In *ACM Computing Surveys*, volume 22(3), pages 183–236, September 1990.

121. Narayanan Shivakumar and Hector Garcia-Molina. Scam: A copy detection mechanism for digital documents. In *Proceedings of International Conference in Theory and Practice of Digital Libraries (DL)*, Austin, Texas, 1995.

122. Arun Swami and K. Bernhard Schiefer. On the estimation of join result sizes. In *Proceedings of the International Conference on Extending Database Technology (EDBT)*, volume 779 of *LNCS*, pages 287–300, Cambridge, UK, 1994. Springer.

123. K.L. Tan, C.H. Goh, and B.C. Ooi. On getting some answers quickly, and perhaps more later. In *Proceedings of the International Conference on Data Engineering (ICDE)*, pages 32–39, Sydney, Australia, 1999.

124. Giri Kumar Tayi and Donald P. Ballou. Examining data quality. *Communications of the ACM*, 41(2):54–57, 1998.

125. Dennis Tsichritzis and Anthony C. Klug. *The ANSI/X3/SPARC DBMS framework*. AFIPS Press, Arlington, VA, USA, 1978.

126. Jeffrey D. Ullman. *Principles of database and knowledge-base systems*, volume II. Computer Science Press, Rockville, MD, 1989.

127. Richard Y. Wang. A product perspective on Total Data Quality Management. *Communications of the ACM*, 41(2):58–65, 1998.

128. Richard Y. Wang and Diane M. Strong. Beyond accuracy: What data quality means to data consumers. *Journal on Management of Information Systems*, 12(4):5–34, 1996.

129. Richard Y. Wang, Diane M. Strong, Beverly K. Kahn, and Yang W. Lee. An information quality assessment methodology. In *Proceedings of the International Conference on Information Quality (IQ)*, pages 258–265, Cambridge, MA, 1999.

130. Web.de, a german search engine. www.web.de.

131. Inktomi WebMap. www.inktomi.com/webmap/.

132. Gerhard Weikum. Towards guaranteed quality and dependability of information systems. In *Proceedings of the Conference Datenbanksysteme in Büro, Technik und Wissenschaft (BTW)*, pages 379–409, Freiburg, Germany, 1999.

133. Gio Wiederhold. Mediators in the architecture of future information systems. *IEEE Computer*, 25(3):38–49, 1992.

134. Gio Wiederhold. Trends for the information technology industry. Technical report, Stanford University under sponsorship of the Japan Trade Organization, October 1999.

135. The Yahoo finance pages. finance.yahoo.com.

136. Ramana Yerneni, Felix Naumann, and Hector Garcia-Molina. Maximizing coverage of mediated web queries. Technical report, Stanford University, CA, 2000. http://www-db.stanford.edu/~yerneni/pubs/mcmwq.ps.

137. C. Yu and W. Meng. *Principles of database query processing for advanced applications*. Morgan Kaufmann, San Francisco, CA, USA, 1998.
138. Z39.50 Implementors Group and Z39.50 Maintenance Agency. Attribute Set BIB-1 (Z39.50-1995): Semantics. `http://lcweb.loc.gov/z3950/agency/defns/bib1.html`, Sep 1995.
139. Wojciech Ziarko. Discovery through rough set theory. *Communications of the ACM*, 42(11):54–57, November 1999.

Lecture Notes in Computer Science

For information about Vols. 1–2209
please contact your bookseller or Springer-Verlag